You look at all those bands throughout history like Fleetwood Mac and The Beatles, there's always so many stories behind the recording process and the people involved. But I love reading about those processes and it's always a part of the really great records. You don't get it without going through it.

– James Lavelle, 1998

Copyright © 2020 by James Gaunt

All rights reserved. No part of this publication may be reproduced, distributed, or transmitted in any form or by any means, including photocopying, recording, or other electronic or mechanical methods, without the prior written permission of the publisher, except in the case of brief quotations embodied in critical reviews and certain other noncommercial uses permitted by copyright law.

Foxteeth Press
www.foxteethpress.com

Printed in the United States of America

First Printing, 2020

ISBN 9781702889346

First Edition

MAKING PSYENCE FICTION

By James Gaunt

Table of Contents

INTRODUCTION	1
JAMES LAVELLE	3
BLUEBIRD AND HONEST JON'S	9
TALKIN' LOUD	17
MO' WAX	19
MAJOR FORCE	27
DJ SHADOW	31
TRIP HOP	41
THE TIME HAS COME	49
MO' WAX EXPANDED	55
ENDTRODUCING…..	65
BELMONDO IN LA	69
ENDTRODUCING…..COMPLETE	87
LONELY SOULS	93

APE SOUNDS	101
RECORDING PSYENCE FICTION	107
TRACK BY TRACK - PSYENCE FICTION	113
"Intro (Optional)"	113
"Guns Blazing (Drums of Death, Pt. 1)" feat. Kool G Rap	116
"UNKLE Main Title Theme"	121
"Bloodstain" feat Alice Temple	124
"Unreal"	130
"Lonely Soul" feat Richard Ashcroft	131
"Getting Ahead in the Lucrative Field of Artist Management"	135
"Nursery Rhyme / Breather" feat Badly Drawn Boy	137
"Celestial Annihilation"	141
"The Knock (Drums of Death, Pt. 2)" feat Mike D	145
"Chaos" feat Atlantique Khan	148
"Rabbit in Your Headlights" feat Thom Yorke	151
"Outro (Mandatory)"	159
"Be There" feat. Ian Brown	161
Unreleased and Unrecorded	164
FINALISING PSYENCE	169
RELEASE	175

TOURING WITH THE NME / BE THERE	189
DOWNFALL OF MO' WAX / NEVER NEVER LAND	193
WHERE ARE THEY NOW	201
SELECT UNKLE DISCOGRAPHY	213
REFERENCES	217
APPENDIX: TIMELINE 1973-2003	275
INDEX	303
ACKNOWLEDGMENTS	311

Introduction

Psyence Fiction is an album I've continued to come back to ever since first hearing it back in 1998 or 1999. At the time I was a massive Beastie Boys fan and I was lent two CD's which featured Mike D from Beastie Boys, one was Handsome Boy Modelling School, and the other was *Psyence Fiction* by UNKLE. Since then I have kept an ear out for anything by UNKLE and they've always impressed me, but *Psyence Fiction* is the one continues to blow me away with each listen.

In 2017 I was reading several books on the creation of classic albums and assumed there would be one about *Psyence Fiction*, but there wasn't. At the same time, I watched an early screening of a documentary about Mo' Wax and I was frustrated that it skimmed over UNKLE's early days prior to DJ Shadow's involvement.

I had never really looked into the pre-Shadow stuff, so I began researching UNKLE which led me to find out not only had there been several UNKLE releases prior to *Psyence Fiction* which I hadn't known of, but there had even been an abandoned album recorded in 1995. I kept researching and then decided to write this book and about three years later it is finished.

Unfortunately, neither James Lavelle nor DJ Shadow were available to take part in this book, as both were recording their respective latest albums at the time when I contacted them. Because of this I have instead relied on an extensive collection of interviews so that you can read their story in their own words.

I have tried to discuss everything relating to the creation of *Psyence Fiction*, from the beginnings of Mo' Wax and trip hop, to Lavelle's Japanese influences such as Major Force and Nigo. Naturally some of these topics could fill their own books and I hope my work will inspire others to write them.

James Lavelle

Born on February 22nd, 1974 in Oxford, England,[1] James Gabriel Leo Lavelle[2] grew up in a house surrounded by art and music. His father, Gabriel Lavelle, was a multi-instrumentalist who played in groups across several genres including classical, jazz, and folk.[3] Gabriel Lavelle had at one time played with the Irish folk band The Dubliners[4] but gave up on his musical career to instead become a lawyer.[5] James Lavelle's mother, Jennifer (née Smith-Parr), was a psychotherapist, dance teacher[6] and stencil artist who created a household which Lavelle described as "very beautiful in its art and design."[7]

Many of James Lavelle's extended family came from a musical background, which served as further influence on him. His grandmother Dorothy Lavelle (née Clifton) was the first Irish woman to be accepted into the Philharmonic Orchestra, and while he never met him, Dorothy's husband Gabriel Lavelle left an impression on the young James through his early career as a singer, where he appeared regularly on BBC Radio 2.[8] Gabriel and Dorothy had two sons, Gabriel (James Lavelle's father) and Michael Lavelle both of whom were multi-instrumentalists.[9] [10]

The Lavelle family influence would not only influence James Lavelle, but also his two younger brothers, Henry (born 1977) and

---

[1] Gregory, A (ed) 2002, p. 295
[2] Companies House 2019
[3] Allen, R 2018, 00:11:00
[4] Greenham, A 2011
[5] Burgess, J 1998, p. 59
[6] Cole, B 1998, p. 152
[7] Williams, E 2017
[8] Greenham, A 2011
[9] Lavelle, A n.d.
[10] Allen, R 2018, 00:11:00

Aidan (born 1979), who later would both find careers in music and the music industry themselves.[11] [12]

With such a pool of musical talent in the family it will come as no surprise that there was always music in the house, and James Lavelle's earliest memories are of listening to his father play records by a wide range of artists such as John Coltrane, Marvin Gaye, Deep Purple, Queen,[13] Stevie Wonder and Art Blakey,[14] as well as a lot of classical music.[15] His mother would also take him on excursions to visit galleries such as the Museum of Modern Art, and the Ashmolean Museum in Oxford,[16] and Lavelle would later describe his childhood as a "constant feed of visual stuff going on."[17]

From the age of eight James Lavelle received cello lessons from his Grandmother Dorothy.[18] Dorothy had attended the Royal Irish Academy of Music where she played both piano and cello. She later began teaching cello in Oxford at the local Dragon School after her husband died in 1960.[19] While James Lavelle would later refer to learning the cello as "amazing",[20] he also found it difficult, explaining:

> I was a kid and it was a very pressurized situation. I was only learning because my family wanted me to. My grandmother was very strict, and for me it was extremely difficult to learn an instrument in such a disciplined environment.[21]

---

[11] Allen, R 2018, 00:11:00
[12] Lavelle, H n.d.
[13] Potato Head 2017
[14] Passey, M 1996, 00:09:00
[15] Allen, R 2018
[16] Williams, E 2017
[17] Ibid.
[18] Greenham, A 2011
[19] Gaunt, J 2019
[20] Greenham, A 2011
[21] Ibid.

In the same year that cello lessons had started, James Lavelle also discovered hip hop culture for the first time when a performance was put on at his school which included hip hop music and a breakdancing demonstration.[22] Lavelle found himself attracted to hip hop, seeing it as a means to be part of something, he recalled: "At my middle school in Oxford, I was a bit of a loner and I had never really felt part of anything, so hip-hop attracted me because it was a whole culture. There was an art form with graffiti, a language, and a dress code."[23]

Soon he began listening to the Street Sounds compilation cassette tapes,[24] a series that had begun in 1983 and collected hip hop and electro tracks such as Rammellzee Vs. K-Rob, and Davy DMX.[25] While Lavelle may have felt like a loner, he wasn't alone in this interest, with other students at his school soon arriving wearing Puma trainers with Tacchini tracksuits,[26] spending their lunchtimes listening to electro and hip hop on cassettes.[27] School was also where Lavelle's love of street art formed, with graffiti books being passed around during art classes.[28] He referred to those books, such as *Spraycan Art* and *Subway Art*, as being like "naughty boy bibles"[29] which would be used as a distraction during boring classes.[30]

At 12, Lavelle's parents separated[31] in a divorce which he would describe as "horrific"[32] explaining, "I had a comfortable upbringing to a certain point and then my family just destroyed itself and exploded...My parents divorced because my father thought my mother was mad 'cause she was in Women Against Nuclear

---

[22] BFI 2018a
[23] Mark, O 1998
[24] Hodgkinson, W 2002
[25] Discogs 2019mmm
[26] Metaxas, N 2014, 00:01:00
[27] Hodgkinson, W 2002
[28] Williams, E 2017
[29] Ibid.
[30] Ibid.
[31] Burgess, J 1998, p. 59
[32] Wright, R 2017

Disarmament and all that."[33] While their father moved out, Lavelle and his younger brothers stayed living with their mother in Oxford[34] and it was during this period that he lost interest in his classes, feeling as though he didn't fit in.[35] He was also being bullied at school at the time because of the glasses he had to wear due to his poor eyesight,[36] and had began taking kung fu lessons as a means of self-defence. Unfortunately, the bullying continued until he was thirteen when he got into a big fight. He won the fight and afterwards was left alone again,[37] but continued his kung fu lessons and began training to become an instructor.[38] By now he was also putting serious thought in to what he would do once he completed school, with two ideas at the time being either to study Greek Mythology[39] or moving to China to further his studies of kung fu and martial arts.[40]

In 1987, aged 13, James Lavelle was watching Channel 4 when a film came on that took his interest. It was *Bombin*, a British documentary directed by Dick Fontaine that focused on the graffiti art world in both the USA and UK.[41] The film would serve as Lavelle's introduction to the street art of Goldie and 3D, who that same year were also featured in *Spraycan*.[42] *Bombin'* also featured a sound system from Bristol called The Wild Bunch, who's members would later go on to form Massive Attack. Inspired, Lavelle now set his sights on becoming a DJ.[43]

---

[33] Cole, B 1998
[34] Ibid.
[35] Burgess, J 1998, p. 59
[36] Burgess, J 2004
[37] Ibid.
[38] Girou, B 2018
[39] Burgess, J 1998, p. 59
[40] Girou, B 2018
[41] BFI 2018a
[42] Chang, J 1998
[43] Jockey Slut 2002

At 14 Lavelle dropped the cello and played his first gig as a DJ with his friend Matthew Puffet.[44] [45] The pair then joined up with Justin Winks, Mark Burgess, Paul McMahon, and Dave Thomson to form a sound system collective of their own, The Underground Movement.[46] [47] The Underground Movement were a collective of DJ's, rappers, dancers and graffiti artists[48] with Lavelle later claiming "I became a DJ because I couldn't Breakdance and I was no good at Grafitti (sic)."[49] The group would put on parties around their local Oxford area, with Lavelle's early sets made up from records taken from his parents collection,[50] he would later explain:

> We had our own DIY sound system that we would play at youth centers and house parties. I borrowed money from my mum, bought myself some decks, and I put on a party, which earned me the cash to pay her back. Those were the gigs where I first started DJing, and music was primarily influenced by bands like Soul II Soul, Massive Attack and The Wild Bunch, a mix of influences from Bristol and London.[51]

After initially listening to the hip hop featured on the Street Sounds compilation tapes,[52] Lavelle's interests began to branch out further towards Public Enemy, A Tribe Called Quest, De La Soul, Grandmaster Flash, Beastie Boys, and Run DMC who were all beginning to enter the UK charts.[53]

Alongside hip hop, Lavelle was still interested in Greek Mythology and Kung Fu, with each competing for his attention. Lavelle continued taking Kung Fu lessons in London several times a week,

---

[44] Rose, C 1994
[45] Gadelrab, R 2017
[46] Cooper, D 2017b
[47] Pustianaz, M 2010
[48] Harris, D 1994
[49] Girou, B 2018
[50] Thompson, A 2002
[51] Greenham, A 2011
[52] Mark, O 1998
[53] BFI 2018a

travelling by coach from Oxford,[54] and it was through these travels that Lavelle discovered record stores. He explained:

> I was going to London to do kung fu...It was in Chinatown and I realised that area, around Soho, is where all the good record shops are. So I started getting the bite to discover records in a different way. Prior to that, I was only buying records that were domestically released. A lot of it on cassette, too; whether it was Street Sounds compilations, or early American and British hip hop. But going to London was like going somewhere alien.[55]

---

[54] Passey, M 1996, 00:01:00
[55] Long Live Vinyl 2017

Bluebird and Honest Jon's

In 1988 at age 14, James Lavelle needed to complete two weeks work experience for school, and with his new passion for records and DJing it made sense that he would apply at record stores for work.[56]

When he told his friends his plan to get work experience at a record store in London though they were dismissive and told him "you're not going to get anywhere."[57] Undeterred, Lavelle applied at Bluebird Records on Edgware Road in London,[58] renowned at the time for their range of the latest imported records across their three stores.[59] Lavelle was accepted and completed the work experience and was then given a permanent position working on Saturdays,[60] reportedly working in exchange for records.[61]

While at Bluebird, Lavelle was introduced to the likes of Pete Tong, Gilles Peterson, Norman Jay, Michael Kopelman and Tim Simenon who were all customers of the store.[62] [63] Working at a record store also opened Lavelle's ears to new sounds such as those being put out by Warp Records which had began in 1989 and released house and techno by groups such as LFO, Nightmares on Wax, Autechre, and The Forgemasters. Lavelle later recalled,

> I remember going to Bluebird on Edgware Road and buying a white label of one of the first Warp releases – *Dextrous* by Nightmares On Wax. It started a sudden influx, hearing that kind of thing. The shops were like clubs…but in the daytime.

---

[56] Passey, M 1996, 00:05:00
[57] Ibid. 00:06:00
[58] Gamble, C 2017, ch. James Lavelle
[59] Greenham, A 2011
[60] Rose, C 1999, p. 146
[61] UNKLE 1998, 00:02:40
[62] Goodhood n.d. a
[63] Rose, C 1999, p. 146

> People smoking joints; everyone in the latest gear; the latest haircuts; the latest trainers.[64]

In 1990 Bluebird's owners asked Lavelle if he would be interesting in managing a new store they were thinking of opening. Lavelle agreed, but then instead all of the Bluebird stores closed down[65] and Lavelle found himself unemployed and unsure what to do with himself,[66] as by now he was no longer going to school.[67] Nearly everyone else in his family had attended university at either Oxford or Cambridge,[68] so James Lavelle enrolled at the Oxford College of Further Education with the hope to complete Business Studies. He soon found that he loathed the course but stuck with it for the time as he still felt he had to do something.[69]

As part of his studies Lavelle was given the opportunity to do work experience again, and once more chose a record store, this time Honest Jon's on Portobello Road in London. Lavelle recalled:

> Jon Clare, who owned Honest Jon's and a few other independent shops, was at the end of his time in the business and had become a therapist…So I had this weird interview with him. He had this hardcore knowledge of jazz records, and I knew fuck all, to be honest with you. But he also asked me: 'Do you ever have sexual fantasies about your father?'[70]

Lavelle passed the interview and soon began work at the store that was described by Honest Jon's later co-owner Alan Scholefield as having "a hard, noisy kind of atmosphere…(with) records being played at high volume all the time, (and) lots of shouting just to be

---

[64] Long Live Vinyl 2017
[65] Passey, M 1996, 00:08:23
[66] Mark, O 1998
[67] Waterman, R 1994
[68] Mark, O 1998
[69] Rose, C 1999, p. 146
[70] Long Live Vinyl 2017

heard."[71] But outside of the noisy atmosphere there were also the customers to deal with, and Scholefield recalled many of the regulars giving Lavelle a hard time when he started, "They ate him for breakfast. They absolutely hammered him. And James, to his credit, took it on the chin."[72]

Lavelle completed the one month of work experience and just like after his experience at Bluebird he was kept on as a permanent staff member.[73] Lavelle began working there three days a week while also continuing his studies until the now 16-year-old James Lavelle decided he was tired of business studies and begged Jon Clare to make him full time. When Clare agreed Lavelle quickly dropped out of college.[74]

Lavelle tasked himself with building up the hip hop section at Honest Jon's, hoping to bring in more contemporary records while also experimenting with putting old and new records together,[75] placing the latest hip hop records next to the records which had been sampled. At the time many hip hop releases were only available on vinyl as promos and white labels, promotional releases not meant for sale[76] [77] but which were often released by labels for DJs to promote. Lavelle became an expert of precuring promos[78] and in 2015 he discussed the promo culture from his time at Honest Jon's:

> We were the kings of promo hip-hop...If you wanted a Diamond D record or a Pete Rock record or A Tribe Called Quest record, you had to get it on a promo...In those days, getting a record was a very important status symbol. If you didn't get the 12-inch, you didn't get to play it as a DJ. So

---

[71] Coultate, A 2015
[72] Ibid.
[73] Passey, M 1996, 00:09:35
[74] Rose, C 1999, p.146
[75] Passey, M 1996, 00:09:25
[76] Hogan, M 2015
[77] Rare Records, n.d.
[78] DMC 2000?

there would be this mad energy in the shop. You would play records and hands would go up and you'd be throwing records across to people and they'd get angry when they couldn't have one…DJ culture in those days wasn't what it is now…It was working class, it was hardcore…It wasn't as refined and intellectualised as it is now.[79]

Lavelle built connections with record labels around the world to help keep Honest Jon's stock fresh, and these connections allowed Lavelle to get his hands on records before anyone else, such as when he became the first person in the UK to own House Of Pain's *Jump Around*.[80] Alan Scholefield for one was unimpressed and questioned the work Lavelle was doing spending time in the shop organising gigs for bands, but his co-worker, and later joint co-owner, Mark Ainley reassured him, telling him "Don't you realise that's the only reason we're busy? Figure it out. He's on the phone to New York and Leeds, making these connections. That's why we're having a really good weekend, not because you want him to sweep up the floor."[81]

In 1991 Lavelle started his own club night in Oxford called *Mo' Wax Please,*[82] with the name meant to reference both the decline of vinyl production at the time, with many hip hop releases in particular hard to find on vinyl at all,[83] and as a direct reference to the 1964 jazz album by Freddie Roach, *Mo's Green Please*.[84] The club was held at The Oxford Venue on Cowley Road[85] in what is now the O2 Academy Oxford.[86] Local Oxford band Radiohead also began playing at there in 1992[87] when it was known as The Zodiac, and later used the location to film the video for their first single *Creep*.[88]

---

[79] Coultate, A 2015
[80] Long Live Vinyl 2017
[81] Coultate, A 2015
[82] The Guardian 1994
[83] Valadez, A 2018, 00:10:00
[84] Didcock, B 1998
[85] Lavelle, J 2014
[86] Hughes, T 2008
[87] Green Plastic Trees n.d. a
[88] Greenwood, C 2014

James Lavelle recalled his time at the club in 1994:

> That was my real breakthrough. We were doing stuff with Galliano, Giles Peterson and that whole acid jazz thing. I hooked up with all sorts of people. That's how it started. I got the support of people. What I was doing was young, fresh, left field; it was doing things that other people weren't and it had the right people involved. They saw the need for a young element in the jazz scene. I got props from people like Giles Peterson and the magazine *Straight No Chaser*. To them it didn't matter who you were, it was what you had to say and what you had to offer.[89]

During the opening night of Mo' Wax Please Lavelle bumped in to an old school friend, Tim Goldsworthy.[90] While they had first met as students at Oxford's Summertown Middle School in 1983, they hadn't got on at the time. But meeting once more at Mo' Wax Please they started talking and realised they had some things in common, primarily their interest in music. The pair soon decided to make their own music together and Goldsworthy helped Lavelle run his club.[91] Tim Goldsworthy described those early Mo' Wax Please nights in 1995:

> It was mad. There was like 800 people getting really pissed up and doin' it to pure jazz. It was strange because the scene hadn't set up as a cool kind of jazz scene, everyone was just having a laugh. Then it got a bit trendy after some magazines caught onto it and people started dressing up and standing around the edge and it just killed it.[92]

Mo' Wax Please nights would also feature guest DJs with Patrick Forge and Gilles Peterson both appearing as part of Talking Loud

---

[89] Waterman, R 1994
[90] Lazarus, D 1995, p. 69
[91] Ibid.
[92] Ibid.

nights, a reference to the pairs own Talkin Loud record label and popular club night held at The Fridge in London.[93]

Lavelle continued to build connections through his work as a DJ and at Honest Jon's, staying in touch with those he had made at Bluebird, such as Gilles Peterson and Pete Tong, and the new regulars he was meeting at his new store including producer Trevor Jackson,[94] Charlie Dark,[95] Tim Westwood, and Paul Oakenfold.[96] It was also through Honest Jon's that Lavelle met Cynthia Rose, an American journalist who suggested he speak to Paul Bradshaw about writing for his magazine *Straight No Chaser*. Lavelle wrote Bradshaw a letter and then went in to meet him at the *Chaser* office for an interview, as he later explained:

> I'd said I wanted to do a column and something that was a bit more eclectic and contemporary. I wanted to talk about what was really going on in the underground side of the music that was happening at that time which was Acid Jazz and Talkin' Loud and a lot of Japanese stuff and also the whole thing that was going on with the Groove Academy in New York, DJ Smash. I just wanted to give a bit of focus for that and that was how the column started. I was also revealing records and tapes; things that I liked and that my friends had given me and things that just weren't getting exposure anywhere else.[97]

Straight No Chaser was started by Paul Bradshaw when the first issue launched in March 1988 after he realised that his then current employer, the *New Music Express* (or *NME* for short), weren't interested in covering music that he was interested in writing about such as African, jazz and hip hop.[98]

---

[93] Peterson, G 2017, 01:30:00
[94] Long Live Vinyl 2017
[95] Cooper, D 2013a
[96] Rage 2017
[97] Goodhood n.d. a
[98] Wang, G 2018

One of *Straight No Chaser's* claims to fame was that it was made entirely on an Apple Macintosh computer, donated by Island Records director Rob Partridge in exchange for a break in advertising space.[99] The Mac became the tool of Ian Swift, aka Swifty, the magazine's art director who gave *Straight No Chaser* a visual identity that won awards,[100] and Swifty's work continues to be acclaimed today.[101]

Swifty later recalled meeting Lavelle on the day of his interview:

> It was his boundless energy and geeky knowledge of all things beats, hip-hop and jazz that secured him a column in the mag... it was as much about the language and style as much as the music.[102]

Lavelle ended his interview with Paul Bradshaw insisting "you need *me*" and received the job,[103] naming his column after his club night *Mo' Wax*, and soon began reviewing the music he loved, signing his column as 'The Holygoof',[104] an adopted pseudonym which Lavelle explained in 2004:

> It was from being into the beat generation thing. It was Neal Cassady from 'On The Road', that was his nickname. I was really into Burroughs and Kerouac when I was 15. I'm still a fan of their view of life, I don't think it's something that leaves you. When did I last use the name? Ten years ago, there was a significant binning of it. It was buried in the garden, given a respectful funeral.[105]

---

[99] Goldman, V 1993, p. 74
[100] Bradshaw, P 2011
[101] Eye Magazine 2017
[102] Cooper, D 2013b
[103] Bradshaw, P 2013
[104] Llewellyn Smith, C 1994
[105] Burgess, J 2004

While he wasn't paid for his column,[106] he started receiving white labels, demos, and promos sent from all over the world in the hopes of getting reviewed or played by Lavelle at his DJ nights. One of those records that found its way to Lavelle was by a group called *Zimbabwe Legit*. While he wasn't that interested in the A Side, *Doin' Damage In My Native Language*, on the B-side there was a remix called *Shadow's Legitimate Mix* which Lavelle found himself going back to again and again over the years.[107]

---

[106] Rose, C 1999 p. 146
[107] Friedman, K 2013

Talkin' Loud

During the summer of 1991 Lavelle was asked if he'd like to DJ at The Fridge, taking over from Giles Peterson and Patrick Forge while they took a summer break.[108] Talkin' Loud had started as a small DJ night at Dingwalls in Camden, West London, before moving to Brixton's The Fridge which offered them a 1000 capacity room and a budget to put on bands with live visuals.[109]

The summer Lavelle joined them, Talkin' Loud was renamed to Talkin' Summer to signify the change over, and Lavelle would play every Saturday for several months, experience that he would consider his big break as a DJ.[110]

During his time at The Fridge, Lavelle would continue to receive promos of albums ahead of everyone else, including Young Disciples' *Road To Freedom* which he would later call "one of the most underrated British records of its time."[111]

This was a time for records that would define who Lavelle was as a DJ and musician, with many releases from this period continuing to be favourites of his for years to come. In particular *Unfinished Sympathy* by Massive Attack which was released in February 1991,[112] and continued to have importance to Lavelle through his life. In 2015 he would praise the song as the holy grail of his youth, explaining:

> This song proved how sophisticated the sound had become. Truly one of the most beautiful records I've ever heard. Sounding as fresh today as it did then. I can't explain how it felt to hear it for the first time, I'd never heard an orchestra

---

[108] Aubrey, E 2017f
[109] Resident Advisor n.d.
[110] Aubrey, E 2017f
[111] Ibid.
[112] MassiveAttack.ie 2019c

and hip-hop beats together before. It was truly revolutionary and made me want to make records.[113]

Unfinished Sympathy was the second single to be released in the lead up to Massive Attack's debut album *Blue Lines*, which was released April 8th 1991.[114] The album featured tracks from when the group were part of The Wild Bunch sound system as well as newer tracks[115] produced by Johnny Dollar and featuring string arrangements by Will Malone.[116] *NME* would call it "the sleekest, deadliest, most urbane, most confounding LP 1991 has yet seen" giving it 10/10,[117] and *Blue Lines* has continued to appear in several Top Album lists ever since.[118]

In 2017 Lavelle described to *The Quietus* the experience of first hearing *Blue Lines*, and the lasting effects it has had on him:

> I just remember when I got the cassette, I got a promo cassette of it...and I was just sitting there on my bed at my mum's house. I must have listened to it about 100 times. I just didn't turn it off, just kept playing it. I can't explain how fucking cool it was and how cerebral it was, and how beautiful it was...This is my favourite album ever made and the most influential record ever. The idea of a record that had multiple voices and engaged in a different way…the production, the cover, the paintings, the photographs, the mystique, everything that about it defined my late teenage years and defined the beginning of Mo' Wax. It was amongst other things a blueprint for where I went with my life.[119]

---

[113] Dummy 2015
[114] MassiveAttack.ie 2019a
[115] Select 1992, p. 51
[116] Discogs 2019z
[117] Fadele, D n.d.
[118] Pitchfork 2003
[119] Aubrey, E 2017d

Mo' Wax

In 1992 James Lavelle had a job in a record store, regular DJ gigs, a column with *Straight No Chaser*, and was also contributing to other magazines such as *I-D*.[120] All of these lead to great connections, enabling Lavelle to have the latest music promos, white labels, and acetates. But what he really wanted was to work for a record label.[121]

Gilles Peterson had started the record label Talkin' Loud in 1990, naming the label after his popular club night at Dingwalls[122] and in 1991 Lavelle spent two weeks interning with the label,[123] but no job came out of it for him.[124] Frustrated that he was unable to get a job at a record label he next tried to set up a sub-label,[125] a small record label which is part of a larger label.[126]

Lavelle had been talking to Island Records about a job potentially working for their Antilles division and starting his own sub-label for them.[127] In fact in 1992 Lavelle announced he was starting a label called Mo' Wax Please Records, making the announcement in his column in issue 15 of *Straight No Chaser*.[128]

In the issue he revealed two new releases would be coming soon, *Strangers* by Sweatmouth and an *Untitled EP* credited to The Venus Project. *Strangers* is described as "fast breakbeats meets jazz vocals with some funku (sic) club business", and was intended as the first release of Mo' Wax Please Records with a release date of March 1992. The Venus Project was also given a release date of

---

[120] Stokes, N 2008
[121] Rose, C 1994
[122] Didcock, B 1998
[123] Davis, J 1999, p. 22
[124] Peterson, G 2017, 01:30:00
[125] Rose, C 1999 p.147
[126] Rutter, P 2016, n.p.
[127] Rose, C 1999 p.147
[128] Lavelle, J 1992a, p. 58

late March and described as "the sounds of new age jazz-funk."[129] Neither of these were released on any label, let alone a Mo' Wax Please Records and it is not clear what happened to them or whether this was the label Lavelle had intended to start with Island Records or not. In the next issue of *Straight No Chaser* Lavelle apologised for the delay, explaining that something would be dropping in mid-June, but no further explanation was given.[130]

Thanks to his column in *Straight No Chaser* readers from all over the world had begun sending Lavelle their demo tapes,[131] especially after he announced he was starting his own label.[132] Lavelle explained, "I had all these records being sent for review, all these records that nobody else could get. I used to search high and low for weird b-sides, hip-hop instrumentals."[133] This fit well with Lavelle's hopes of Mo' Wax mirroring record labels such as Hollywood BASIC, who were releasing music by a wide range of international artists.[134]

One of the groups who sent a tape to *Straight No Chaser* were called Repercussions,[135] a group from Brooklyn in the USA who Lavelle had begun talking to and hoped to sign once his deal with Island Records was finalised. Unfortunately, the deal with Island fell through but one of the members of Repercussions suggested Lavelle could put it out himself if he gave them £1000 in cash.[136] Borrowing the money from Mark Ainley at Honest Jon's, Lavelle flew to New York with the £1000 in an envelope and made the deal.[137] Mo' Wax Records was then formed, taking the name he'd been using for his column and club night, because he "couldn't think of another name for a label."[138]

---

[129] Lavelle, J 1992a, p. 58
[130] Lavelle, J 1992b, p. 62
[131] Metaxas, N 2014, 00:04:17
[132] Davis, J 1999, p. 22
[133] Burgess, J 1996, p. 57
[134] Ma, D 2017, p. 74
[135] Metaxas, N 2014, 00:04:44
[136] Rose, C 1999 p. 147
[137] Bradshaw, P 2014a
[138] Rose, C 1999 p. 147

While most sources credit Mo' Wax Records as having been founded by Tim Goldsworthy and James Lavelle together,[139] this is incorrect and it was created solely by James Lavelle,[140] with Goldsworthy later joining and helping Lavelle with some of the business side such as A&R,[141] or Artists and Repertoire which is essentially talent scouting, overseeing the recording process and assisting with marketing.[142] Goldsworthy was also tasked with delegating design work to Swifty for potential artwork on Mo' Wax's releases.[143] Swifty, who worked with Lavelle at *Straight No Chaser* and had also been designing flyers for Lavelle's club nights, was brought in as the Mo' Wax Art Director, and he designed the initial Mo' Wax cover art and the original Mo' Wax logo which would evolve slightly over time until settling in 1994.[144]

The very first Mo' Wax release was the 12" record for Repercussions' *Promise* of which an initial one thousand copies were pressed,[145] and Lavelle made sure to promote the record in his own column within *Straight No Chaser*, announcing:

> D-Day! The launch of Mo' Wax Records coming atcha with NYX's, the Repercussions massive. Straight outta Brooklyn 'n' lettin' off the vocal 70's funk influenced 'Promise' and 'Field Trippin' - a the native tongues new wave hip-hop summer groove. Massive music droppin' live 'n' sample free.[146]

The announcement was reproduced word for word on the cover for the Repercussions 12" as linear notes. This first release would be

---

[139] Geoghegan, K 2014
[140] Tubbs, Christopher 2013, 00:01:00
[141] Discogs 2019mm
[142] Music Careers 2019
[143] The Mo'Wax Vaults: The Lost Men from Unkle 2018, 00:12:00
[144] Cooper, D 2013b
[145] Bradshaw, P 2014a
[146] Lavelle, J 1992c p. 58

followed up by two more before the end of the year which also featured a review on their covers. The second Mo' Wax release was Raw Stylus *Many Ways* which featured the following linear notes:

> Raw Stylus come from a growin' new vibe-- London Soul, Beats, Bass, phunki break downz 'n' strong 'n' musical contentz. Arrivin' on the scene in 1989 with "Bright Lights Big Cities". Raw Stylus came on a breaks 'n' beats tip, hittin' the U.K. 'n' U.S. on a large underground tip. After an abcense of 2 years the boyz came back with the prolific "Pushin' Against The Flow" bustin' boom boxes from London to LA. Now the RS massive drop another piece of soul flavoured London funk. So lick up a fat blunt 'n' support the new soul massive.[147]

Followed by Palm Skin Productions *Getting Out Of Hell*:

> Working harder to bring you hands-on music: hands on the decks, hands on the mix, hands on the drum. Music made not by style of clothing but SKIN OF PALM. Inside the deep lick, running things, the sound of the PALM SKIN coming easy on the downlow. Working with a clear conscience 'cos PALM SKIN do it LIKE BROTHERS every time. Too often the brother's a chameleon, he leaves you dry with the change of season, so when your'e GETTING OUT OF HELL you need A LITTLE SKIN to put you on the primrose path. PALMSKIN PRODUCTIONS: building a fat blunt for your ears. We Come in Peace. Release.[148]

Each of these early Mo' Wax releases stood out thanks to the distinctive design of the record sleeves, a plain white cover with a strip of colour down one side full of information about the record such as the descriptive linear notes. The initial three releases featured this strip stuck on as a sticker, but from then on they were

---

[147] Mo' Wax Discography 2011a
[148] Mo' Wax Discography 2011b

printed on to the cover instead[149] due to it becoming too expensive to pay someone to put the stickers on.[150] This design was inspired by the obi strips seen on Japanese imports of albums Swifty and Lavelle had around them. Swifty explained:

> There was no money for expensive sleeves and packaging then – it was all done on a shoestring and a lot of belief! The idea of the stripe came from the belly-wrap which we'd seen on Japanese imports, particularly the Blue Note LPs which were floating around the *Straight No Chaser* office at the time. It was my idea to do something that could be knocked out quickly. [151]

Lavelle continues:

> The identity we created was initially based on a love for those Japanese records, which had an obi wrapped around original British or American artwork. The obi would have a Japanese language explanation. We based the idea of the early sleeves on those wraps. And at the time, everybody had a million logos. Originally with Mo' Wax it was 'A Men From U.N.K.L.E. Production'[152]

The 'Men From U.N.K.L.E. Production' logo featured on the back of every Mo' Wax 12" sleeve for the next few years, but at the time it was just a logo. Lavelle had also used the name when creating charts, such as the *Honest Jon's Mo' Wax Please 20 chart*[153] which was credited to The Men From U.N.C.L.E. with the acronym standing for "United National Command For Long Playing Electro."[154]

---

[149] Foakes, K 2015
[150] The Mo'Wax Vaults: Asthetic Origins 2018, 00:05:20
[151] Cooper, D 2013b
[152] Bradshaw, P 2014a
[153] Lavelle, J 2014
[154] Bradshaw, P 2014a

The first actual music credited to Men From U.N.K.L.E. came out in 1992 as a remix on United Future Organization – *Loud Minority*, entitled *Moondance "(Moon Chant: Hip Sensibility Mutates....)"* which acted as the B Side to initial CD's put out by Zero Corporation,[155] and the 12" released in 1993.[156] The remix featured programming credited to Tim "Tibbs" Goldsworthy, while James "Holygoof" Lavelle was credited with the arrangement. The remix also featured Simon Richmond of Palm Skin Productions and received a write up in Lavelle's Mo' Wax Please column where he described it as "eight and a half minutes of musical deepness. Check the 808! Boom!"[157]

While this was UNKLE's first released remix, Lavelle and Goldsworthy had previously created a remix for Ronny Jordon after Lavelle convinced someone at Island Records to give them the job, Goldsworthy explained:

> [Lavelle] knew someone at Island Records who was looking after Ronnie Jordan and he told them I knew everything there was to know about working in studios - when all I really knew how to operate was my Casio. We remixed *'Get to Grips'* but the end result was never released. It may have had something to do with the fact that we didn't like Ronnie's guitar solo so we took it out. With Ronnie being a guitarist, it obviously didn't go down too well.[158]

The track never came out and Lavelle has said it will never be heard as it was "horrible".[159]

Lavelle and Goldsworthy would release two more remixes as The Men From U.N.K.L.E. before retiring the name in favour of the shortened U.N.K.L.E.. *Vibe P.M. (Stranger Things Have Happened - Brazil On A Jimmy Hill Mix)* was a remix off Mondo Grosso's 1993

---

[155] Discogs 2019vv
[156] Discogs 2019ww
[157] Lavelle, J 1993, p. 53
[158] Lazarus, D 1995, p. 69
[159] Metaxas, N 2014, 00:23:28

Marble mini album, which also featured remixes by Norman Cook.[160] Their second remix was Men From U.N.K.L.E. Featuring Marden Hill - *Come On (2010 Version)* which featured on the compilation *Mo' Wax Presents Mo' Groove Vol.1*. This was a remix of Marden Hill's *Come On*, which featured exclusively on the *Mo' Groove* compilation and released only in Japan by Avex Trax.[161]

The remixes were created at Goldworthy's house along with some "dodgy techno"[162] the pair created for fun. Initially Goldsworthy only owned a Casio keyboard, but after the first few remixes he decided he wanted to better commit himself to making music, and he bought himself a sampler and soon "started experimenting with the likes of Alice Coltrane, Miles Davis and mad jazz stuff sampled on top of dark beats."[163]

While the UNKLE name came from Lavelle and Goldsworthy's love of 1960's television programs, namely *The Man From U.N.C.L.E.*,[164] the origins of the initial UNKLE logo are thanks to Swifty. Lavelle was visiting Swifty at his home while they were planning the first Mo' Wax releases and seeing that he had some toys from the TV series *The Man From U.N.C.L.E.* Lavelle became inspired. There Lavelle insisted that a Men From U.N.K.L.E. Productions logo be put on the Mo' Wax 12" sleeve's, with Swifty taking the original U.N.C.L.E. TV series logo and changing the gun into a "dooby".[165]

During this time, Lavelle had been taking a coach from Oxford to London each day, but now that he had his own label, and a fulltime job at Honest Jon's, it was time to move. One of Honest Jon's regulars was Fraser Cooke, a writer for culture magazine *The Face*, and when Lavelle one day asked if he knew of any places to stay Cooke offered him a room. Cooke had a place just off Portobello

---

[160] Discogs 2019bb
[161] Discogs 2019iii
[162] McLean, C 1995a, p. 106
[163] Lazarus, D 1995, p. 69
[164] Ibid.
[165] Cooper, D 2013b

Road, close to Honest John's, and Lavelle took him up on the offer, with Goldsworthy becoming a regular visitor at the flat as well, crashing on their couch with his Casio.[166] [167] The meeting was fortuitous as Cooke was not only working at *The Face*, but also within the music industry as a distributor, and so was able to help Lavelle license tracks for early Mo' Wax releases. He would also help out by making t-shirts and bags for the label, which were sold through ads in *Straight No Chaser*, and other magazines.[168]

---

[166] Goh, G 2012
[167] Lazarus, D 1995, p. 69
[168] Goh, G 2012

Major Force

While working at Honest Jon's if a customer came in looking for a hard to obtain record James Lavelle would make a deal with them. He'd tell them he would get them their record if they would bring him some Major Force releases, which were hard to find at the time in London.[169][170]

Major Force was a Japanese record label set up in 1988, initially releasing Japanese house and hip hop music by artists such as Kan Takagi and Fujiwara Hiroshi under their Tiny Panx and TPO monikers, Nakanishi Toshio (aka Tycoon To$h) and Masayuki Kudo under their Major Force Productions moniker, and DJ Milo from the Wild Bunch.[171]

Nakanishi Toshio had been an original member of Japanese New Wave band Melon who released their debut album *Do You Like Japan?* in 1982. During the recording sessions in New York the band had seen Afrika Bambatta performing and became interested in hip hop,[172] with the album featuring record scratching at the end their song *Optimistic Depression*. At the time in Japan hip hop was still considered underground, but musicians from overseas would occasionally visit and Kan Takagi would later recall taking Chuck D and The Jungle Brothers record shopping on separate occasions.[173]

Masayuki Kudo visited London in 1985 where he met with The Wild Bunch, and Melon joined him in 1986 to record their next album, this time with Kudo as a contributing member. During 1986 Kudo spent more time with DJ Milo and Nellee Hooper from The Wild Bunch and they played him demos for their single *The Look of Love*

---

[169] Metaxas, N 2014, 00:24:50
[170] UNKLE 1998, 00:06:00
[171] Yoshioka, K 2018
[172] Egaitsu, H 2014
[173] Yoshioka, K 2018

and introduced him to Soul II Soul and Jazzy B.[174] One of Kudo's strongest memories of this time was seeing Run DMC at the Hammersmith Odeon where he was shocked to see the group perform with only two turntables and two microphones. This was the first time he had seen such a set up and he deciding that Melon should tour with a similar system once they returned to Japan.[175] By 1987 Melon's second album *Deep Cut* was released with a hip hop infused sound,[176] taking the influence that the group had found in New York and London and channelling it in to what would next become Major Force.[177]

Like Kudo, Tiny Panx member Fujiwara Hiroshi had an early taste for hip hop when had spent time in London during the 1980's. Originally he had been drawn there due to a love of punk rock[178] but while in London Hiroshi had stayed with producer Malcolm McLaren who introduced him to hip hop and suggested that Hiroshi visit New York.[179] At the time McLaren was completing his hip hop fused *Duck Rock* album which featured New York hip hop crew World's Famous Supreme Team alongside production by members of British experimental group Art of Noise. McLaren's album would release in 1983 and feature the singles *Buffalo Gals* and *Double Dutch*.

After visiting New York and seeing early pioneers such as Afrika Islam, and Kool Lady Blue[180] Hiroshi had returned to Japan and formed Tiny Panx with Kan Takagi , releasing their 12" *Last Orgy* in 1988[181] and opening for the Beastie Boys during their Japanese tour[182] in Tokyo.[183] This was followed by Hiroshi + K.U.D.O. Featuring D.J. Milo's *D.J.Mix*, which featured *Return Of The Original Art Form* on the B-side, which became a favourite of

---

[174] Takayama, Y 2013
[175] Ibid.
[176] Tycoon To$h Kingdom n.d.
[177] Takayama, Y 2013
[178] Li, R 2019
[179] Cooke, F 2010
[180] Ibid.
[181] Yoshioka, K 2018
[182] Yu, S 2019
[183] Li, R 2016

producer Howie B in England, where he used it to close his DJ sets.[184]

In 1992,[185] Nakanishi Toshio and Masayuki Kudo (usually referred to as Toshi and Kudo respectively)[186] had moved to London with the intention of recording a Love TKO album,[187] and one day wandered into Honest Jon's record store where James Lavelle was working. Lavelle had become a big fan of Major Force releases, but they were hard to get in London and when Toshi and Kudo came in asking about some records Lavelle answered with his usual "Sure I can get it, if you can get me some Major Force records",[188] to which the duo replied "we ARE Major Force!" and the group soon became friends.[189]

It wasn't just Japanese music which interested Lavelle, as he had also become a fan of Japanese street fashion thanks to Michael Kopelman, who in 1991 had been put in charge of distribution for the fashion brand Stüssy, and created the "International Stüssy Tribe", a group of tastemakers around the world who would be sent boxes of streetwear as a means to promote the brand.[190] The two had become friends while Lavelle had been working at Bluebird, and Kopelman had given Lavelle his first Major Force record.[191] At the time Kopelman was also distributing brands such as Bape, Neighborhood, WTAPS, and Supreme, and Lavelle credits Kopelman with helping him discover Japanese clothing culture, thanks to him giving Lavelle t-shirts whenever he would stop by Kopelman's office.[192]

---

[184] Muzik 1995, p. 85
[185] Takayama, Y 2013
[186] Metaxas, N 2014, 00:24:00
[187] Takayama, Y 2013
[188] Metaxas, N 2014, 00:25:00
[189] Darby, A 2013
[190] Deleon, J 2015
[191] Dike, J 2017
[192] Ibid.

Lavelle was becoming more and more interested in Japanese music and culture[193] but it wasn't until December 1993 that he would get a chance to visit the country which had held his fascination. The trip was made possible thanks to *Straight No Chaser* arranging a tour to Japan, with Paul Bradshaw taking some of his staff along, including Lavelle. During the tour Lavelle visited fifteen cities across the country and would take in the design and style of Japanese streetwear and records.[194] [195] Kudo arranged a meeting for Lavelle with Kan Takagi and Fujiwara Hiroshi from Major Force,[196] and he also meet with DJ Krush who was preparing his debut album for its January 1993 release on Chance Records in Japan.[197] [198]

Lavelle had heard some demos that Krush sent Paul Bradshaw at *Straight No Chaser* and had become interested in signing him to Mo' Wax.[199] Gilles Peterson also heard the demos, and both he and Lavelle made offers to release an album in the UK, with Krush unsure which label to choose. Conveniently for Lavelle, he was able to visit Krush in Japan, and after meeting one another in person Krush became convinced by Lavelle's enthusiasm and soon signed with Mo' Wax.[200] [201]

While Mo' Wax's early releases would feature an acid jazz sound, Lavelle was taking in wider influences and moving on as he had become more interested in downtempo instrumental hip hop. The record that is most often attributed with this shift is Mo' Wax's 14th release, 1993's *In/Flux / Hindsight* by DJ Shadow.[202] [203]

---

[193] Butler, A 2014
[194] Williams, E 2017
[195] Darby, A 2013
[196] Ibid.
[197] Winston, D 2017, p. 53
[198] Discogs 2019d
[199] Winston, D 2017, p. 53
[200] Ibid.
[201] Omae, K 2018
[202] Pemberton, A 1994
[203] Cooper, D 2014

DJ Shadow

Joshua Paul Davis, aka DJ Shadow, was born on June 29, 1972[204] and grew up in Davis, California.[205]

After first hearing Grandmaster Flash and the Furious Five's *The Message* in 1982,[206] Davis became interested in hip hop due to how many of the songs were created from sampling other music. While he became more involved in the culture of hip hop, similar to James Lavelle, Davis wasn't able to breakdance so he chose to focus on music and DJing.[207] In 1984 he received his first record player,[208] a $99 Sears combination turntable which included a radio and dual cassette tape decks, allowing Davis to make copies of records and record songs off the radio.[209] He also began experimenting with scratching, after having seen it demonstrated on TV in music videos for Run DMC, and Grandmaster Flash. In 1985 he began calling KDVS, a college radio station in Davis California, where a DJ named Oras Washington had a hip hop show. Davis began calling in to request hip hop records and in 1987 he asked another favour, whether Washington could play a mix he'd made at home.[210] Washington agreed, requesting a 20 minute mix, and in 1988 Davis left him a cassette tape before returning home to record the show on to another tape.[211] The recording was later released as an MP3 called *Josh Davis - Spinning Live At KDVS '88*.[212]

By the late eighties Davis had sold all of his comics and was using the money earnt from a paper-route to fund his new obsession of

---

[204] Levine, M 2019
[205] Wilder, E 2017 p. 24
[206] Spine Magazine, n.d.
[207] Grundy, G 1997, p. 252
[208] Wilder, E 2017 pp. 34-35
[209] Fox, K 2016
[210] Ma, D 2017, p. 65
[211] Wilder, E 2017 p. 41
[212] Discogs 2019u

buying records.[213] He was buying used soul and rock records such as James Brown and Bobby Byrd and soon noticed that these old records had also been sampled by the hip hop artists he was listening to such as Eric B & Rakim, and Public Enemy.[214] At the time several hip hop records were created by sampling the break from another record, such as James Brown's *Funky Drummer*.[215] The 'break' being a short instrumental section of the record, often a drum solo, which could be sampled and looped or cut up to create a larger backing track.[216] In 1989 Davis saw Public Enemy perform and noticed they weren't just sampling the same breaks that everyone else was, but they were using records which even his dad owned, such as Isaac Hayes.[217] This was a breakthrough moment for Davis as he realised he could potentially make this music too.[218]

In high school, Davis saved up $300 for a four track cassette recorder,[219] the Yamaha MT-100 4-Track,[220] and began creating his own hip hop music, sampling songs from his record player on to the four track by recording a drum break, rewinding the tape, and then recording scratches over the top.[221] Many of these songs were eventually given an official release by Davis in 2007 and then collected in 2009 as *DJ Shadow: The 4-Track Era Collection*.[222]

Now that he had become serious about making music a DJ name was required. Some early names included DJ Motivator,[223] DJ White Lightning, and DJ 24KT[224] (24 Carat),[225] before settling on DJ Shadow. The name was in reference to his preference for DJ's who

---

[213] Grundy, G 2012
[214] Ibid.
[215] Scott, D 2017
[216] Toop, D 1991, pp. 113-115
[217] Hermes, W 2002, p. 98
[218] Grundy, G 2012
[219] DJShadow.com 2010
[220] Discogs 2019h
[221] Rule, G 1997
[222] DJShadow.com 2010
[223] Grundy, G 1997, p. 253
[224] Ma, D 2017, p. 65
[225] Grundy, G 1997, p. 253

stayed in the shadows behind the turntables, whereas he felt that in 1989 there was a trend towards having the DJ or producer step in to the spotlight.[226] When speaking to *The Face* about the origins of the name, DJ Shadow likened it to being a movie director because "people know their names, but they don't need to know their face."[227]

Around 1991 DJ Shadow met with the program director for KMEL, a radio station located in San Francisco,[228] where he told them "you need me," and he was hired to create mixes.[229] Shadow would spend 2-3 weeks creating intricate one hour mixes on his four track recorder, and began using the fact he had a show on KMEL as a means of getting promo records from labels.[230] These record labels, such as Tommy Boy and Profile, were eager to get their records heard and so would send Shadow records, posters, stickers etc. and in return he would feature their records on his mix tapes.[231]

In early 1991 Shadow sent two tapes to *The Source*, one of the few hip hop magazines at the time, with one addressed to Dave Klein, a writer whose work Shadow had enjoyed, and the other addressed to Matty C for his Unsigned Hype column[232] dedicated to giving recognition to hip hop artists who were yet to be signed to a record label. The tape was a 90 minute mix, featuring original remixes created by Shadow, and was featured in the June 1991 issue of *The Source* where they suggested readers "check him out for production, or if you seek new flavor for a remix."[233] This wasn't Shadow's first appearance in the magazine either, as he also had a letter printed in the May 1991 issue where he laments MC's who disrespect each other based on the colour of their skin.[234]

---

[226] Ma, D 2017, p. 65
[227] Grundy, G 1997, p. 253
[228] Wilder, E 2017, p. 49
[229] Bradshaw, P 2014b
[230] Ibid.
[231] Wilder, E 2017 p. 50
[232] SLurg, 2006
[233] C, M 1991, p. 22
[234] Shadow 1991, p. 10

Dave Klein, better known as Funkenklein,[235] also got in touch with Shadow telling him "I think I have a job for you, if you're interested in earning $ 3,000."[236] At the time Shadow was working for a pizza shop earning a minimum wage of $3.55 an hour[237] while also studying Communications at Davis University. He was blown away by the offer which resulted in his first releases on Funkenklein's label Hollywood BASIC, a hip hop focused subsidiary of the Disney owned Hollywood record label. Funkenklein's vision was for the label to feature an international roster of artists, and included acts from Japan, Netherlands and Africa.[238] While this vision wasn't commercially successful, it would influence others such as James Lavelle and his own vision for Mo' Wax Records.[239]

Later in 1991 Shadow had his first record released on Hollywood BASIC, *Lesson 4*,[240] a megamix combining samples from various records.[241] The title was a reference to the Lessons series which had been released by Double Dee & Steinski, starting in 1983 with *Lesson One (The Payoff Mix)*,[242] with the series pausing in 1985 after the completion of *Lessons 3*[243] before Double Dee & Steinski later returned with their own *Lesson 4* in 2018.[244]

Shadow recorded his *Lesson 4* in 1991 on the Yamaha 4-Track,[245] and when it came time to release it Shadow was asked to list all of the songs sampled. At this time record labels were starting to get sued for the use of uncleared samples and when Hollywood BASIC saw the list of 80 samples they decided to release *Lesson* Four as

---

[235] Ma, D 2017, p. 73
[236] SLurg, 2006
[237] Ma, D 2017, p. 73
[238] Ibid.
[239] Ma, D 2017, p. 74
[240] Discogs 2019v
[241] Wilder, E 2017 p. 55
[242] Christgau, R 1986
[243] Double Dee 2017
[244] Double Dee & Steinski, 2018
[245] Rule, G 1997

a promo only, rather than release it to the public,[246] and it was made the B-side of Lifers Group *Real Deal (Shadow Remix)*.[247] This was followed in 1992 by another megamix similar to *Lesson 4, Basic Mega-Mix*,[248] and his remix of Zimbabwe Legit *Doin' Damage In My Native Language (Shadow's Legitimate Mix)* also from 1992.[249]

Shadow had also provided production for the local Californian rapper Paris.[250] Paris' second album *Sleeping With The Enemy* was released in America on November 23 1992[251] after some delay due to its controversial themes. Shadow is credited as providing samples on three tracks, *Make Way For A Panther*, *The Days of Old*, and *Funky Lil' Party*,[252] though DJ Shadow's website credits Shadow as providing co-production and/or scratches for eight songs on the album.[253] These including *Bush Killa*, one of the songs which led to his record label Tommy Boy refusing to release the album forcing Paris to release it on his own Scarface Records.[254] The possible reason for this discrepancy in credits is that Shadow created demos for Paris which Paris then resampled as a way to get around giving Shadow credit for production, leading Shadow to later thank Paris for teaching him "the game".[255]

While his mixes were well constructed, Shadow wanted to move beyond the limitations of his four track and had been looking into samplers after a producer named Mr. Niceguy showed him his Emu SP-1200,[256] a sampler released in 1987.[257] By the time Shadow had saved enough money to buy a sampler of his own, he was told by Stretch Armstrong aka Adrian Bartos, that he should look in to the

---

[246] Wilder, E 2017 p. 55
[247] Discogs 2019v
[248] Discogs 2019ff
[249] Discogs 2019qqq
[250] Wilder, E 2017, p. 47
[251] AllMusic.com 2019a
[252] Discogs 2019ee
[253] DJShadow.com n.d. c
[254] Kellman, A 2019
[255] DJShadow.com n.d. c
[256] Rule, G 1997
[257] Vintage Synth Explorer 2020

Akai MPC-60 mkII,[258] a sampler designed by Roger Lin and released by Akai in 1991 as the follow up to the original MPC-60 released in 1988.[259]

On May 26th, 1992, Shadow became the owner of his first sampler, the Akai MPC-60 mkII. The unit was purchased at Guitar Center on Mission Boulevard, San Francisco for $2,821 including tax,[260] thanks in part to money lent by his Dad,[261] but he also had his friend Paris come with him to better negotiate a discount as he was a regular at the store.[262] He would later tell *Keyboard Magazine* about his excitement for the MPC:

> By the time I got the MPC, I was so ready for something new. I mean, I'd taken the 4-track to the limit, doing everything from putting the tape in on the other side for reverse loops, to everything I could possibly think of, and there was nothing more for me to do with it, and it was really depressing...I was so ready. I'd fantasized about it for so long that when I got it, I took it home and I was shaking and sweating. I stayed up all night reading the manual front to back. I had to use it immediately because I was bursting with all these ideas. The first record I actually made on the MPC was the very first SoleSides record.[263]

But moving from a four track to the MPC wasn't easy, as the MPC could at times be unintuitive. Shadow spent his first night with the MPC learning how to program it. He explained:

> ...it took a long time because I couldn't figure out certain things. The menus were not very intuitive, and there were a lot of limitations to what they could show you and the amount of information they could give you at any one time.

---

[258] Doyle, T 2017
[259] Polynominal, n.d
[260] DJShadow.com 2009a
[261] SLurg, 2006
[262] Wilder, E 2017, p. 61
[263] Rule, G 1997

You had to scroll through menus. There was a lot of referring back and forth to the manual and making little asterisks in the manual. I don't think I went to sleep until about 6am that day because I just really wanted to complete a beat.[264]

After three releases on Hollywood BASIC Shadow was now struggling with getting his music released as the label was on the decline due to Funkenklein's deteriorating health. Shadow was sending work to labels such as Tommy Boy and Profile, but they preferred a more recognisable hip hop sound, and they didn't release any of the music he sent them.[265]

Meanwhile back in England, after repeatedly listening to *Shadow's Legitimate Mix*, curiosity eventually got the better of James Lavelle and in late 1992 he called Albee Ragusa at Tommy Boy and asked if they knew anything about Shadow. Tommy Boy had been trying to work with Shadow for a while but were finding his style didn't suit their sound, so they gave Lavelle Shadow's phone number and told him he seemed a better fit for Mo' Wax.[266] Calling out of the blue in November 1992,[267] Lavelle and Shadow immediately bonded, talking for hours about records, labels, and movies they each enjoyed. In fact, Shadow already knew who Lavelle was thanks to his interest in British music magazines such as *NME* and *Melody Maker*, where Lavelle occasionally popped up.[268] Lavelle took the opportunity to tell Shadow to keep doing his own thing, and asked for something to put out on Mo' Wax.[269]

Lavelle and Shadow then met in person in 1993, with Shadow introducing Lavelle to the sounds of David Axelrod as they drove around LA,[270] before Shadow joined Lavelle on a Mo' Wax

---

[264] Doyle, T 2017
[265] Ma, D 2017, pp. 76-77
[266] Aubrey, E 2017b
[267] Ma, D 2017, p. 74
[268] SLurg, 2006
[269] Ma, D 2017, p. 77
[270] Wilder, E 2017, p. 61

European tour in November,[271] playing in Germany[272] and then joining Lavelle as a guest of That's How It Is at Bar Rumba in England.[273]

Lavelle had also continued to encourage Shadow to submit something to Mo' Wax, and he was eventually sent the track *In/Flux / Hindsight*.[274] But prior to the release of *In/Flux*, Shadow released another solo track as DJ Shadow & The Groove Robbers in February 1993, entitled *Entropy*.[275] This was still a solo record, with the Groove Robbers being a reference to Shadow's two turntables.[276]

Entropy marked the first release on Solesides, an independent label set up in 1991 by Blackalicious (Chief Xcel & Gift of Gab), Lyrics Born, Lateef the Truthspeaker, and DJ Shadow,[277] with assistance from DJ Zen.[278] *Entropy* featured *Send Them* by Lyrics Born on the B-side, known as Asia Born at the time,[279] and while the release attracted little notice in America at the time[280] (with one of the few reviews coming from *Spin Magazine* in December 1994)[281] it was later considered an underground classic.[282]

In/Flux / Hindsight was released by Mo' Wax in November 1993 under the moniker DJ Shadow & The Groove Robbers,[283] and had been recorded across the Spring and Summer of 1993[284] at Dan The Automator's studio.[285] The Automator, aka Daniel M.

---

[271] unkle98 2019
[272] Wilder, E 2017, p. 61
[273] Swift, I 2013
[274] Wilder, E 2017, p. 60
[275] Discogs 2019m
[276] Kirwin, P 2003
[277] HipHopCrack, nd
[278] Chennault, S 2005
[279] Discogs 2019m
[280] Fine, J 1997, p. 61
[281] Aaron, C 1994, p. 110
[282] Reeves, M 1999
[283] Cooper, D 2014
[284] Discogs 2019l
[285] Wilder, E 2017 p. 60

Nakamura, had a home studio in his parent's attic[286] which was known as The Glue Factory,[287] and had invited Shadow to use it after meeting and realising they had a mutual love of hip hop, with *In/Flux* being the first thing Shadow recorded there.[288]

In 1993 when Lavelle had first received *In/Flux* from DJ Shadow he played it to people at Mo' Wax and they were confused by how Lavelle was going to market an instrumental record. Lavelle made sure the right DJ's played it and soon the press took off[289] with *Melody Maker* calling it "the most delicious sound of the week, a colossal feast tipped straight in to the open mind."[290] While *NME* enthused that it was "undoubtedly one of the musical highlights of a confused but eclectic 1993."[291]

Both *In/Flux* and it's B-side *Hindsight* were sample heavy explorations different from what hip hop fans were used to hearing, but Shadow was not alone in his sonic explorations with DJ Krush soon releasing his own record on Mo' Wax which featured a similar sample-based style.[292] These releases would serve as hints of a new sound which Mo' Wax would be at the forefront of, and there was still more to come.

---

[286] Wilder, E 2017, p. 78
[287] Doyle, T 2017
[288] Wilder, E 2017, p. 60
[289] The Mo'Wax Vaults: Extended interview with James Lavelle and DJ Shadow 2018, 00:26:35
[290] Parkes, T 1993
[291] NME, 1994
[292] Sutherland, A 1994, p. 32

Trip Hop

Trip hop as a term has not always been popular, with many of the acts associated with the trip hop sound unimpressed by it,[293] while music fans have likewise found themselves arguing over what is and isn't trip hop, and what exactly makes someone trip hop anyway.[294] While people will argue over whether a descriptive term is really a genre, or just pigeonholing by the press, in their 1995 article on acid jazz, *Fly* described the use of terms like trip hop as a "necessary evil" that helps sell records and "in turn keeps musicians afloat."[295] Regardless, trip hop as a term has stuck around and is still applied to music today, generally to describe slower hip hop songs.[296] But where did this hip hop inspired genre spring up from?

Hip hop began in the United States of America, specifically New York City during the 1970's and as a culture it came to comprise of four main elements: DJ, MC (Rapping), Graffiti and Breakdance.[297] Some of the originators and founders of hip hop included DJ Kool Herc who introduced the Jamaican sound systems to parties in America, as well as DJs such as Grandmaster Flash who used two turntables to seamlessly extend the instrumental breaks on a record which created the breakbeat, and Afrika Bambaataa[298] who's 1982 single *Planet Rock* would include samples from Kraftwerk[299] mixed with Roland TR-808 Drum Machines.[300]

In England new sounds were also brewing in the 1970's with punk becoming a subculture of its own thanks to the popularity of groups such as The Sex Pistols and The Clash. But while punk was still developing there weren't many Punk records for DJ's to play so they

---

[293] Reynolds, S 1994c
[294] Zen <solesides@aol.com> 1996
[295] Phenian, 1995
[296] Twells, J and Fintoni, L 2015
[297] Tate, G and Light, A, 2019
[298] Ibid.
[299] Reighley, K 1999 p. 72
[300] Anderson, J 2008

began playing dub reggae instead.[301] Punk groups were also reggae influenced, with The Clash featuring a cover of a reggae song, *Police and Thieves*, on their 1977 self-titled debut album and former Sex Pistols frontman John Lydon's group Public Image Ltd. featured a noticeable dub influenced sound. With punks listening to reggae they started going to Jamaican sound system parties as well as their own punk shows.[302]

Sound systems had become popular in Jamaica during the 1950's with the idea being that instead of hiring a large band to play at your event you have a DJ play records instead.[303] The records played included styles such as ska, rock steady, reggae, dancehall, and dub.[304] Dub music is often bass heavy in nature, and strips reggae back to its essence, and dub mixes were created as an early form of remix where artists such as King Tubby, Scientist, and Lee Perry began adding reverb, delay and other effects[305] to give dub its own trippy soundscape like sound.[306] Another element of the sound system was toasting, or MCing, where the DJ would rhyme and hype up the crowd, in what is seen as a natural precursor to rap.[307] Sound system culture found its way to England in the 1970's[308] and gained popularity with several sound systems set up[309] and competing across the UK.[310]

At the time American hip hop had also entered the British Music Charts, with the Sugarhill Gang's *Rapper's Delight* reaching #3 in the UK Singles Chart in December 1979,[311] and The Rock Steady Crew peaking at #6 in the charts with their single *(Hey You) The Rock Steady Crew*, which became the 50th Best Selling Single

---

[301] Howe, R 2019
[302] Ibid.
[303] BBC, n.d. c
[304] Ibid.
[305] BBC, n.d. b
[306] BBC, n.d. a
[307] BBC, n.d. d
[308] Dagnini, J 2010
[309] NME 1981
[310] Fearon, R 1981
[311] May, C 2015

release of 1983.[312] For many people their introduction to hip hop in Britain wasn't until 1982 and 1983 when British artists began releasing their own take on the genre such as Malcolm McLaren's *Buffalo Gals* and DJ Newtrament's *London Bridge Is Falling Down*[313] the latter of which is considered to be the "first authentic British hip hop tune."[314]

1983 also brought the first *Street Sounds Electro* compilation, released on 12" record and cassette by the Street Sounds record label,[315] featuring an assortment of hip hop infused tracks licensed from America.[316] The *Electro* series would extend for 22 volumes,[317] lasting until 1988,[318] and electro as a genre had now taken off in the UK[319] with its robotic sound described in 1984 as a fusion of "street funk and hip-hop mixed with influences from British synthesizer groups, Latin music and Jazz fusion - all thrown into the robot dancing, breaking and moonwalking meltdown."[320]

Meanwhile in 1982, Grant Marshall became resident DJ at The Dug Out,[321] a club in Bristol often described as a melting pot of cultures where DJs played various genres such as punk, soul, hip hop, reggae, funk, and jazz,[322] and the crowds were built up of "Punks, Soul boys and girls, Rastas, Afro-Caribbeans, students and 'Clifton trendies'; artists and musicians."[323] In 1983 Grant Marshall was joined by The Wild Bunch,[324] a sound system generally credited for birthing what was termed the Bristol sound, and in particular they became famous for the parties held in the Bristol neighbourhood of

---

[312] Wikipedia 2020
[313] May, C 2015
[314] Dabydeen, D, Gilmore, J, & Jones, C 2007, p. 549
[315] Discogs 2019nnn
[316] Titmus, S 2013
[317] Street Sounds, 2015
[318] Discogs 2019ooo
[319] Toop, D 1984, p. 40
[320] Ibid. p. 48
[321] Webb, P 2007, p. 39
[322] Murray, R 2018
[323] Dubplate To Dubstep, n.d.
[324] Pride, D 1995 p. 80

St. Pauls.[325] Influenced by the Jamacian sound system culture, the group played an assortment of genres including punk,[326] hip hop, reggae, funk, rap and R&B.[327] The group was founded by Miles Johnson (DJ Milo) but grew to include Nellee Hooper, Grant Marshall (Daddy G), Claude Williams (Wille Wee), Robert Del Naja (3D), and Andrew Vowles (Mushroom). Other collaborators included Adrian Thaws (Tricky), though reportedly their members effectively included anyone "who could be trusted to distribute flyers or sell a few cans of lager."[328]

The group released two singles, *Tearin Down The Avenue* in 1987 and *Friends And Countrymen* in 1988, the latter of which was described by James Lavelle as "The record that started it all... This is the blueprint of British sound system soul."[329]

By 1988 The Wild Bunch had broken up, Nellee Hooper began producing Soul II Soul, DJ Milo had moved to Japan to work with Major Force, and Daddy G, 3D, and Mushroom formed Massive Attack, releasing *Any Love* in 1988, featuring co-production from Smith & Mighty.[330]

By the late 1980's hip hop had gone mainstream in the UK with the Beastie Boys album *Licensed To Ill* bringing hip hop back in to the British music album charts,[331] and artists such as Public Enemy,[332] Beastie Boys and Run DMC extended their tours in to the UK, giving British fans a chance to experience hip hop live.[333] British hip hop likewise continued to strive with many local artists making the mainstream charts, but they rarely made the cultural impact that many of their American contemporaries would.[334] Two

---

[325] British Council, n.d.
[326] Dubplate To Dubstep, n.d.
[327] British Council, n.d.
[328] Red Lines, n.d.
[329] Dummy, 2015
[330] Dubplate To Dubstep, n.d.
[331] Official UK Charts Company 2019f
[332] Mccray, JL 2013
[333] Phillips, M 2017
[334] Love, L 2018

documentaries were created in 1987 focusing on British hip hop and the respective scene, Tim Westwood's BBC documentary *Bad Meaning Good*,[335] and Channel Four's *Bombin'* which featured The Wild Bunch's 3D.[336] But while hip hop was going mainstream other new genres were popping up in the UK as well.

In 1987 the Acid Jazz record label was formed by Giles Peterson and Eddie Piller.[337] Peterson had also been part of BGP Records[338] which released a series of compilations entitled *Acid Jazz* which collected old jazz and funk songs.[339] Acid jazz soon became considered a genre in its own right, through it was never truly defined, and in the liner notes from *Acid Jazz Vol. 2* Chris Bangs states, "When you've finished listening to this album, you probably still won't be sure what Acid Jazz really is. That's exactly what Acid Jazz is all about. It's new music, old music, it's esoteric music."[340]

By the early 1990's the name acid jazz had become the buzzword for a scene made up of new music by bands such as Brand New Heavies, Galliano, and The Young Disciples, but artists and fans continued to argue over what acid jazz really was, and if it was a genre at all.[341] Early Mo' Wax releases were considered part of the acid jazz scene[342] before they became more hip hop focused,[343] and Lavelle began describing these as "progressive electro"[344] and "abstract musical science."[345]

In 1993 a new British sound had reached America bearing the electro name, with *Billboard* reporting that electro is "one name for a multifaceted scene that many in the British music business are

---

[335] BBC 2019
[336] Spray Daily 2014
[337] Acid Jazz 2018
[338] Ace Records 2019
[339] Discogs 2019fff
[340] Discogs 2020h
[341] Phenian, 1995
[342] Twells, J and Fintoni, L 2015
[343] Davis, E 1996, pp. 72-74
[344] Discogs 2019l
[345] Discogs 2019n

busting to define."[346] Some of the suggested definitions include "jazz but not jazz" and "street soul", but *Billboard* explained it was "the mutant child of what used to be called rare groove, 70's funk, and acid jazz."

Electro groups began to enter the charts in the UK, with Gabrielle's *Dreams* hitting the #1 spot in 1993, where it stayed for three weeks and remained in the charts for a total of fifteen.[347] Another big hit for the scene was Jamiroquai, who in 1992 reached #52 in the charts with *When Your Gonna Learn* released by Acid Jazz.[348] He then signed to Sony and his debut album *Emergency on Planet Earth* reached #1.[349] This eclectic melting pot of styles led many to doubt electro would have any success in America, with Paul Bradshaw explaining to *Billboard* in 1993, "America doesn't understand what's going on at all."[350] As an example, they highlighted how The Brand New Heavies had their album's American release delayed by fifteen months, by which time the lead singer had left the band.[351] *The Guardian* further theorised that America's lack of understanding stemmed from the fact Britain's distinctive take on hip hop was "so thoroughly mutated that they're unrecognisable to American hip-hop audiences."[352] Notably in an interview with *Dazed & Confused* in 1994, 3D admitted Massive Attack's *Blue Lines* album, widely heralded in UK, had not done well at all in America.[353]

Massive Attack's *Blue Lines* was followed by more albums featuring similar downtempo beats such as Björk's 1993 *Debut*, produced by Nellee Hooper, and Portishead's *Dummy* released in 1994. To the British press by now it was clear a new sound had evolved in England, and in June 1994 an article in the British magazine

---

[346] Goldman, V 1993, p. 1
[347] Official UK Charts Company 2019d
[348] Official UK Charts Company 2019e
[349] Official UK Charts Company 2019c
[350] Goldman, V 1993, p. 74
[351] Ibid.
[352] Reynolds, S 1994c
[353] Leedham, R 1994, p. 47

Mixmag suggested a new term to describe the sound, trip hop. Describing the genre as:

> Slow and crunching hip-hop beats, no vocals, just strange swirling noises over the top...a deft fusion of head-nodding beats, supa-phat bass and an obsessive attention to the kind of otherworldly sounds usually found on acid house records. It comes from the suburbs, not the streets, and with no vocals you don't need to be American to make it sound convincing.[354]

While the record *Mixmag* held up as the pinnacle example of trip hop, DJ Shadows' *In/Flux*, was technically created by an American, the point the article tried to get across was that British hip hop had suffered in comparison to the sounds coming from America, and trip hop was the answer.

At the time in the 1990's British hip hop wasn't respected, with Lavelle explaining "British Hip-hop lacks the lyrical skills of US counterparts, but British kids have got the musical side. They know about records. That's the step forward. Now they can do their own style, they don't have to copy anything."[355]

But while fans ate up the music, the artists weren't impressed with being slapped with the trip hop name, as it lumped together artists such as DJ Shadow, Massive Attack, Tricky, Portishead, Björk and even The Chemical Brothers. Lavelle has spoken out on the term several times when pressed in interviews, stating in 1998:

> The whole trip hop thing was odd. It was great to receive attention for what we were doing, but the term was horrific. Neither the bands on the label or myself had really decided what we were doing and we got put into the same category as people who weren't really on the same course as us. We'd always get mentioned along with the Chemical

---
[354] Pemberton, A 1994
[355] Ibid.

Brothers and the whole big beat scene. I'm sure they were equally upset about being compared with a mellow hip-hop label![356]

DJ Shadow also had an opinion on trip hop, telling *Spine Magazine* in early 1995:

> What I can't stand - and find most difficult about being on Mo'Wax - is that in America almost any kind of new music that comes out of Britain is considered 'acid jazz'. Jungle is considered acid jazz. The type of records I do back home are considered as following in the lineage of acid jazz. I didn't even know what acid jazz was 'til James (Lavelle) called me before the release of *'Influx'*. I don't know what that is... I don't know what 'ambient' is... I wasn't even influenced by dub. If you're into hip-hop it's hard enough keeping up with the latest shit without having to buy all this other stuff. A lot of people I'm down with know that what I do is my interpretation of hip-hop, it's not my interpretation of 'ambient-meets-hip-hop-meets-techno'…But anyway this whole trip hop thing is just dumb.[357]

The term trip hop wasn't the first time someone had tried to place a new label on this style, with other examples including "Ambient Hip-Hop"[358] and "The Bristol Sound"[359] originating from journalists trying to contextualise Massive Attack and those that had also come from or been influenced by Bristol such as Nellee Hooper, Tricky and Portishead.

Massive Attack's 3D has given the most relaxed attitude to the term, telling *Melody Maker* in 1994 "If you're doing anything in music, you've got to have some kind of category so that people can get a handle on you. It's like helping people find what they want."[360]

---

[356] Thatcher, D & Lavelle, J 1998, p. 66
[357] Spine Magazine n.d. c
[358] Reynolds, S 1994c
[359] Pride, D 1995, p. 1
[360] Reynolds, S 1994a

The Time Has Come

June 1994 saw the first release by UNKLE, at the time stylised as *U.N.K.L.E.* and featuring James Lavelle, Tim Goldsworthy, Masayuki Kudo and Nakanishi Toshio as members. Released on both Mo' Wax and Major Force as *Mo Wax Vs. Major Force : Time Has Come*, the 12" EP contained two tracks, Major Force vs. UNKLE *The Time Has Come*, and Howie B. vs. Major Force *Martian Economics [unified planet theory]*.[361]

Previously UNKLE were primarily a remix or production outfit, with only Lavelle and Goldsworthy appearing on the credits of UNKLE and Men From UNKLE releases. Lavelle would bring in ideas and samples, while Goldsworthy would put everything together and make the actual music,[362] with UNKLE being Lavelle's way of getting the records he wanted to hear made by bringing people together who had the skills to realise his ideas.[363] Kudo and Toshi had moved to London in 1992 as a means of exploring new sounds and recording an album as Love TKO,[364] which became the album *Head Hunter,* released in 1994 and featuring co-production by Howie B.[365]

At this time James Lavelle was moving his Mo' Wax offices to a new building and offered a space for Kudo and Toshi, giving them a studio and forging a new partnership, Major Force West,[366] a record label run by Kudo and Toshi from the Mo' Wax office which put out a handful of releases in 1994, each featuring hand drawn artwork by Toshi.[367] The label released the *Head Hunter* album, as well as EP's by Love TKO, Howie B, and Major Force vs. UNKLE's *Time Has Come*.

---

[361] Discogs 2019jjj
[362] Lazarus, D 1995, p. 69
[363] Ma, D 2017, p. 75
[364] Takayama, Y 2013
[365] Discogs 2019x
[366] Takayama, Y 2013
[367] Mo' Wax Discography 2011d

The Time Has Come was largely built around a sample of Sun Ra's *Twin Stars of Thencei,* from his album *Lanquidity*, recorded and released in 1978 on Philly Jazz.[368] Vocal samples from a 1967 soundtrack by Dr. Timothy Leary for the documentary film *Turn On, Tune In, Drop Out*[369] are inserted across the track, beginning with "Are you ready to die, and be reborn?", screams for help, and the source of the title "The time has come." Lavelle described the recording as stemming from "a session in the studio for a day just mucking around", after he'd convinced Kudo to let him come into his studio.[370]

David Toop, reviewing *The Time Has Come* for *The Times London*, called the track "like music heard through a dream" and concluded "Reviews so far have emphasised what it is not. What it is, nobody knows".[371]

In 1995 *Dazed & Confused* magazine asked Tim Goldsworthy about the use of "astro, weirdo, boingy noises" that feature in UNKLE's songs and Goldsworthy explained:

> When you're listening to the tunes, sitting on the window ledge, looking out on the world with a spliff and a cup of coffee, mad noises can add a new dimension, an unmusical dimension which adds something to the entire thing. Looking for sounds can become an obsession. For example the other day my girlfriend Samantha was in bed with a slightly blocked up nose and she was snoring but she was doing this really full on banging beat. I just had to get to work.[372]

The Time Has Come B-side, *Martian Economics [unified planet theory]l,* was provided by Howie B and described by *The Wire* as "a

---

[368] Sun Ra 2014
[369] Discogs 2019o
[370] UNKLE 1998, 00:06:55
[371] Toop, D 1995
[372] Lazarus, D 1995, p. 69

wacked-out, Sun Ra-meets-The Orb affair they knocked up in five hours,"[373] and which Howie described as "like me doing a tune with Jimmy Smith, even though he wasn't there."[374] He explained the release of the track, saying "We took it to James Lavelle and said "what do you think?'. Five weeks later I was in a club and I heard it, thought "Fuck, what's going on?!" James'd released it without telling us!"[375]

Howie, Toshi and Kudo would continue their collaboration as Skylab, recording and releasing *Skylab#1* in late 1994, with the *Seashell* 12" preceding it, releasing on July 1994.[376] In his review of *Skylab#1 The Times'* David Toop again likened this release to music heard through a dream, asking "How many more remarkable albums can be released before the end of the year?"[377]

While Nakanishi Toshio created the visual style for Major Force West's record covers, James Lavelle was also looking for new visual ideas and collaborators on Mo' Wax. The first twenty releases on Mo' Wax featured the familiar obi strip design, but then for the twenty first release, Deep Joy's *Make Some Sense of This*, the cover featured a colourful Mo' Wax logo as its artwork, which then featured across the next two releases in slight variations.[378]

These were followed by DJ Shadow & DJ Krush's split release *Lost and Found (S.F.L) / Kemuri*, and DJ Krush's album *Strictly Turntablized*. These last two releases not only epitomized the new Mo' Wax sound, but also showcase a new visual style for Mo' Wax introducing people to the work of graffiti artist Leonard Hilton McGurr, better known at the time by his graffiti tag Futura2000, and later simply as Futura. Futura and Lavelle met while they were both in Berlin in 1993 while Lavelle was performing at triebWerk as part of a Mo' Wax party on August 27th, and Futura was taking part in

---

[373] Reynolds, S 1996 p. 26
[374] Ibid. p. 27
[375] Ibid. p. 26
[376] Discogs 2019ii
[377] Toop, D 1994
[378] Mo' Wax Discography 2011c

the first Cycle Messenger World Championships where he raced and took part in a live art performance with Stash.[379] The Championship was held in Berlin from August 27-29, with Futura reportedly placing 82nd out of 400 in one of the events.[380] Lavelle was already a fan of Futura's work, and they had a mutual friend in artists Stash and Eric Haze.[381] Lavelle introduced himself to Futura[382] and asked if he had any paintings Lavelle could buy to use as album artwork,[383] and Lavelle later visited Futura in his Brooklyn studio. He would discuss their meeting to *Graphotism* in 2000:

> I went to his studio and, from then on, it was pretty quick. I bought paintings used for the original DJ Krush covers. The first sleeve I bought was used on DJ Shadow's and Krush's split record, *Lost & Found / Kemuri*, and then the UNKLE sleeve for *Time Has Come*...I don't get him to design specific things. I go and look at his work and then choose things because I prefer to have that choice. I'm very picky about what I want, so I found that if you commission people it's sometimes not as good as when you have an opportunity to look through a selection of work. So most of Mo' Wax covers have been paintings he's just done or what he's doing the time. I'd have a specific thing in mind for what I'd want on the cover, and you'd either see it or you wouldn't.[384]

Futura was not new to the world of music, having toured with The Clash in 1981, and he had even released a 12" of his own *The Escapade of Futura 2000*. In 1982 he joined Afrika Bambaata, Rammellzee, the Rock Steady Crew, and Fab Five Freddie on the The New York City Rap Tour in Paris, where he performed[385] and

---

[379] Messenger 2011
[380] McLean, C 1998, p. 65
[381] Cooper, D 2013c
[382] Bradshaw, P 2014a
[383] Cooper, D 2013c
[384] Graphotism 2000
[385] Le Républicain Lorrain, 2019

painted on stage,[386] and also met his future wife.[387] He also supplied artwork for several vinyl releases in the early 1980's for artists such as Fab Five Freddie and Cabaret Voltaire.[388] By the mid-80's he had settled down somewhat and moved away from graffiti to became a bike messenger while also working various jobs to support his family.[389] During this period Futura was still exhibiting artworks[390] but in his own words had "basically just abandoned the whole art world"[391] but began returning to art seriously once more after teaming with James Lavelle. In 1994 Mo' Wax began releasing records featuring artwork by Futura, which introduced the artist to a new audience as well as future collaborators.[392]

Their first collaboration, the split release of DJ Shadow and DJ Krush – *Lost and Found (S.F.L.) / Kemuri*,[393] was released in September 1994,[394] and also served as the first Mo' Wax release worked on by Ben Drury, who had joined Mo' Wax as their new Art Director, sitting alongside Will Bankhead and Swifty on the graphic design team.[395]

This was followed in December by UNKLE's *The Time Has Come EP*, a remixed version of the previous Mo' Wax v.s. Major Force 12". This new 12" featured a fresh rendition of *The Time Has Come* by UNKLE entitled, *If You Find Earth Boring (UNKLE Mix)*, which opens with an answering machine message from Shadow rapping.[396] Lavelle had asked Shadow to come in and work on a remix for the track, serving as the first time Lavelle and Shadow would appear together under the UNKLE name,[397] though

---

[386] Schwartzberg, L 2015
[387] Bird, G 1996, p. 6
[388] Discogs 2019p
[389] Spine Magazine 2002?
[390] Artnet, 2019a
[391] Spine Magazine 2002?
[392] Ibid.
[393] Graphotism 2000
[394] Discogs 2019n
[395] Discogs 2019b
[396] Discogs 2019rr
[397] Ma, D 2017, p. 75

The new EP was subtitled "A tribute to Sun-Ra and all things fucked up" and took its song title of *If You Find Earth Boring* from Sun Ra's *Outer Spaceways Incorporated* where "If You Find Earth Boring…" is part of the repeated lyrics.[398] Alongside the UNKLE remix, the EP featured remixes and reinterpretations by Adrian Utley of Portishead, Howie B, and two by Plaid.[399]

The artwork was another piece created by Futura, but unlike the previous abstract graffiti styles, *The Time Has Come* featured his pointmen characters which would continue to be utilised as the logo for future UNKLE projects. Lavelle had first spotted the pointmen when visiting Futura's studio after their meeting in Berlin. Futura described their meeting:

> So we met in Brooklyn, he comes in to my studio and I had a painting on the wall that was one character. They've been called Pointmen, just because their heads are pointed, that was a subtle shout out to HR Giger, who was a bit of an influence on me. So James goes, 'Who's that little bloke over there?'…I thought a bloke was a guy, a man. So I said, 'I don't know what you're talking about', so he said, 'Oh, the little bloke with the ears' and I realised he was talking about my character and it just made me laugh. It was funny how my guys were my guys but nobody really ever looked at them. So the artwork had been there…but it was really James who embraced them. They went on to symbolise, initially, U.N.K.L.E.—and...they just appropriated those characters as an identity.[400]

Their collaboration would continue, and in 1995 Futura travelled to London to work on paintings at the Mo' Wax offices, with Lavelle picking out the ones he wanted for future releases.[401]

---

[398] Burega, G-M 2014
[399] Discogs 2019rr
[400] Donners, B 2018
[401] Graphotism 1995, p. 4

Mo' Wax Expanded

In 1993 Mo' Wax was losing money[402] but had been able to stay afloat thanks to an international distribution deal in Japan, worth £25,000.[403] London Records had offered James Lavelle a £25,000 licensing deal, but he turned it down,[404] and it wasn't until March 1994 that the label turned their first profit, with the release of Federation's album *Flower to the Sun*,[405] released March 30, 1994.[406] This was followed by the *Headz* compilation in November 1994,[407] which sold 40,000 copies by the end of 1996[408] making Mo' Wax a £20,000 profit, close to the amount of money Lavelle had turned down from London Records.[409]

The *Headz* compilation was spread across three 12" records, and would be followed later by an even larger sequel.[410] Both instalments contained tracks by artists such as Attica Blues, Nightmares On Wax, Le Funk Mob, Autechre, DJ Shadow, and Howie B, combing Mo' Wax artists with licensed tracks from other labels Lavelle admired.[411]

Headz signalled a new direction for Mo' Wax as a label, as it stepped away from the acid jazz sounds that defined the label, and *Melody Maker* called it "Arguably the most radical redefinition of hip-hop since De La Soul's birth of the Daisy Age".[412] *Headz* is the release Lavelle would credit for putting Mo' Wax on the map,[413] and at the time Radiohead's Thom told *NME* the album was a favourite

---

[402] Passey, M 1996, 00:21:00
[403] McLean, C 1995b, p. 156
[404] Halasa, M 1996, p. 15
[405] Mark, O 1998
[406] AllMusic.com 2019b
[407] The Guardian 1994, p. 45
[408] Halasa, M 1996, p. 15
[409] McLean, C 1995b, p. 155
[410] Hermes, W 1997, p. 160
[411] Yellow Peril, 1995
[412] Bush, C 1994, p. 37
[413] Long Live Vinyl 2017

of his, which made Lavelle consider a future collaboration with the band.[414]

Lavelle's lack of business focus led to the release of another Mo' Wax's compilation, *Royaltie$ Overdue*, so named because the label had run out of money to pay their artists.[415] The album served as an overview of the label and their various acts at that point in mid-1994, and while it spent five weeks in the UK Compilation Charts[416] it also received very mixed reviews,[417] with *Melody Maker* commenting "the Mo Wax roster is evenly divided between the brilliant and the bland."[418]

In 1994 Lavelle was moving Mo' Wax away from the labels acid jazz roots and was looking towards finding its own niche, or as he explained at the time, "Mo' Wax isn't the label that puts out the biggest records, it's the label with the fattest concepts."[419] Some of those concepts included a follow up to Headz and *Mo' Wax Vs Grand Royal*, a compilation featuring artists from Lavelle's Mo' Wax and the Beastie Boys Mike D's record label Grand Royal.[420] But beyond music Lavelle also planned to expand in to publishing books on graffiti, art gallery shows, a range of clothes, videos, films, soundtracks, a magazine and CD-ROMs.[421] [422] In terms of the future sound of Mo' Wax, Lavelle explained at the time, "I think when people see the next load of records come out, people will see it's changing."[423] Some of these releases included La Funk Mob, DJ Shadow, and DJ Krush, with Mo' Wax showing it was leaving acid jazz behind as the label embraced a greater hip hop influence.

Lavelle discussed the differing sounds of Mo' Wax in early 1994:

---

[414] Burgess, J 1998, p. 60
[415] The Mo'Wax Vaults: The Lost Men from Unkle 2018, 00:03:50
[416] Official UK Charts Company 2019h
[417] Penman, I 1994, p. 66
[418] Reynolds, S 1994b
[419] Crysell, A 1994, p. 53
[420] Diamond, M 1995
[421] Crysell, A 1994, p. 53
[422] Gray, L 1994, p. 32
[423] Crysell, A 1994, p. 53

> We've got two sides to the label. There's the live jazz thing which is basically soul, funk and jazz orientated music - bands like Federation, Step, Mistura and to an extent, Palm Skin, which fits into the normal acid jazz criteria. And then we've got a progressive, head music sound which is DJ Shadow, Attica Blues, Revolution Per Minute, Men From Unkle and various things that are coming soon.[424]

Further to this distinction was Lavelle's plan not to just emulate labels such as Hollywood BASIC with their international hip hop aesthetic,[425] but to include a wider range of genres as well,[426] with hopes to include techno, jazz, abstract hip hop, as well as a rock / hip hop band in the future.[427] Lavelle explained that last point in further detail in 1994, "We are gonna launch a mad hip-hop/thrash fused band, a young Beastie Boys kind of thing. I'm into the total energy of the Beasties and that whole kind of skate thing. I want that energy and total madness surrounding the whole idea."[428]

By the end of 1994 Mo' Wax had also started entering the charts, with DJ Shadow and DJ Krush's *Lost and Found (S.F.L.) / Kemuri* split release entering the UK Top 100 Singles Chart in October where it spent a week at #84. This was just a taste though of what was to come, with DJ Shadow's *What Does Your Soul Look Like* entering the Singles Top 100 at #59 on 25th March 1995, before dropping to #97 in its second week, and then out of the charts. While UNKLE's *The Time Has Come* EP was the first Mo' Wax release to enter the Album Charts on January 21st 1995, spending one week at #73 before dropping out again.[429] At the time Lavelle noted now that UNKLE had reached the charts he felt an immense pressure for the next UNKLE release to live up to expectations. *The Time*

---

[424] Harris, D 1994
[425] Ma, D 2017, p 78
[426] Gray, L 1994, p. 32
[427] Waterman, R 1994
[428] Ibid.
[429] Official UK Charts Company 2019l

Has Come was recorded in two days, [430] and Lavelle felt that UNKLE had previously been more of a fun, spontaneous, "it'll just be a laugh, we'll go and see what happens"[431] type of project between Tim Goldsworthy and himself. But now Lavelle felt he had to take UNKLE more seriously.[432]

But at the time Lavelle's main focus was on Mo' Wax and in 1995 Lavelle had big plans, explaining:

> We're one of the biggest independent labels...Most people on that scene will sell 4,000 records, whereas we'll sell 10-12,000. Which means that I know we've gone beyond the trainspotting thing. There's the real underground market, then there's your market that us and Warp have got. Then you've got that market where people buy Björk and Massive Attack and Portishead. That's the next market you've got to get into.[433]

Lavelle was at a crossroads with Mo' Wax Records, and the major labels were starting to steal his acts. Groups that had been released on Mo' Wax via licensing agreements were now getting snatched up before Lavelle could sign them himself. Or worse, groups that he had hoped to sign were being wooed to the major labels because Mo' Wax couldn't offer as much money. Two of those better-known acts were Portishead and Tricky.[434] Lavelle had approached Portishead about releasing their single *Sour Times* as a 12", with the intention of having it released jointly through Massive Attack's Wild Style and Lavelle's own Mo' Wax. While this didn't occur, it did lead to Lavelle meeting 3D in person which led to future collaborations.[435] Portishead's *Sour Times* was released in 1994 by Go! Discs, and would reach #13 on the UK Singles Charts spending

---

[430] Passey, M 1996, 00:56:00
[431] UNKLE 1998, 00:09:00
[432] Passey, M 1996, 00:56:00
[433] McLean, C 1995a, p. 106
[434] Thompson, B 1995
[435] Lavelle, J 2019, 00:44:45

a total 8 weeks in the charts.[436] While Tricky's debut 12" *Aftermath* had its records pressed by Mo' Wax before the deal fell through,[437] eventually being released by 4TH & BROADWAY it would reach #69 in the UK charts and stay in the Top 100 for two weeks.[438]

To counter this, Lavelle had begun talks with London Records to start a new sub-label for them called S.F.T., or Smoke-Filled Thoughts.[439] Steve Finan, who had started managing Lavelle as an artist, laughed when he saw the deal with London, telling Lavelle it was ridiculous to start a new label that would eat in to what he was doing with Mo' Wax.[440] Instead Finan introduced Lavelle to three major label execs from Deconstruction, Virgin, and A&M, who each made offers for Lavelle and Mo' Wax to join them. The deals from A&M and Virgin were similar and Lavelle was leaning towards Virgin, due to their connection with Massive Attack,[441] and in November 1994 *New Statesman & Society* made the announcement that Lavelle had signed a deal with Virgin where he would be starting new record labels for them, both major and independent.[442] This appears to have been premature, as when Steve Finan announced to Lavelle that he was going to work for A&M Lavelle decided he wanted to follow, and so told A&M he would sign with them if they bought him an artwork by Jean-Michel Basquiat.[443] They agreed,[444] and he signed a three year deal to A&M[445] for £350,000,[446] and received Basquiat's 1981 drawing *Untitled (The sky is the limit)*, which features the text "Cowards will get rid of you, the sky is the limit."[447] [448]

---

[436] Official UK Charts Company 2019i
[437] Metaxas, N 2014, 00:11:00
[438] Official UK Charts Company 2019k
[439] Rose, C 1999 p. 147
[440] Rose, C 1999 p. 147 (IBID)
[441] Bradshaw, P 2014a
[442] Gray, L 1994, p. 33
[443] Williams, E 2017
[444] Ibid.
[445] Farsides, T 1998
[446] Horan, T 1999
[447] Bradshaw, P 2013, p. 129
[448] Artnet, 2019b

Finan then began to manage the business side of Mo' Wax,[449] and became a 50% owner of the label,[450] split with Lavelle as co-owners.[451] Reassuring the press that Mo' Wax wouldn't change, Lavelle told *The Independent,* "We are still independent in practice...I still sign all the acts, we distribute and market ourselves and design all our own packaging."[452]

The deal with A&M brought in larger budgets so Lavelle was now able to sign and release a broader range of acts such as Money Mark, Andrea Parker,[453] and Dr Octagon, a hip hop project from Dan The Automator and Kool Keith.[454] Lavelle stated after the deal that Mo' Wax likely would have gone bankrupt if they hadn't signed with a major,[455] but he would also later describe signing to A&M as "the worst decision I ever made".[456]

At the time, James Lavelle wasn't interested in the business side of the label, which meant Mo' Wax often lost money,[457] but with Finan taking over the business side Lavelle was now free to focus on other interests.[458] In 1996, Ashley Newton, the Virgin Records Deputy Manager who Lavelle almost signed Mo' Wax with, and who famously signed Massive Attack, had this to say: "Success has changed James. As soon as you plug into a corporate system, there is a certain demand that comes with that."[459]

Previously, Lavelle would release records it whenever suited him, and if they sold that was great, but if they didn't then they would

---

[449] Wilder, E 2017, p. 66
[450] Companies House 2019
[451] Heimlich, A 1998
[452] Sturges, F 1998, p. 15
[453] Thompson, B 1995
[454] Burgess, J 1996, p. 57
[455] Ibid.
[456] Sturges, F 2014
[457] Passey, M 1996, 00:21:00
[458] *The Man from Mo' Wax* 2018, 00:23:00
[459] Halasa, M 1996, p. 15

move on to the next one.[460] Under A&M though, there was pressure to adhere to a schedule, and for records to sell.[461] Before the deal, Lavelle was also very hands on with the acts he signed, allowing them to call him at all hours[462] and take the time needed to experiment in the studio, but this was not the case so much afterwards.[463] [464] Attica Blues were one of those affected groups who felt they were being pressured in to creating a "radio friendly sound".[465] The group had joined Mo' Wax in 1992 when Lavelle suggested Charlie Dark record something for the label. They would release a handful of EP's between 1994-97 before Mo' Wax released their self-titled debut album. The band would then depart Mo' Wax and sign with Sony / Columbia Records for their next album released in 2000.[466]

Andrea Parker was another artist affected by the A&M deal. While she released two EPs in 1996 after signing with Mo' Wax, the A&M deal reportedly caused her debut album *Kiss My Arp* to be delayed for three years, eventually releasing in 1998.[467]

While the deal with A&M would later be viewed as something which lead to a dip in quality for Mo' Wax,[468] at the time it was seen to have saved Mo' Wax financially.[469] Business was booming, and while Mo' Wax had put out almost 50 releases in 1995, this would jump to over 100 in 1996, counting records, CDs, and promo items.[470] It led to comparisons being made between Lavelle and Virgin Records founder Richard Branson which had begun in 1994 due to Lavelle's age when he had started Mo' Wax,[471] but after the

---

[460] Duyn, E 1996
[461] Cooper, D 2013a
[462] Patterson, S 2007, p. 53
[463] Cooper, D 2013a
[464] *The Man from Mo' Wax* 2018, 00:24:00
[465] Berry, D 2009b
[466] Ibid.
[467] Berry, D 2009a
[468] Sturges, F 2014
[469] Burgess, J 1996, p. 57
[470] jimmyjrg 2020
[471] Rose, C 1994

A&M deal the comparisons became more frequent and Lavelle was less fond of them, in 1996 telling *The Guardian*:

> I don't want to be Richard Branson. Virgin cola is about contributing to a market, I'm about creating something new. Mo'Wax is an attitude that encompasses a whole culture - music, style, design. I want to change the way people perceive commercial and accessible music.[472]

After Mo' Wax's deal with A&M, Lavelle moved Mo' Wax to new offices on Caledonian Road and surrounded himself with new people. He later explained his feelings from the period:

> I felt very lost at the time because I was 18 and everybody else was a lot older. The scene didn't seem to be about young kids, it seemed to be about 28 year olds. I needed to appeal to people my own age. I hooked up with Slam City Skates because I was into all the clothes and I met Will who designs all my sleeves now and he was my age.[473]

It was around this time that Swifty left[474] and Will Bankhead and Ben Drury stepped in as Artistic Directors when they were asked to take over the design of the label, with Drury later recalling the change:

> James encouraged us to source new materials, use special printing processes, develop new packaging solutions and to experiment across the range of formats, his mania for novelty and the profuse output of the label made this both an instructive and intense period and some of these sleeves are among my personal favourites.[475]

---

[472] Halasa, M 1996, p. 15
[473] Burgess, J 1996, p. 57
[474] Cooper, D 2013b
[475] Drury, B 2001

The collaboration between Bankhead and Drury continued for a year until Bankhead left to develop his own work, and Drury remained on as Art Director of Mo' Wax.[476]

The new Mo' Wax offices were soon decorated by Lavelle's *Star Wars* memorabilia,[477] and the Major Force West studios were also moved with Masayuki Kudo and Nakanishi Toshio located in the basement. Kudo later described the studio to *Wax Poetics Japan* as being dark and cold, with a low ceiling, which initially didn't leave a good impression. But he continued working none the less.[478]

---

[476] Drury, B 2001
[477] Burgess, J 1996, p. 56
[478] Takayama, Y 2013

Endtroducing.....

Following the releases of *In/Flux* in 1993, Mo' Wax wanted an album from DJ Shadow. Both 1993's *In/Flux* and 1994's *Lost and Found* 12" singles had been well received by the press and the obvious next step was to release an album. Shadow for his part had been working on one, spending four months on a series of tracks entitled *What Does Your Soul Look Like*,[479] a title Shadow discovered when flipping through an old psychology book and one of the chapters featured that title.[480]

Shadow presented the collection of tracks to James Lavelle as a work in progress to give an idea of how the album was progressing, but Lavelle felt this would do better as an EP and released it as such in June 1994[481] to great acclaim, leading to more high praise from the press for Shadow and Mo' Wax.[482]

What Does Your Soul Look Like would later be re-released in 1995 and enter the UK Singles Top 100 at the #59 spot on March 25th 1995, before dropping to #97 in its second week, and then out of the charts.[483] Meanwhile the release of his album in progress meant that Shadow was forced to start again, and Shadow feared he had "missed the boat" as albums by Portishead were being released which the press positioned as competitors to the sound Shadow had developed.[484]

Shadow decided for his debut album that he wanted to make a statement, with the proposed title *Endtroducing* meant to signify the end of the sound he had been associated with so far. He explained in early 1995:

---

[479] Fader, L 2012
[480] Bright, M 1995, p. 37
[481] Discogs 2019k
[482] Kulkarni, N 1995
[483] Official UK Charts Company 2019n
[484] Bradshaw, P 2014b

> The album's going to be called 'Endtroducing'. Side one's called 'Build' and side two's called 'Destroy'. The last song's called 'The Phoenix', because it's all about destroying the thing that you've created.[485]

The album was also intended as a statement regarding the state of sample-based music in hip hop at the time, he later told *WestWorld*:

> What I was trying to do was push the art of sampling forward because, as I was starting to make mixes in '89 on a four track and got my MPC in '92, all throughout that time frame, the manipulation of samples was becoming more and more intricate and challenging and people were pushing the boundaries.
> Then around '93 and '94, sampling took a turn a little bit to the stylings of what Dr. Dre was doing with adding keyboards over the top and having live instrumentation played over just a couple of samples...By '95, when I was really working on Endtroducing heavily, I was very much trying to make a statement about, "Why are we all abandoning this artform? What everybody else is doing is great, but I feel like there's a lot of work left to be done in this discipline." And I wanted to create a record that pushed that conversation forward. That was then and I've tried to do that through the year at various times still, just sort of be like, "Well this little moment on the record I'm going to try to blow people's minds.[486]

Songs for the album were created from samples discovered while digging for records at Rare Records in Sacramento, a record store which had a basement overflowing with records which the owner Ed Hartman allowed Shadow access to.[487] The store was opened by Hartman in the 1970's and remained in its location on the 700

---

[485] Spine Magazine n.d. c
[486] Murphy, T 2013
[487] Doyle, T 2017

block of K Street, Sacramento until the mid-2000's when it moved to 1618 Broadway, before closing in 2016.[488] One of the records Shadow had found there was David Axelrod's 1969 album *Songs Of Experience*.[489] Axelrod had produced several albums for David McCallum, an actor and musician who starred in the TV series *The Man From U.N.C.L.E.*, before Axelrod went solo.[490] He would release several albums across the 1970's which would be heavily sampled as they were later discovered by hip hop producers during the 1990's with artists such as De La Soul, Dr Dre,[491] and Kool G Rap[492] all using elements of Axelrod's productions in their work.

For DJ Shadow, Axelrod's *The Human Abstract* featured a piano which fit perfectly with a breakbeat Shadow had created from *Life Connection*, a 1968 song by Rotary Connection.[493] Shadow then added samples from *Sower of Seeds* by Baraka, *Sekoilu Seestyy* by Pekka Pohjola, *Releasing Hypnotical Gases* by Organized Konfusion, *Dolmen Music* by Meredith Monk, and *California Soul* by Marlena Shaw, which together became *Midnight In A Perfect World*.[494]

Shadow would record the samples in to his MPC and an ADAT machine.[495] DAT is short for Digital Audio Tape and was a format created by Sony which was used by many musicians in the studio due to the higher quality of audio in comparison to regular audio cassettes,[496] while ADAT was Alessis' take on DAT which was a more affordable alternative.[497] Once a track was complete, Shadow would record from the MPC to ADAT and then take the tapes to Dan

---

[488] Macias, C 2016
[489] Doyle, T 2017
[490] Kreps, D 2017
[491] Weiss, J 2017
[492] WhoSampled 2019f
[493] Doyle, T 2017
[494] WhoSampled 2019l
[495] Rule, G 1997
[496] Shambro, J 2019
[497] White, P 2010

The Automator's studio where they would be copied across to DAT for further mixing.[498]

In the middle of the *Endtroducing* sessions, James Lavelle had arranged with A&M for a budget to allow Tim Goldsworthy, Masayuki Kudo, and himself to travel to LA[499] and record the first UNKLE album at producer Mario C's studio, with Shadow also invited to contribute.[500]

---

[498] Rule, G 1997
[499] O'Connor, F 1995
[500] McClean, M 1995, p. 106

Belmondo in LA

In 1995, while James Lavelle was finalising a deal between Mo' Wax and A&M Records, UNKLE had continued to record, remix and release tracks including two which saw release in March of that year.

March 16th saw the release of *Dewback*, a new UNKLE song produced by Tim Goldsworthy and Lavelle, featuring D'Afro (Charlie Dark of Attica Blues) and Patterson aka David Patterson. *Dewback* was released on a compilation of trip hop entitled *110 Below - Trip To The cHIP sHOP Vol-2*.[501] The title *Dewback* is a reference to the Dewback creature from the original *Star Wars* film, where the Dewback are thick-skinned reptiles native to the planet Tatooine seen in the film mounted by sandtroopers.[502] At the time Lavelle was well known for his collection of *Star Wars* memorabilia which filled the Mo' Wax offices,[503] and the Dewback toy was considered to be quite rare during Lavelle's childhood[504] with many fans assuming it was only a rumour,[505] but Lavelle eventually found one by chance in a shop when he was 18.[506]

The second UNKLE track released in March 1995 was a remix of Massive Attack's *Karmacoma*, released on the *Karmacoma EP* on March 20th, featuring production from Tim Goldsworthy, Masayuki Kudo and Lavelle as well as scratches by DJ Shadow.[507] The remix, entitled *Karmacoma (U.N.K.L.E. Situation)*, contains samples from Doctor John's 1968 song *Gris-Gris Gumbo Ya Ya*, and was featured next to remixes by Ben Young, Blacksmith, and Portishead.[508]

---

[501] Discogs 2019eee
[502] Wookieepedia 2019
[503] Burgess, J 1996, p. 56
[504] Darby, A 2013
[505] Veekhoven, T 2014
[506] Darby, A 2013
[507] Discogs 2019aa
[508] MassiveAttack.ie 2019b

James Lavelle was also continuing with plans for an UNKLE album, and in June 1995 MC Rammellzee was flown to the UK by Lavelle to record something in the Major Force West Studio.[509]

Rammellzee aka RAMM:ΣLL:ZΣΣ was born in 1960, though his birth name and exact date of birth have not been made public.[510] He entered the graffiti art scene in the 1970's, tagging trains in the New York City subway, and appeared in the hip hop films *Style Wars* and *Wild Style*. He would also appear as "Man with Money" in *Stranger Than Paradise*, Jim Jarmusch's second feature film released in 1984.[511] Rammellzee exhibited his visual art around the world, working initially in painting and later focusing on intricate sculpture pieces.[512]

In 1983 Rammellzee appeared on the 12" *Beat Bop*, a hip hop single by Rammellzee and K-Rob released in 1983 and featured in the documentary *Style Wars*.[513] Notably the cover of *Beat Bop*'s initial release was designed by the artist Jean-Michel Basquiat, who is also credited with producing the song,[514] and James Lavelle has stated that it is one of his favourite album record covers.[515]

After the release of *Beat Bop* Rammellzee continued to release music, working with Death Comet Crew in 1985,[516] Sly & Robbie in 1987,[517] and as part of Gettovetts with Nicky Skopelitis and Shockdell (Charles Howard) who released the album *Missionaries Moving* in 1988.[518] During the 1990's Rammellzee became the first artist to collaborate with clothing brand Supreme[519] but was

---

[509] Gill, E 2014
[510] Ray, J 2018
[511] IMDB 2019a
[512] Gavin, F 2019
[513] Ray, J 2018
[514] Ray, J 2018 IBID
[515] Nagshineh, A 2013
[516] Discogs 2019c
[517] Discogs 2019hh
[518] Discogs 2019q
[519] Hsu, H 2018

exhibiting less, preferring to spend his time in his studio, the Battle Station, creating new artworks from scavenged materials.[520]

In June 1995 Rammellzee recorded vocals for UNKLE's *Rock On*, with Rammellzee's appearance intended as a homage to *Beat Bop*.[521] Production on *Rock On* was handled by Tim Goldsworthy while DJ Shadow was brought in to perform scratches on the song,[522] with John King of The Dust Brothers also brought in to remix the track, creating the *Nutcracker Mix* and *Nutcracker Dub* mixes respectively.[523]

Rock On is built around a sample from *Lovefingers* by Silverapples from their 1968 self titled album.[524] The instrumental sections of *Lovefingers* have then been cut up and layered with scratches and Rammellzee repeating the phrase "rock on to the break of dawn," making *Rock On* sound more like a remix of *Beat Bop* or Shockdell's *Gangster Lean* which also featured similar "rock on" vocals from Rammellzee.

Rock On would first see release in 1996 on a compilation called *Header #1*[525] which also included CD-ROM content featuring a video of James Lavelle explaining that a different version of *Rock On* would be appearing on the forthcoming UNKLE album, with the Header #1 version described as being an outtake.[526] The CD-ROM elements also included the ability to remix songs, described as follows:

> Header is an independently produced 'enhanced CD' combining 30 minutes of standard audio CD with CD-ROM multimedia. The ROM section is twelve tracks presenting different techniques for de-constructing and re-constructing

---

[520] Gotthardt, A 2018
[521] James Lavelle Interview 1996
[522] DJShadow.com n.d. d
[523] Discogs 2019qq
[524] WhoSampled 2019i
[525] Discogs 2019ggg
[526] James Lavelle Interview 1996

musical pieces from dance and reggae artists, plus occasional interviews in Quicktime video clips...On the Mo Wax piece you can grab the sound track with the mouse and move it like a scratch record deck. On the Unkle piece different tracks can be found, iconised, adrift on a background that slides across the screen at a speed and direction determined by the location of the cursor. Their level in the mix is determined by the distance of their icon from the cursor. So as the graphic landscape glides past, the tracks fade in and out seamlessly. This representation of the source music content is sometimes more physical and sometimes more abstract than we are used to. As opposed to the abstraction that turns music into staves in traditional notation, the Header abstractions — into space and graphic effects — have the potential to create new synaesthetic effects for the user.[527]

Header was created by Tui Interactive Media, and was followed in 1998 by *Header #2*, one version of which contained *Header #1* as a bonus disc with the full original tracklist including UNKLE's *Rock On*. Tui would go on to work with Mo' Wax again, creating their website in the early 2000's,[528] and won several awards for their work with Daft Punk, creating the DaftClub webportal where fans could download exclusive free tracks.[529]

Back in August 1995 the Mo' Wax and A&M deal had been finalised, with Mo' Wax Records now part of the major label, and Lavelle was granted a budget to fly to LA to record the debut UNKLE album. On August 14th Frances O'Connor of A&M sent Lavelle a letter explaining, "The budget will exhaust your total recording budget for Album 1. Any additional funds spent over and above this budget will be treated as an additional label advance, and deducted from royalties due to you."[530]

---

[527] Jennings, D 2003
[528] Ibid.
[529] Tui 2001
[530] O'Connor, F 1995

The budget has been mythologised over the years, and exact numbers are unknown, though it was reportedly £30,000 at the time,[531] with A&M also putting the group up in a house owned by Meatloaf which featured a bat-shaped swimming pool. The album was to be recorded over four weeks, then brought back to England to be completed, with a February 1996 album release date announced to the press.[532]

Lavelle spoke to *The Face* at the time and told them he planned to collaborate with Plaid, Baby Ford and Photek as part of further recording sessions in London once the LA sessions had been completed, with the album set to be complete by December 31, 1995.[533]

In September 1995 Lavelle, Goldsworthy, Kudo, and Money Mark met at producer Mario C's home studio to begin recording the UNKLE album, with some recordings also being made at the Beastie Boys' G-Son studio nearby.[534] Graffiti artist Futura also joined the group and began creating artwork for the album, a collaboration with DJ Spooky which was announced would be a comic called *Loopz*.[535] The recordings meanwhile were nicknamed *Belmondo* after an article about the sessions appeared in the December 1995 issue of UK Magazine *The Face*, which explained the album would be released as "UNKLE/Belmondo, the new extended name for the ensemble project."[536]

Belmondo was a name that Tim Goldsworthy had come up with, named after the French actor Jean-Paul Belmondo who starred in several films which were part of the French New Wave of the 1960's. Originally, before releasing songs as UNKLE Lavelle and Goldsworthy wanted to name their band Belmondo but by then had

---

[531] Bradshaw, P 2014b
[532] Burgess, J 1998, p.57
[533] McLean, C 1998, p. 65
[534] Lazarus, D 1995, p. 69
[535] McLean, C 1995a, p. 105
[536] Ibid.

already produced tracks as UNKLE, and when UNKLE started to take off Belmondo was forgotten.[537] According to Lavelle, "Unkle was supposed to be the fun stuff and Belmondo the more serious project."[538] He later further explained that UNKLE was intended to be more spontaneous and alternative sounding, while Belmondo would feature more vocals, and be their "adventure in to singer songwriter" type of music.[539]

Mario Caldato Jr., aka Mario C, was at the time primarily known as the producer for the Beastie Boys, having met them during the recording of 1989's *Paul's Boutique* album, and subsequently continued working with them through to their *Hello Nasty* album in 1998.[540] He had a home studio set up at his house in Los Angeles, California and Lavelle had arranged to record there with Tim Goldsworthy and KUDO co-producing, DJ Shadow producing his own tracks, and Money Mark appearing as a guest.[541] With so many contributors taking part Money Mark's manager Max Burgos was brought in to work A&R for the sessions, working as a go between for Lavelle and Mario C, as he confirmed to me in a telephone conversation in 2019.[542]

I spoke with Mario C via video chat in late 2017 where we discussed UNKLE's LA sessions from 1995:

> I do remember the enthusiasm about the project and putting together all these different musicians, and producers, to create this...y'know...nobody really knew what it was going to be...beats with instrumentals, with funky sounds and things, so we kind of just got together and kind of winged it. We recorded at my house. Everyone would show up and I think Tim was mainly the one in charge of some of the stuff that they had and running the samplers at the time...and

---

[537] Cooper, D 2013c
[538] Burgess, J 1998, p.57
[539] UNKLE 1998, 00:09:00
[540] Hilleary, M 2017
[541] Mario C 2017, video conversation August 23
[542] Max Burgos 2019, telephone conversation May 28

Mark [and] Kudo were just throwing up ideas and stuff, and I had some instruments around the house. We were just putting two and two together...We had the MPC60s and the SP1200 and then Tim had the computer, I believe they were doing stuff off some other programs. At the time it was ...Studio Vision I believe. So, it was kind of a machine type [of recording]. I don't think we did anything to tape, though I did have...a tape machine, but I don't think we used that.[543]

DJ Shadow's contribution included recording tracks with Zoe Bedeaux, who was at the time an aspiring singer and stylist who worked for *The Face* and *I-D Magazine*.[544] In 1999 she would appear under the pseudonym Aurora Borealis singing as part of The Baby Namboos on *Ancoats 2 Zambia*,[545] a trip hop infused album led by Tricky's cousin Mark Porter, and also featuring Claude Williams of The Wild Bunch as a member.[546] Tricky signed the group to his Durban Poison label[547] [548] and also appears on three tracks.[549] Bedeaux's contributions were hailed as the shining star of many of the tracks, with press describing her singing as an "incredibly unique and haunting voice,"[550] and "like a cross between Martina and Breakbeat Era's Lennie Laws. Occasionally, she's slyly enticing, sometimes maternally comforting. Often, she's the incarnation of female anguish and excruciatingly maintained pride."[551] Bedeaux was brought in to The Baby Namboos album sessions after the music was already produced, spending two days improvising and recording lyrics for them after Tricky felt it would be a good idea to have her contribute.[552]

---

[543] Mario C 2017, video conversation August 23
[544] National Portrait Gallery, n.d.
[545] Discogs 2019kk
[546] McLeod, K 2000
[547] Benson, D 2000
[548] Chart Magazine 2000
[549] Benson, D 2000
[550] Ibid.
[551] Goldberg, M 2000
[552] Nowinski, A 1999

Back in 1995, it is unclear how Zoe Bedeaux became involved with UNKLE's album recording in LA, but at least two tracks were recorded between her and DJ Shadow. *Anything You Like*, and *Where Do You Go?* are both named in 1995's *The Face* article detailing the recording sessions.[553] *Anything You Like* opens with some sonar blips and a distorted voice before Zoe Bedeaux's vocals begin and they are joined by some instrumentation similar to that which opens Massive Attack's *Paradise Circus* from their 2010 *Heligoland* album. The track then becomes what Mario C calls "the signature Shadow [sound]...the drum machine just bugs out."[554] When I spoke with Mario C he didn't know about a song called *Where Do You Go?*, but remembered *Anything You Like* which he described as an idea that was left unfinished, he told me, "we literally did one mix, we didn't go back and refine it...[we] never really finished it."[555]

Keyboardist Mark Ramos Nishita, aka Money Mark, also contributed to some songs, notably *Berry Meditation* and *Garage Piano*. Mark had begun working with the Beastie Boys in 1992 initially as a carpenter, but when the band realised Mark could play keyboards he joined the Beastie Boys as they recorded their album *Check Your Head*.[556] James Lavelle had signed Mark to Mo' Wax and across 1995 he had two singles in the UK Singles Chart,[557] followed by his debut album *Mark's Keyboard Repair* which entered the UK Album Charts while UNKLE were recording in LA,[558] peaking at #35 on September 9 and spending two weeks in the Top 100.[559] The album featured a sleeve designed by Ben Drury and Will Bankhead, as well as photography by producer Mario C.[560]

---

[553] McLean, C 1995a, p. 105
[554] Mario C 2017, video conversation August 23
[555] Ibid.
[556] Willmott, B 1996, p. 46
[557] Official UK Charts Company 2019g
[558] McLean, C 1995a, p. 106
[559] Official UK Charts Company 2019g
[560] Discogs 2020b

UNKLE's *Garage Piano* would later be heard in 1996 when it appeared on the *Headz 2A* compilation.[561] Considered by *Alternate Press* as a high point of the compilation, they describe it as a "Woozy, 4 a.m. come-down track enlivened by fat kettle drums, DJ Kudo's scratches, theremin and Money Mark's keyboard."[562] Garage Piano opens with scratching and a big drum beat before the main samples arrive from Esquivel's *Harlem Nocturne*, taken from their *Infinity in Sound* album released in 1960.[563]

Mario C recalled recording *Garage Piano*:

> The beats were mainly programmed based, y'know sample. And then some of them might have a musical element to it, and then there would be layers y'know, and Mark would play a keyboard, or somebody would play some vibes. Obviously, The Garage Piano, that one there actually used, the drum beat was the drums at my house that were in the garage, and it was super roomy. I think Mark played it, and then Tim just cut it up and then programmed something. And the piano was my piano as a kid growing up in my house that was kind of in my garage. It's an old English piano that I never imagined would be used, and it's completely out of tune and dusted. Mark opened it up and then just played something and they just recorded it and it sounded crazy. They cut it up and then I mixed it...*Garage Piano*, that's it.[564]

Berry Meditation also saw a release, initially as a test pressing in 1996,[565] and then on the soundtrack from the film *SubUrbia* in February 1997,[566] followed in March by a release as a 12" single by UNKLE which features two different mixes and a remix by Attica Blues.[567] *Berry Meditation* received its title after Money Mark

---

[561] Discogs 2019hhh
[562] Heimlich, A 1998
[563] WhoSampled 2019d
[564] Mario C 2017, video conversation August 23
[565] Discogs 2019oo
[566] Discogs 2019ppp
[567] Discogs 2019pp

suggested they name the songs from the sessions after fruits,[568] and the song features vocal samples taken from a meditation record.[569] *Berry Meditation* opens with a sample from *Riversong* by Tonto's Expanding Head Band[570] and is then taken over by breakbeats and effects, eventually ending after seven minutes.

Another instrumental recorded at the time was titled *Cherry Pie*. There were three versions of the track created during the LA sessions, named *Cherry Pie Part 1, Cherry Pie Part 2, and Cherry Pie Part 1 and Part 2 edit*, which as the name suggests was an extended version which joined up parts 1 and 2. *Cherry Pie* starts with a piano and keyboard jam over a breakbeat and also features a Theremin, with several breakdowns. According to Mario C the song was a jam between Kudo and Mark, which he describes as a song that "just goes on and on"[571] with the *Part 1 and 2 edit* extending for 8 minutes.[572]

Two more instrumentals, *Abstract Soul* and *Soup or Salads*, likewise both had multiple versions recorded in the studio, with dub versions of both tracks created featuring extra effects on top the track. *Abstract Soul* was produced by Kudo and featured Goldsworthy, Kudo and Mark on the track. While *Soup or Salads* was produced by Goldsworthy, and was a collaboration between himself and Mark, with engineering from Mario.[573] This was a favourite of Kudo's from the recording sessions and he continued to praise it, later saying "It is still wonderful to hear."[574]

Soup or Salads begins with a Stylophone-like keyboard playing over a cut-up beat, and apart from the occasional breakdowns there isn't much more to it. *Abstract Soul* meanwhile features a slow Money Mark Harpsichord-like keyboard over backwards drums, a

---

[568] Burgess, J 1996, p. 60
[569] Ibid.
[570] WhoSampled 2019bb
[571] Mario C 2017, video conversation August 23
[572] Ibid.
[573] Ibid.
[574] Takayama, Y 2013

saxophone, and various dub effects. It is the more fully realised of the tracks and is more jazz than hip hop sounding of all of the tracks recorded.

Chico Jam was also recorded at the time and later played publicly for the first time in 2019 by James Lavelle during his January 23rd *Living In My Headphones* show on SoHo Radio.[575] It starts off with a double bass and horn accompanied by a drumbeat and various effects which overall sound similar to what was explored on *Abstract Soul*. *Chico Jam* featured Lavelle, Goldsworthy, and Kudo, with the song's title apparently a reference to a percussionist working with the Beastie Boys.[576]

While Kudo and Goldsworthy are credited with production on these tracks, and Money Mark's contributions can easily be heard thanks to his distinctive keyboard sounds, less clear is what James Lavelle brought to the project. Lavelle's role is self described as "the creative controller, the concept person...I envisage what it should be like and everyone else puts it together."[577] While Goldsworthy described his contributions as coming up with "the breaks and ideas" but noted Lavelle "hates the studio."[578] Speaking to *Dazed & Confused* in 1995 he further explained what it's like working with Lavelle:

> [It's] Insane. It can get frustrating at times because he like has 1,000 ideas in his head and he wants them done immediately. Kudo and I are such perfectionists that there have been a few pitched battles around the samplers. The most annoying thing James does is, when you're fucking around with a sample, trying to get it right and it's not quite there, James will come in and say 'That's good, I like that, keep it'. I try and get around it diplomatically by saying 'We can't, its got a different time signature' or something like that

---

[575] Lavelle, J 2019b, 00:44:36
[576] Ibid. 01:02:55
[577] Burgess, J 1996, p. 56
[578] McLean, C 1995a, p. 103

which will blind him with science. Generally though, we are very like-minded. He is the creative director as far as U.N.K.L.E. is concerned and fortunately we are on the same tip.[579]

Outside of those mentioned there were other songs recorded as part of the sessions, with a reported 15 tracks brought back to London once the LA sessions had completed,[580] and plans for more to be recorded in London, with future collaborations with Deborah Anderson,[581] Plaid, Baby Ford and Photek planned.[582] But after arriving back in London, Lavelle listened to everything that they had recorded in LA and was dismayed, "I was at a point of sort of disbelief...Nothing sounded the way I was thinking. I was pissed off and not happy with things at all."[583] Lavelle felt that, apart from *Berry Meditation*, nothing from the LA sessions represented how he wanted UNKLE to sound.[584]

The sessions had been quick, and while Lavelle had spent a month in America, he didn't spend all of that time in the studio. There had been a trip to Las Vegas with Goldsworthy and Futura, while Kudo stayed in the studio, and Shadow later admitted that nothing was done during the first two weeks.[585] Then there had been Meatloaf's house, which had so many people staying at it that Shadow slept on the couch while Futura made a bed in the laundry. At various times the housemates included James Lavelle, Tim Goldsworthy, Money Mark and his manager Max Burgos, Futura, DJ Spooky, Mario C, DJ Shadow, Kan Takagi, Kudo and his family, Zoe Bedeuax, Will Bankhead, Donovan Leach and Amanda de Cadenet, and visits from Lavelle's girlfriend Janet Fischgrund, with Lavelle later describing the experience as like a travelling circus.[586]

---

[579] Lazarus, D 1995, p. 69
[580] McLean, C 1995a, p. 106
[581] Burgess, J 1996, p. 58
[582] McLean, C 1998, p. 65
[583] URB, 1998
[584] Ibid.
[585] Smith, A 1998
[586] Burgess, J 1998, p. 57

One name that is a notable exclusion from the list is Mike D of the Beastie Boys who Lavelle had wanted to work with on the UNKLE album, either as a producer or guest artist, but according to Goldsworthy "it all got a bit rushed and we never hooked up."[587]

The party atmosphere of the house was a possible contribution to things not getting done, with Lavelle complaining, "everybody was just having a laugh rather than focussing on the record."[588] While Shadow gave a similar description of the sessions, explaining, "in the summer of 1995, James wanted to do an album of remix-type stuff, but really fast, in a month...He asked me to do two tracks, but it was not a good experience because I felt like nobody was grabbing the reins." Shadow became frustrated at the time as he felt he could have been working on his own album since no one was doing any work there.[589] He would elaborate to *NME* in 1998:

> I left after that experience feeling like, 'I don't want to be any part of this'...There were all these people coming in and out and having a laugh and doing this and that, and I got fucked off with it to the point that eventually I just locked the studio door and wouldn't let anyone in. Every now and then I would see the top of someone's head peering over looking concerned and I would be like, "No, go away!". I wasn't sure who was supposed to be running the show, so I got on with stuff but I wasn't really sure anything would come of it.[590]

Mario C later recalled the recording sessions as almost over before they started, describing them to me in 2017:

> It was interesting, it was a busy time. Everyone had projects, [they'd say] "let's just try something together" and we did it. It kind of went quick and then we didn't get a chance to elaborate on it...I don't know if it was one week, or two

---

[587] McLean, C 1995a, p. 104
[588] Burgess, J 1998, p. 57
[589] Bradshaw, P 2014b
[590] Cigarettes, J 1998, p. 14

weeks...We probably did like an idea a day, or one or two ideas a day."[591]

But back in London Lavelle decided to shelve the LA sessions,[592] later explaining that he "wasn't hearing what he wanted to hear through the music. The idea of recording an album in a month was ridiculous, it was just never going to happen."[593]

While *Garage Piano* and *Berry Meditation* both saw releases by UNKLE, Shadow abandoned his tracks with Zoe Bedeaux and they have yet to see release. Kudo for his part didn't want to throw out some of the tracks he and Goldsworthy had been working on,[594] and both *Abstract Soul* and *Soup or Salads* would appear on the Major Force West compilation *93-97*, a collection of tracks worked on as part of Nakanishi Toshio and Masayuki Kudo's Major Force West projects in London.[595] The album was described by *The Wire* as "bizarre without being 'trippy', and pretty cool without trying to hard."[596] While Mo' Wax released the album in 1999, it is notable that James Lavelle shares no credits on the album.[597]

While it is never mentioned explicitly in any press, it appears that Kudo left the UNKLE project around the time that the LA sessions were abandoned. This was not the end of their partnership though as Kudo maintained the Major Force West studio in the Mo' Wax basement, where he continued contributing to production and remixes for James Lavelle such as on Hurricane #1's *Only The Strongest Will Survive (James Lavelle Remix)* released in 1998.[598]

With the LA sessions abandoned, Lavelle and Shadow ended 1995 by flying to Australia for a Mo' Wax tour along with Money Mark and

---

[591] Mario C 2017, video conversation August 23
[592] Burgess, J 1998, pp. 57-58
[593] UNKLE 1998, 00:10:30
[594] Takayama, Y 2013
[595] Discogs 2019y
[596] Shapiro, P 1999, p. 68
[597] Discogs 2019y
[598] Discogs 2019r

Charlie Dark. After the tour ended at the beginning of 1996, Shadow would return home to complete his debut album,[599] while Lavelle continued DJing through the new year, and contributed a mix CD as part of Cream Live Two, part of a 3 CD package which also featured mixes by Paul Oakenfold, and Nick Warren.

Lavelle noted there was controversy at the time over his inclusion, as he was not seen as a club DJ in the same way Oakenfold was, saying:

> A lot of people told me not to do it but then thanked me for putting their records on it...Cream is so much a part of northern club culture, it's important for those people to hear those records. I can't really get into that thing where you're so hardcore that you have to keep everything in its shell and nobody will hear what you do. If Shadow could sell as many copies as M People then great. It's good music at the end of the day.[600]

Eyebrows were further raised when it was noted that on the Cream mix The Psychonauts were credited with performing most of the mix work for Lavelle's CD. Lavelle for his part acknowledged that his skills as a DJ were more geared towards track selection and reading a crowd, as opposed to mixing, so he asked the Psychonauts to help out in that respect. Speaking about the mix in an interview he said:

> I wanted it to be technically the bollocks...I've never touted myself as the best DJ in the world. People will listen to it because of my name so you may as well get the best people in to work on it and have good cuttin' up, have it mixed well, edited properly. It was more like James Lavelle presents... I chose the records.[601]

---

[599] Ma, D 2017, p. 78
[600] Burgess, J 1996, p. 56
[601] Ibid.

The Cream mix would also feature a new UNKLE track, *Spinners*, which is primarily made of samples from the *Blade Runner* soundtrack by Vangelis, alongside drums sampled from Bernard Purdie's 1968 song *Soul Drums*, as well as dialogue from Bruce Lee's 1973 movie *Enter The Dragon,* and sound effects from the 1991 videogame *Street Fighter II*.[602] Reportedly created solely for this release,[603] the song has not been featured anywhere else and ends abruptly as it mixes into the next song of the mix. Lavelle considers the *Blade Runner* soundtrack to be the greatest soundtrack ever, and an inspiration, telling *The Quietus*:

> It's one of the most perfect albums ever made. It's an instrumental piece of music and one of the greatest electronic records ever made. The film was incredible and the way it was made for the film was amazing. Just perfection to me.[604]

The title, *Spinners*, is a nod to the name of a flying car from the *Blade Runner* series. The car was designed by Syd Mead and built by Gene Winfield,[605] with the cars becoming fan favourites and later appearing in the background of other science fiction films such as the *Star Wars* prequels and *The Fifth Element*.[606]

UNKLE's *Spinners* is also notable for being one of the early collaborations between Lavelle and Pablo Clements, of The Psychonauts. Lavelle had been given a mixtape of The Psychonauts by Tim Goldsworthy while UNKLE were recording in LA during 1995, where it was played on repeat. Lavelle loved the tape and quickly signed the group to Mo' Wax after arranging a meeting with the group.[607] Clements soon became one of the rotating artists who Lavelle would pull in to apply turntable scratches

---

[602] WhoSampled 2020c
[603] shivo 2018
[604] Aubrey, E 2017e
[605] Willoughby, G n.d.
[606] McLellan, M 2017
[607] The List 1996

on various UNKLE songs through the 1990's, and would also apply scratches to UNKLE remixes of *Pepper* by Buthole Surfers, and Palm Skin Productions' *The Beast,* both in 1994, as well as UNKLE's remix of Tortoise's *DJed* in 1996, before Clements become a full time member of UNKLE during the early 2000's.

Meanwhile as Lavelle continued to DJ and work on UNKLE project in 1996, DJ Shadow had been putting the final touches on his debut album which was preparing for a release by Mo' Wax.[608]

---

[608] Ma, D 2017, p. 78

Endtroducing…..Complete

After touring Australia with James Lavelle, DJ Shadow went back to finishing his debut album, dedicating January to June 1996 to completing the final touches.[609]

While the album was mostly completed in June 1995 Shadow had continued to work on it, telling *Rolling Stone*:

> I usually tweak it right at the end to bring me up to date in terms of what's inspired me lately…If I'm going to live with something that has my name on it for the rest of my life, I have to like it six months or a year later. If it still takes me somewhere, then in my mind I know it's a classic for me.[610]

During the third week of May 1996 Shadow mastered the album and returned to England so he would be available for the album's release.[611] Lavelle would later recall the day he received the DAT of *Endtroducing* in the post and he kicked everyone out of the Mo' Wax office so he and Will Bankhead could listen to the album undisturbed. He explained, "I sat down with Will Bankhead and we played the album and it was just one of those moments when you thought "Ok, fuck, this is a masterpiece.""[612]

Shadow had tried to make his album well rounded, with songs such as *Organ Donor* meant to lighten the mood set by the heavier *What Does Your Soul Look Like* sections as he felt he needed to mix things up for an album length release. While Shadow had been afraid *Organ Donor* was too light and that no one would like it, he was happy to hear Lavelle tell him that when he and Will Bankhead first heard the song they started jumping around the office.[613] *Organ Donor* would later be extended with the *Organ Donor (Extended*

---

[609] Ma, D 2017, p. 78
[610] Margasak, P 1996
[611] Wilder, E 2017, p. 79
[612] Bradshaw, P 2014b
[613] Wilder, E 2017, p. 74

Overhaul) created at the request of James Lavelle so he could use it in his DJ sets,[614] and later released on the *High Noon* single in August 1997.[615]

Endtroducing was released in September 1996 in England,[616] followed by it's American release in November of the same year.[617] On September 28 *Endtroducing* entered the UK Album Charts at #17, spending four weeks in the charts before dropping out of the Top 100,[618] making it Mo' Wax's highest charting album at the time.[619] *Endtroducing* would go on to be certified as a Gold Record in the UK during 1998,[620] having sold 100,000 copies,[621] and would go on to sell over half a million copies as of 2019.[622]

Endtroducing was also awarded a Guinness World Record for the first album released which was completely made up of samples,[623] though it has been noted there are snippets of live recordings from Shadow's friends. Lyrics Born and Gift of Gab appear on songs, as does Shadow's girlfriend at the time Lisa Haugen, whom Shadow had recorded talking to herself.[624] Shadow had previously named one of his songs *Lost And Found (S.F.L.)*, released in 1994, with the S.F.L. standing for Song For Lisa.[625] On *Entroducing* Haugen's monologue about Darth Vader and Zanadu featured on the track *Mutual Slump.*[626] Whether or not these can be considered samples is up to the individual, though Shadow himself referred to these bits as "not samples."[627]

---

[614] Billboard, 2015
[615] DJShadow.com n.d. b
[616] Discogs 2019f
[617] Discogs 2019g
[618] Official UK Charts Company 2019b
[619] Cooper, D 2015
[620] BPI 2019b
[621] BPI 2019a
[622] Wustemann, L 2019
[623] Guinness World Records 2019
[624] Doran, J 2010
[625] Discogs 2019w
[626] Hirway, H 2016, 00:06:08
[627] Roeder, M 1999

One of Lyrics Born's contributions was to the song *Why Hip-Hop Sucks in '96*,[628] which Shadow spent several interviews explaining the meaning behind over the next few years.[629] [630] [631] In the song the only lyric serve as an answer to why Shadow felt hip hop sucked in 1996, "It's the money". He would explain that it was meant somewhat tongue in cheek,[632] but also as a criticism of where hip hop was moving. Shadow felt at the time that mainstream rap music was ruining hip hop, and in particular that as rap became more popular that the more militant fans of hip hop were beginning to invent rules on how hip hop should be made as a means to preserve its authenticity. But these were rules Shadow wasn't interested in following.[633]

The instrumental sound of the album was heavily praised by the press, with *MTV* writing, "Without using any rapping or featured vocals, Shadow unearths the blues that are buried deep in hip-hop."[634] While *NME* awarded the album 8/10 commenting "DJ Shadow calls it hip-hop. We'll settle for groovy."[635] The lack of vocals had initially been a point of worry for some people who questioned Lavelle about releasing an album of instrumental hip hop, but while Lavelle wasn't worried, he couldn't anticipate the album's popularity and impact.[636] Lavelle would later call the album "the most important record on Mo' Wax,"[637] and commented that "If you can put out a record that defines a culture you're very lucky."[638]

Shadow would later comment himself on the sound of this album, and how it built upon his previous work:

---

[628] Inoue, T 2002
[629] Chang, J 2006
[630] Roberts, M 1997
[631] Vaziri, A 2006
[632] Ma, D 2017, p. 78
[633] Stubbs, D 1996, p. 29
[634] Bremser, W 1998
[635] NME, 1996
[636] Kane, D 2014
[637] Long Live Vinyl, 2017
[638] Ibid.

> I felt like I was on to something when I was doing "*Influx*,"…and the *What Does Your Soul Look Like* EP. All of that preceded *Endtroducing......*, and the reason why it's spelled with an "E-N-D" is because it signified the fourth and final chapter in a series of pieces that I was doing for Mo' Wax with a certain sound, a certain tone, a certain atmosphere. And I feel like my work really changed after that. It was the summary of this sound, and [the album] wrapped up the series. I had this vision at the time that every album I did after that would be completely different, and that's something I've been trying to be adamant about—maintaining that autonomy from record to record.[639]

Further explaining the END in the title Shadow told *The Telegraph* in 1996:

> I don't intend to keep making the same sort of records for ever...You have to create and then destroy - because if you don't destroy what you've done, someone else will, and then you'll be left saying, 'Now what do I have? I don't have anything!'[640]

The title was originally *Endtroducing......*, with five periods for the Mo' Wax edition, but in the US this was shortened to three periods. Future releases have alternated between the two.[641] No specific explanation for the periods, or the reason some editions have less, seem to be apparent.

At the same time as he was working with Mo' Wax, Shadow had continued working with his Solesides label mates, contributing production to several releases by Blackalicious, Latyrx, and Lateef. As Shadow's popularity grew, so did the rest of the Solesides members as people sought out other work by Shadow. But in 1996

---

[639] Fader, L 2012
[640] Llewellyn Smith, C 1996
[641] Discogs 2019e

the group decided to close the Solesides label down. Several members of the label felt they had become known as "DJ Shadow's supporting cast" and while they had been making a name for themselves, they weren't actually making any money on Solesides.[642] Shadow later commented:

> We collectively sat down there and said, 'Well, this is six years old and it's done more than we could have imagined, but now we want to try a different thing.'[643]

For Shadow trying something different included the release of *High Noon*. The non-album track was his first release following *Endtroducing* and was meant as a response to how he felt pigeonholed by the trip hop tag that had been applied to him.[644] Shadow followed the release by returning to work with James Lavelle on UNKLE[645] in late 1996 as Lavelle also sought to try something different with the project.[646]

---

[642] Chennault, S 2005
[643] MTV News, 1998
[644] DJShadow.com n.d. b
[645] Wilder, E 2017, p. 90
[646] McClean, C 1998, p. 66

Lonely Souls

With the LA recordings abandoned Lavelle put the UNKLE project on hold as he considered the direction he wanted to move in, telling a reporter "...apart from '*Berry meditation*' there wasn't anything that represented how I wanted UNKLE to sound."[647]

Up until now the UNKLE sound had been that of slow and laid-back hip hop beats, typical of trip hop which was popular at the time. The sound had earned UNKLE several fans, with the *The Time Has Come EP* being one of the few Mo' Wax releases to enter the UK charts.[648] But Lavelle was becoming uninterested in the sound as the trip hop genre had grown in popularity, with artists like Massive Attack, Portishead and Tricky perfecting the sound.[649]

For several years Lavelle had held up Massive Attack's *Blue Lines* as the blueprint and holy grail of what he wanted to achieve,[650] but it was clear that for Lavelle to achieve his goal he would need to find a new direction rather than simply emulate his idols. Lavelle commented, "I was looking around thinking, 'I can't make records like this, I've got to move on, even if the ideas are similar and I'm trying to work in a similar area,'"[651] later adding, "My frustration was that I didn't want to make weird instrumental hip-hop records. We could've easily achieved that but I wanted songs."[652]

The previously announced February 1996 release date for UNKLE's debut soon passed as Lavelle sought a new direction for the group.[653] Lavelle explained he needed to re-evaluate the project and think about the sound he wanted to pursue. From the abandoned LA sessions Lavelle went back to the two songs

---

[647] Burgess, J 1998, p. 57
[648] Cooper, D 2015
[649] NME, 1998e
[650] Burgess, J 1996, p. 60
[651] NME, 1998e
[652] Burgess, J 1998, p. 57
[653] Ibid.

Shadow had recorded with Zoe Bedeaux, which Lavelle described as "song-led, melodious and contained beats and scratching",[654] and "hardcore, but it was really emotional."[655] These became the blueprint for UNKLE post-LA,[656] as Shadow was creating music which Lavelle felt represented the sound he had been looking for,[657] and now that he had decided on the albums sound, Lavelle started to develop some ideas about possible vocal contributors for the album.

While in LA, Tim Goldsworthy had lent Lavelle a cassette of The Verve's *A Northern Soul* album,[658] which had been released earlier in 1995. Lavelle listened to the album repeatedly, telling *The Independent:*

> I heard this tape of The Verve, which we used to play every day when we left the studio. Two tracks really inspired me: *'History'* and *'Life's an Ocean'*... After hearing those songs, I got much more of an idea of what I could do with UNKLE if I could get together somebody like Richard Ashcroft and DJ Shadow.[659]

Richard Ashcroft had formed The Verve in 1990, then known simply as Verve, with guitarist Nick McCabe, bass guitarist Simon Jones and drummer Peter Salisbury.[660] Their debut album, *A Storm in Heaven*, was released in 1993 and featured a psychedelic rock influence which garnered them praise from the press.[661] In 1995 they had renamed themselves as The Verve and released a second album, *A Northern Soul*, which moved away from their previous improvised and psychedelic sound[662] and incorporated a greater

---

[654] Burgess, J 1998, p. 57
[655] UNKLE 1998 00:11:00
[656] Ibid.
[657] Burgess, J 1998, p. 57
[658] Higgins, M 1998
[659] Ibid.
[660] BBC 1998b
[661] Abdallah, R 2016
[662] Ibid.

rock influence across the album.[663] Ashcroft's singing was particularly praised by the press,[664] and was what inspired Lavelle to enquire about a possible collaboration for the UNKLE album, as Lavelle later told the *NME*:

> When I heard Richard Ashcroft sing it just really hit me in my heart. I wanted to get the same emotion on the record I was making. I just felt that the guy was speaking to me.[665]

Hearing Ashcroft was a revelation to Lavelle during the unsuccessful LA sessions as he realised what was missing from the sound he was searching for. He would later recall, "I thought, 'If I could bring that ilk of singer in with what I was hearing from Shadow I'll crack it'."[666] Shadow on the other hand was neither here nor there about the idea, as he later explained, "James felt he had something special and I was like, 'whatever, yeah, OK, get him in here.' "[667]

Back in England during the Summer of 1996, Lavelle contacted The Verve's management to enquire whether Richard Ashcroft would be interested in appearing on the UNKLE album, but he was told Ashcroft was unavailable due to the group having just split up.[668]

While recording *A Northern Soul*, The Verve had numerous personal issues, from relationship breakups[669] to nervous breakdowns[670], and even included Ashcroft disappearing for several days at one point.[671] Following the release of the album the band toured America, an experience which is said to have only compounded their problems, but upon returning to the UK they

---

[663] Folb, M 1995
[664] Ibid.
[665] NME 1998e
[666] Burgess, J 1998, p. 57
[667] Kaufman, G 1998
[668] Burgess, J 1998, p. 60
[669] Ellis, L 1995
[670] Simpon, D 1995
[671] NME 1995

continued to tour, playing T In The Park on August 6 1995.[672] The following day Ashcroft phoned Nick McCabe telling him he was breaking the band up, with the announcement reaching the press in September.[673]

Lavelle wasn't aware of this when he had first tried to call Ashcroft, but one day in 1996 he received a call out of the blue from Ashcroft[674] telling him "The band's over, I want to do something different."[675]

A meeting was soon arranged between Ashcroft, Lavelle, Tim Goldsworthy[676] and The Verve's bassist Simon Jones at a pub in Hampstead where they spoke about music.[677] [678] Ashcroft discussed his recent interest in New York hip hop, and Lavelle explained what he wanted from the UNKLE album by referring Ashcroft to Shadow's recently released album, *Endtroducing*. Ashcroft was enthusiastic about the idea and agreed to the collaboration, telling Lavelle "Let's make a piece of history!"[679]

Some weeks later in August, a recording session was arranged at Milo Studios in Hoxton Square, East London for Lavelle, Shadow and Ashcroft to meet and record a demo. When Ashcroft arrived he had some lyrics prepared, telling Lavelle and Shadow "I've just written this thing down…'God knows you lonely soul'".[680] Shadow had created an instrumental beat for the session and Ashcroft recorded a guide vocal over the top, a rough demo meant to give an idea of what the final song would sound like with the intention of coming back at a later date to record a final take. The initial session was over quickly, and at the end of September Ashcroft returned to

---

[672] The Face, 1997
[673] NME 1995
[674] Burgess, J 1998, p. 60
[675] Higgins, M 1998
[676] UNKLE 1998, 00:13:00
[677] Burgess, J 1998, p. 60
[678] Mclean, C 1998, p. 66
[679] Ibid.
[680] Ibid.

Milo Studios to record a new take of the vocal, taking off his shoes and recording the song in one go.

Both Lavelle and Shadow were very impressed with Ashcroft, and Shadow later fondly recalled the sessions:

> He was very charismatic and very genuine. I started bonding with him when we talked about music. He wanted to do a Marvin Gaye-type vocal, an 'answer back' type thing. He was there (in the studio) for about an hour-and-a-half. He did it in one take and, even though he came back twice, it was that guide vocal we ended up using.[681]

Lavelle was equally impressed, "It was a real spiritual moment for me recording that song...There was this sense we could go so far with the song which was exciting. There was this outro that Josh had left on and Richard sang over it so we thought 'Let's make this bigger, more extreme and bring this back out'. It became a benchmark because it was so inspiring."[682] He later added "For someone like myself who hasn't exactly got a rock history there was something about it that transcended the music. It was the attitude. Richard had this raw strength of character and he gave a soul to it that I hadn't heard for ages in somebody's voice."[683]

A few days after the second session at Milo, Ashcroft and Shadow met at Matrix Studios in West London to listen to the recordings of Ashcroft's vocals paired with the instrumental created by Shadow.[684] While they had planned to record a fresh take of the vocals, after listening it over they decided to stick with the original, only recording a few 'answer back' parts on top. These can be heard where Ashcroft sings "There's no secret to living" and it is followed by him repeating the lyric at a lower volume, almost speaking it rather than singing. This is repeated across the song

---

[681] NME 1998e
[682] Burgess, J 1998, p. 60
[683] NME 1998e
[684] Mclean, C 1998, p. 66

with Ashcroft 'answering' different lyrics in the song, acting almost as his own backup singer.

With the recording sessions complete, Ashcroft played Lavelle some new songs he had written entitled *The Drugs Don't Work* and *Bitter sweet Symphony*.[685] At the time Ashcroft had been planning to release a solo album, but then had became unsure of himself and instead decided he'd rather release it with The Verve.[686] One week after the session at Matrix Studios Ashcroft would reform The Verve[687] and go on to release their most successful album at the time, *Urban Hymns*.[688]

While Lavelle had been aware that The Verve had broken up, it was news to Shadow who would later recall:

> I didn't even know at that point The Verve had split up, I can't remember if James had told me but I was like, 'Oh, OK. Whatever'. The impact of a lot of people like Ashcroft and Thom Yorke, fortunately, came later. Not to be rude, but in a way I don't think we would have asked Richard after the success of *'Urban Hymns'*, 'cos it would have seen (sic) like we were grabbing the biggest name around.[689]

Lavelle agreed, telling *Jockey Slut* in 1998, "If I had to record with him now I don't know whether I'd be able to do it because I know so much about him on a media level. If I'd read all about him before meeting him I would've got strung out."[690]

With the vocals complete for *Lonely Soul*, Shadow continued working on tracks which would become *Bloodstain* (featuring Alice Temple), *Unreal*, and another that wouldn't end up on the album,

---

[685] Adams, C 1998
[686] Sturges, F 2003
[687] McLean, C 1998, p. 66
[688] Abdallah, R 2016
[689] NME 1998e
[690] Burgess, J 1998, p. 57

called *Untitled Heavy Beat (Part 1 & 2)*.[691] At the time Tim Goldsworthy was still a member of UNKLE along with Lavelle and Shadow, with Lavelle bouncing ideas between the two producers. But by the end of the year Shadow had grown tired of UNKLE again and feeling like a third wheel he decided he'd had enough and quit the project. Talking about it later he stated:

> While people were playing video games and smoking and hanging out in the other room I just locked myself in with a sampler, and that's where the demo for *"Lonely Soul"* was done, the Alice Temple track and *"Unreal"*. But again, I left thinking, 'I'm never going to do that again'. This time for sure.[692]

Likewise, Tim Goldsworthy had similar feelings. With Shadow seemingly put in charge of producing the project Goldsworthy decided he would leave as he had lost interest in the more rock orientated direction the UNKLE album was moving towards with collaborations between musicians such as Richard Ashcroft. While he had sat in on the *Lonely Soul* sessions, by December 1996 he had officially left UNKLE,[693] explaining to NME in 1998:

> James had a vision for this record, and it soon became clear that I wasn't a part of it. I guess the creative friction started when Mo' Wax took off and I would be working for a week at a time with Kudo, and then he comes in and says, 'Hmmm, it's not quite right...' There's a couple of albums of stuff which we scrapped because he decided it wasn't what he wanted. I was doing the programming, then he brought Shadow in, who's a genius programmer, and I kind of felt redundant. I also didn't like the idea of depending on people for whole tunes, just putting down a backing track and bringing people like Richard Ashcroft or Thom Yorke in for the rest – I think that sucks to be honest...we went out a

---

[691] DJShadow.com n.d. e
[692] Cigarettes, J 1998, p. 14
[693] Roberts, M 1998

couple of times when our relationship was at its worst, and came to a more amicable conclusion. Which was for me to go, because he explained what he wanted, and I didn't want to be part of it.[694]

Lavelle for his part admitted fault for the fallout telling *Jockey Slut,* "It had been going on too long. I was perhaps too overpowering and I wanted to do something different, something bigger. I think maybe he did as well but I think he thought it was all getting a joke." [695]

With his co-producers DJ Shadow, Tim Goldsworthy and Masayuki Kudo having all left, UNKLE was reduced to James Lavelle as the sole member, and the album was once again put on hold.

---

[694] Cigarettes, J 1998, p. 14
[695] Burgess, J 1998, p. 59

Ape Sounds

Outside of his work with the label Major Force, Fujiwara Hiroshi was also the author of a column called Last Orgy which he contributed to the Japanese magazine *Takarajima,* and where he discussed various topics such as the latest music, clothing brands, and skateboarders.[696] The column, which was co-edited by Hiroshi and his Tiny Panx bandmate Kan Takagi since 1987,[697] was considered a bible for Japanese youth, and this influence led him to become one of the original members of the International Stüssy Tribe.[698] Last Orgy also spun off in to a TV series which was watched religiously by a young Tomoaki Nagao[699] who soon earned the nickname Nigo, meaning "Number 2" and meant in reference to the fact he looked up to, as well as looked like, Fujiwara Hiroshi.[700] Nigo soon began working for Hiroshi as well as the Japanese magazine *Popeye*, where he started his own column called Last Orgy 2.[701]

Nigo was born December 23 1970 in Japan,[702] and while studying fashion in 1990 he met his future business partner Jun Takahashi.[703] In 1993, with help from Fujiwara Hiroshi,[704] Nigo and Takahashi opened a clothing store called Nowhere, located in Urahara near Tokyo's Harajuku district.[705] Initially selling select boutique items,[706] the pair soon began selling t-shirts under their own brand's, with Jun creating Undercover and Nigo creating Bape,[707] or A Bathing Ape, a reference to a Japanese saying "a

---

[696] Trebay, G 2016
[697] Tuzio, A 2020
[698] Yu, S 2019
[699] Li, R 2016
[700] Yu, S 2019
[701] Li, R 2016
[702] Famous Fashion Designers, 2019
[703] Li, R 2016
[704] Li, R 2019
[705] Li, R 2016
[706] Ibid.
[707] Yu, S 2019

bathing ape in lukewarm water."[708] Nigo explained the name was intended sarcastically, "It's a reference to the young generation being spoiled, pampered and too complacent...It wasn't really meant as a social message. It was just something that I felt was right at the time."[709] The branding made use of imagery inspired by the *Planet of the Apes* series of films, with Bape's logo of an ape head as well as slogans such as "Ape Shall Never Kill Ape" borrowed from the film series.[710]

In 1995, Nigo visited London and stopped by the Mo' Wax offices to pick up some records from Masayuki Kudo and Nakanishi Toshio who introduced him to James Lavelle.[711] Lavelle explained their meeting:

> I originally met Nigo in London through K.U.D.O and Toshio, who I was working with, from Major Force. Most of the Japanese musicians and designers would come and see those guys because they were OG and kinda helped set it all up in Japan. It was the first time Nigo had come to London and he came to the studio and I was given a t-shirt. I was then in Japan, a couple of months later, and had a phone number. I was told to go to a 'Wendy's' burger bar in Harajuku, make a phone call and someone would come and meet me. I went to their first office and they were just screen-printing t-shirts in quite a small space and he didn't really say very much – he just bowed and gave me some clothes and we built a relationship from there.[712]

The two bonded over their mutual interests in toy collecting, *Star Wars*, art and clothes, and would go out shopping together in London and Tokyo.[713]

---

[708] Hahn, L 2006
[709] Ibid.
[710] Edelson, S 2004
[711] Nigo 2000, 00:00:30
[712] Wilson, R 2014
[713] Dike, J 2017

In 1997 Lavelle started Mo' Wax Japan, a collaboration with the Japanese record label Toy's Factory, and also had a residency at a club there, so he was visiting Japan often giving himself and Nigo a chance to spend more time together.[714]

Lavelle discussed his friendship with Nigo to *The Hype Beast* in 2017:

> We were just similar age, very into toy collecting, really into *Star Wars*, really into contemporary modern art, especially street art and clothes. So we just started to build a relationship...We just used to go around Tokyo buying records, sneakers and toys. He'd come to London and we'd hang out, I'd take him poster shopping. I got him all the original Planet of the Apes posters from all the real poster galleries.[715]

Lavelle and Nigo's first collaboration was a double CD compilation entitled *James vs. Nigo - A Bathing Ape Vs Mo'Wax* where they each had a CD containing a mix of songs they had selected for inclusion.[716] It would be released in Japan only in October 1997, with artwork by Futura featuring characters representing both Lavelle and Nigo.[717] Lavelle introduced Futura and Stash to Nigo in 1995, and they too began collaborating, faxing t-shirt designs to Nigo.[718] In 1997 Bape released a series of t-shirts designed by Futura entitled *Bathing Ape VS Mo' Wax Japan* which featured Futura's artwork from the *James vs. Nigo* album. Toys based on Futura's designs were also released in 1997, with two figures representing Lavelle and Nigo each.[719] Their collaboration on toys would be taken a step further in 1998 when Nigo partnered with Japanese toy company Medicom to create 12" action figures of

---

[714] Ibid.
[715] Dike, J 2017
[716] Nigo 2014
[717] Discogs 2019s
[718] Marx, W 2015 n.p.
[719] Curtis, N 2017

Lavelle and himself, with the Nigo figure featuring an ape mask, while Lavelle's contained an UNKLE pointman mask.[720]

Back in 1997, Nigo had begun visiting London and the Major Force West Studios regularly and each time he visited he would record a song.[721] One of the tracks recorded was *March of The General*, a *Planet of the Apes* inspired track produced by Kudo, and featuring Lavelle, and Tony Vegas of the Scratch Perverts.[722] The track is almost seven minutes long and filled with *Planet of the Apes* samples from Jerry Goldsmith's score of the 1968 film and dialogue from its sequels, 1970's *Beneath the Planet of the Apes*, 1971's *Escape from the Planet of the Apes*, and 1973's *Battle for the Planet of the Apes*. The song mixes samples from everything from Titanic's *Love Is Love* to Ramsey Louis's cover of The Beatles *Back in the USSR*, and ends with a loop from Rick James' *Fire it Up* over scratches provided by Tony Vegas.[723]

March of The General was released on the *James vs. Nigo* album in 1997 and credited to UNKLE.[724] It saw a further release in 1998 when it was released as a single with a series of remixes, the song was now retitled *Ape Shall Never Kill Ape* but otherwise remained the same.[725]

In 1999 it appeared again as part of Nigo's debut album *Ape Sounds*. Produced by Kudo, the album featured contributions from Money Mark, Toshi, Kan Takagi , Ben Lee, and Shawn Lee. The Japanese and UK releases of this album are quite different, with the Japanese version released on the 21st of November 1999 on Toy's Factory,[726] and the Mo' Wax version released in the UK on 25th of September 2000.[727] Each edition features different artwork as well

---

[720] Beastiemania, 2009
[721] The Fashion Post, 2013
[722] Discogs 2019tt
[723] WhoSampled 2020a
[724] Discogs 2019s
[725] Discogs 2019tt
[726] Discogs 2020c
[727] Discogs 2020d

as minor tracklist differences, with the most notable being that while UNKLE's *Ape Shall Never Kill Ape* appears on both albums, it was remixed and renamed for Japan's Toy's Factory release, now titled *Symphony No. 25910 -Escape From Planet Of The Apes-*.[728] While the Mo' Wax version retained the original version as heard on the single, but gave it back the original title from 1997, *March of The General*.[729]

The *James vs. Nigo* album also saw the release of a second new UNKLE track, *Last Orgy 3*. The title refers to the song *Last Orgy* released in 1988 on Major Force by Tiny Panx, aka Fujiwara Hiroshi and Kan Takagi,[730] as well as the Last Orgy 2 column by Nigo.[731] [732] *Last Orgy 3* by UNKLE is similar to the original Tiny Panx song, and like the original it features a rap by Kan Takagi. The UNKLE version was produced by Kudo, and features Tony Vegas again providing scratches. While an exact date for the *Last Orgy* session is unknown, the credits for the release give one hint stating that the vocals were recorded "high in the Hollywood hills"[733] and Takagi was present during the 1995 UNKLE recording sessions in LA,[734] [735] while the rest was recorded at the Major Force West studios in England.[736]

Finally, *James vs. Nigo* saw the first commercial release of *Rock On*, the UNKLE collaboration with Rammellzee that had been recorded back in 1995. Alongside *Ape Shall Never Kill Ape,* and *Last Orgy 3*, *Rock On* was later released as a single in February 1998 as part of the *Trilogy Remix Series*, and then all three singles were combined into one *Trilogy Box Set* on both CD and 12" vinyl in March 1998.[737] The releases feature artwork designed by Stash

---

[728] Discogs 2020c
[729] Discogs 2020d
[730] Discogs 2019nn
[731] Yu, S 2019
[732] Toy's Factory, 2000a
[733] Discogs 2019ss
[734] Toy's Factory, 1999
[735] Kan, T 2014
[736] Discogs 2019ss
[737] Ibid.

and Art Direction by Nigo,[738] and the CD's feature bonus remixes not available on the 12" releases. These Japan only releases weren't widely heard outside of Japan and frustrated many fans as rumours of their releases circulated the internet with no clear way to purchase them.[739]

Each of the singles featured a handful of remixes, with *Ape Shall Never Kill Ape* accompanied by the *Twin Tower Mix* by Shinco from Scha Dara Parr, Keigo Oyamada (aka Cornelius), LaB LiFe, and Natural Calamity.[740] *Rock On* featured *the Nutcracker Mix* and *Nutcracker Dub* by John King of The Dust Brothers, as well as two alternate mixes, the *95 Edit* and *99 Dub*. *Rock On* also featured a remix by DJ Yas, and the CD release also contained the *UNKLE Homebass Mega Mix,* a megamix of the Trilogy songs.[741] *Last Orgy 3* was accompanied by remixes by Dan The Automator, Sound Hero (aka Kan Takagi and Yamatsuka Eye), and Trugoy of De La Soul.[742]

De La Soul had previously worked with Kan Takagi on their third album, 1993's *Buhloone Mindstate*, with Takagi appearing on the track *Long Island Wildin* alongside fellow Japanese rappers Scha Dara Parr. Trugoy later discussed recording with Takagi, noting "I could not understand Kan's lyric at all, but I knew that he was a genuine MC."[743]

---

[738] Discogs 2019uu
[739] Flynn, Sean <sflynn@pobox.com> 1998
[740] Discogs 2019tt
[741] Discogs 2019qq
[742] Discogs 2019uu
[743] Toy's Factory 2000a

Recording Psyence Fiction

During March 1997 DJ Shadow had toured North America with Jeru The Damaja, and he also brought along his MPC loaded with the UNKLE demos to play during his set.[744] At the time Shadow had demos of *Lonely Soul*, *Bloodstain*, and *Unreal*, and mixed them in to his live show along with his solo songs, new and old.[745]

Meanwhile, James Lavelle was still trying to organise UNKLE recording sessions. Radiohead's Thom Yorke had been on Lavelle's mind as a potential collaborator almost as long as Richard Ashcroft, but due to Radiohead's busy schedule, touring their album *The Bends*, then recording and touring their next album *OK Computer*, Lavelle had struggled to find time to get Yorke into a studio.[746]

Lavelle initially deciding on the collaboration after Yorke had listed the *Headz* compilation as a favourite of his, and they met up soon after.[747] Likewise, Radiohead had gone on record crediting DJ Shadow as an influence for their songs *Airbag*[748] and *Paranoid Android* from 1997's *OK Computer* album,[749] and the band had told reporters they hoped to bring Shadow on tour with them.[750] Lavelle had wanted to work with all of Radiohead, but Thom Yorke wanted to use their collaboration as a means to step away from the band and try something different as Radiohead's popularity was increasing with their latest album being their most well received yet.[751]

---

[744] Saeed, A 2012
[745] Ibid.
[746] Burgess, J 1998, pp. 59-60
[747] Burgess, J 1996, p 58
[748] Dalton, S 1997, pp. 57-58
[749] NME, 1997
[750] Douridas, C 1998
[751] Burgess, J 1998, pp. 59-60

Another problem for Lavelle was that Shadow had quit UNKLE again at the end of 1996, as Shadow would later explain, "I was asked to do this album twice - in 1995 and 1996. Both times I walked away from it. Both times I swore that I would never work on it ever again."[752] But playing the UNKLE demos while touring had made him reconsider, as he explained to *NME:*

> ...by the time May '97 came around I listened to the tapes and I thought, 'This is too good to turn my back on'. And by this time James had decided he wanted me to do the whole thing, which appealed to me because then I knew I could just get on with it. So to do justice to those three demos the rest of the record came about.[753]

With Shadow now agreeing to produce the UNKLE album, A&M decided to grant Lavelle a new budget, hoping for the same success that had met Shadow's debut album, *Endtroducing*.[754]

In June 1997, Shadow met with Thom Yorke and plans were made to record something together for the UNKLE album. Studio time was arranged for July,[755] during a break in Radiohead's US tour between their July 27 set at Warfield in San Francisco and their July 31 set at The Rage in Vancouver, Canada.[756] Lavelle had previously stated he one day hoped to record in Skywalker Sound Studios due to the studio being used for the sound recordings of the *Star Wars* films,[757] and that dream came true somewhat with the recording of what would become UNKLE's *Rabbit In Your Headlights*. While the song was actually recorded across the road from Skywalker, Lavelle was given a tour of the Skywalker studio and the staff told him how they admired his work, which Lavelle credits as the reason he was never sued for Mo' Wax's uncleared samples from the *Star*

---

[752] Future Music 1998
[753] Cigarettes, J 1998, p. 14
[754] Adventures in Psyence Fiction 2019, 00:07:20
[755] Burgess, J 1998, p. 59
[756] Green Plastic Trees n.d. b
[757] James, M 1997, p. 145

Wars series.⁷⁵⁸ The Skywalker team would also ask if Shadow could remix the *Star Wars* theme for the next film in the series, though this never materialised.⁷⁵⁹

Shadow drove Thom Yorke to the studio for their UNKLE recording session, while Yorke wrote down lyrics for what would become *Rabbit In Your Headlights*.⁷⁶⁰ Once in the studio, Yorke recorded the vocals in one take,⁷⁶¹ and then stayed for two days as they had booked the studio for 48 hours, with Yorke recording some extra bass parts, as well as tuning the pianos in the studio.⁷⁶²

In September 1997 Radiohead's tour arrived in the UK, and Shadow joined them as their support act, opening for their sets in England. Just as he had on the Jeru tour earlier in the year, Shadow brought his MPC with him and played some unreleased UNKLE demos to the crowd next to his solo work.⁷⁶³

Shadow had recorded his album *Entroducing* on the MPC sampler, using an MPC 60 MK II, but for the UNKLE album he upgraded to the MPC 3000 which had been released in 1994 by Akai. The upgrade meant larger samples could be recorded as the MPC 3000 was capable of recording sixty seconds of stereo, while the MPC 60 MK II was only capable of recording twelve.⁷⁶⁴ Pro Tools was also used for the recording of the UNKLE album, with Shadow first gaining experience using the software thanks to Dan The Automator, who had it in his studio while *Entroducing* was recorded. He would explain the process to *Tape Op*:

> The only time I use Pro Tools is for the editing and sequencing of the album. For Unkle, it was just used to de-click some of the really noisy samples. At the very beginning

---

⁷⁵⁸ BFI 2018b, 00:09:00
⁷⁵⁹ Gadelrab, R 2017
⁷⁶⁰ McLean, C 1998, p. 66
⁷⁶¹ Ibid.
⁷⁶² NME, 1998e
⁷⁶³ DJShadow.com 2009b
⁷⁶⁴ Ma, D 2017, p. 75

> of making the Unkle record, I was feeling very self-conscious. I was hearing all these chops on drum and bass records that I couldn't do on the 3000. I played around with Cubase a little but then I decided that I already had my sound and that I'd stick with it for a while…Endtroducing was recorded to ADAT because that was all that we could afford back then. The Unkle album was multi-tracked to 2" analog. Jim Abbis did the actual mixing but James and I were there for every minute of it.[765]

At the end of 1997, engineer Jim Abbiss was brought in by Lavelle to help Shadow with mixing the various samples used in to one cohesive sound. Initially Abbiss was hired for only two weeks, but he ended up staying for nine months as he saw the album through to completion.[766] Abbiss explained his experience to *NME*:

> Everything is sampled in Josh's music. He's got the most unique and brilliant way of cutting up sounds from some old seven-inches from 1974 or somewhere. But making that all sound like one record rather than a variety of scratchy vinyl is a bit of a headache. Then on top of that people were supposed to come in and write their own lyrics and vocal melodies on top. That caused problems and frustrations for some writers, 'cos they're just not used to working like that.[767]

Shadow for his part told *Remix Magazine,*

> I didn't think I was up for the challenge and the responsibility of having to mix those songs with those vocalists…So from the beginning, I said to Jim, 'Look, having just mixed *Endtroducing*, I know that there are some gaps in my knowledge.' And we just got along really well. I'd have these really intangible words to describe what I was feeling and

---

[765] Stenman, E 1998, p. 17
[766] Tingen, P 2006
[767] Cigarettes, J 1998, p. 16

hearing, and he would actually know how to make it happen.[768]

Abbiss who had worked as an engineer on Björk's *Debut*, and Massive Attack's *Protection* albums enjoyed the challenge the UNKLE project brought, telling *Mix Online*:

> I found DJ Shadow inspirational to work with. His attention to detail was incredible. He did not know any technical terms or how the desk worked, so he would ask for sounds that gave him a feeling. He'd say things like, "When it comes to the middle section, it should have the feeling of an airplane coming over and nearly deafening you." The way he approached music made me completely rethink the way I did sound.[769]

In the end there were twelve songs on the album, with some demos not making the cut. Each one of these has its own story, from the samples used to the guest appearances that scatter throughout the album. Together they make up the album that became *Psyence Fiction*.

---

[768] Swenson, K 2002
[769] Tingen, P 2007

Track By Track - Psyence Fiction

"Intro (Optional)"

A bonus track on the Japanese[770] and Australian editions of the album,[771] with the subtitle "Intro by Heroes and Vilains. Please do not violate",[772] the song contains an assortment of samples collected together featuring small excerpts from songs which represent the inspirations behind the making of *Psyence Fiction*.[773] The track is a pregap hidden track, only accessible if you use the rewind function of a CD player and are often undetected by computers.[774]

UNKLE's *Intro (Optional)* features a slew of uncleared samples, so it's no wonder that when he was asked about it at the time of release Lavelle pretended not to know about the track, saying "What song? That's an accident, it must have ended up on our album when something went wrong at the pressing plant."[775]

The following songs are featured:[776]

- Quannum MCs – "Blue Flames"
- Massive Attack – "Teardrop"
- Air – "All I Need"
- Invisibl Skratch Piklz – "Invisibl Skratch Piklz vs. Da Klamz Uv Deth"
- Timbaland and Magoo – "Clock Strikes" (Remix)
- The Chemical Brothers – "Elektrobank"
- Jurassic 5 – "Jayou"

---

[770] Discogs 2019rrr
[771] Discogs 2019aaa
[772] Discogs 2019rrr
[773] Spencer, R 2012, p. 14
[774] Smith, E 2017
[775] Adams, C 1998
[776] Snaporaz100 2010

- Cornelius – "Mic Check"
- Radiohead – "Just"
- Oasis – "Wonderwall"
- Portishead – "Numb"
- The Verve – "History"
- Peshay – "The Nocturnal (Back on the Firm)"
- DJ Krush – "Kemuri"
- Björk – "Human Behaviour"
- Nirvana – "Come as You Are"
- Innerzone Orchestra – "Bug in the Bassbin"
- A Tribe Called Quest (featuring Leaders of the New School) – "Scenario"
- Young Disciples – "Apparently Nothin'"
- Orbital – "Chime"
- Gang Starr – "Just to Get a Rep"
- 808 State – "Pacific State"
- Ice Cube – "Get Off My Dick and Tell Yo Bitch to Come Here (Remix)"
- Main Source – "Looking at the Front Door"
- Massive Attack – "Unfinished Sympathy"
- Soul II Soul – "Keep on Movin'"
- De La Soul – "The Magic Number"
- The Stone Roses – "I Wanna Be Adored"
- Talk Talk – "The Rainbow"
- Ultramagnetic MCs – "Give the Drummer Some"
- M|A|R|R|S – "Pump Up the Volume"
- Public Enemy – "Public Enemy No. 1"
- Major Force West – "Kiss FM Radio Promo"
- Depeche Mode – "Stripped"
- Beastie Boys – "The New Style"
- Metallica – "Welcome Home (Sanitarium)"
- Eric B. & Rakim – "Eric B. Is President"
- Frankie Goes to Hollywood – "The Last Voice"
- Newcleus – "Jam on It"
- Jamie Jupitor – "Computer Power"
- UTFO – "Roxanne"
- Art of Noise – "Beat Box"

- Run-DMC – "30 Days"
- New Order – "Blue Monday"
- Afrika Bambaataa & the Soulsonic Force – "Planet Rock"
- Malcolm McLaren & the World's Famous Supreme Team – "Buffalo Gals"
- Rammelzee and K-Rob – "Beat Bop"
- Grandmaster Flash & The Furious Five – "The Message"
- Kraftwerk – "It's More Fun to Compute"
- Zapp – "More Bounce to the Ounce"
- Grandmaster Flash & The Furious Five –"Superrappin'"
- John Oswald – "Brown"
- Sound taken directly from the opening scene of *Contact*
- Juice – "Catch a Groove"
- Herbie Hancock – "Chameleon"
- Sun Ra – "Space Is the Place"
- James Brown – "The Payback"
- Incredible Bongo Band – "Apache"
- Silver Apples – "Lovefingers"
- Terry Callier – "Dancing Girl"
- The Doors – "The End"
- Mickey & the Soul Generation - "Get Down Brother"
- The Meters – "Cissy Strut"
- David Axelrod – "Holy Thursday"
- The Beatles – "Tomorrow Never Knows"
- Jimi Hendrix – "Happy Birthday"
- Velvet Underground – "Venus in Furs"
- Nina Simone – "Feeling Good"
- The Elvin Jones/Jimmy Garrison Sextet - "Half and Half"

"Guns Blazing (Drums of Death, Pt. 1)" feat. Kool G Rap

The song begins with the sound of static like that from an old TV set, and a bleep which sounds like R2D2 from *Star Wars* though it hasn't been verified. These are followed by a long fade in of strings and beeps sampled from Alan Hawkshaw's *Countdown,* off the 1978 album *Terrestrial Journey.*[777] A voice then announces, "Somewhere in space, this may all be happening right now." This voice belongs to the French actor Malachi Throne, and was sampled from the original *Star Wars* preview trailer released during Christmas 1976 in anticipation for the first *Star Wars* film in 1977 (later renamed *Star Wars Episode IV: A New Hope*).[778] Malachi Throne incidentally also guest starred on an episode of *The Man From U.N.C.L.E.* TV series ("The Four-Steps Affair" from 1965).[779]

Lavelle explained the idea of the sample:

> We were inspired by archetypal narrative structures so we open with his track, '*Guns' Blazing*' because, to use *Star Wars* as a common reference point, it starts out with the rebel being attacked by the Empire. *Star Wars* also starts out with 'A long time ago in a galaxy far far away' and we have our little statement 'Somewhere in space this may all be happening right now'.[780]

Once the voiceover ends we hear a sudden flurry of fast drum beats cut up and sampled from Tullio De Piscopo's *Medium Rock* off their 1974 album *Suonando La Batteria Moderna*,[781] while the rest of the track contains drums from Frank Zappa's *Apostrophe* from the 1974

---

[777] WhoSampled 2019p
[778] De Lange, S 2015
[779] IMDB 2020b
[780] Burgess, J 1998, p. 60
[781] WhoSampled 2019s

album of the same name,[782] and Wizzard's *Buffalo Station/Get On Down To Memphis* taken from 1973's *Wizard Brew* album.[783]

Following the beats comes the voice of two characters, one who is named U.N.K.L.E. 77 and is being attacked by two fighter jets, while the other is Mission Control.[784] Though this may sound like a sample from an obscure movie it was actually scripted,[785] and served the purpose of creating a slight narrative for the album as the characters return briefly later. *The Independent* described the U.N.K.L.E. 77 character as "a kind of Major Tom for the Nineties, whom the album's artwork actually reveals to be a sweet-looking alien with a natty satchel."[786]

Following this introduction, the first of the albums many guest artist appears, Kool G Rap (a.k.a. Nathaniel Wilson),[787] sometimes shortened to G Rap, is an American rapper from Queens. He released his first single in 1986 and was brought in to the Juice Crew by Marley Marl who then produced Kool G Rap's debut album with DJ Polo, 1989's *Road To Riches*.[788] G Rap is considered one of the original MC's who introduced gangster and mafiaso themed rap to East Coast hip hop in America.[789] His albums have continued to influence his contemporaries, including Jay-Z, Nas and Eminem.[790] DJ Shadow was also a fan, having grown up listening to G Rap he considered him a legend[791] and had even sampled him for his album *Endtroducing*.[792]

---

[782] WhoSampled 2019q
[783] WhoSampled 2019t
[784] Maconie, S 1998
[785] Lavelle, J 2014
[786] Higgins, M 1998
[787] Kaufman, G 1998
[788] Ekpo, I 2018
[789] Birchmeier, J 2019
[790] Weingarten, C 2017
[791] MTV News, 1998
[792] WhoSampled 2019j

Kool G Rap recorded his vocals in one hour[793] in October 1997, after Shadow sent a beat for him to rap over.[794] Shadow likened G Rap as being akin to the Terminator "because he's so aggressive compared to everyone else on the record."[795] Shadow later discussed featuring G Rap on the album:

> I wanted someone involved who I grew up listening to. He was one of my favorite lyricists and probably a rapper most people wouldn't choose. He was given a breakbreat and the only instruction he was given, which were the same ones we gave to everybody else, were 'just be yourself'. The only thing I said he should try and avoid was the killer hoe type material. But then if you're gonna ask for Kool G Rap you're gonna get Kool G Rap![796]

Kool G Rap also described the session, telling *MTV*, "[DJ Shadow] wanted me to do, like, an old version of G rap...but not with a lot of curses, just hard-core freestyle stuff where I'm talking about money and mob stuff."[797] On the album track most of the cursing is censored by effects, but another version titled *Guns Blazing (Vocal Street)* was made available as a promo with the swearing intact.[798]

While the rest of *Psyence Fiction*'s guest artists were brought in by Lavelle, Kool G Rap was included at the insistence of Shadow, who explained,

> We agreed on who should be on the record...Except I had to put my foot down over Kool G Rap, because James was saying things like. 'Mike D represents the hip-hop side of the record'. and I was like, 'Well he doesn't really to me...' I

---

[793] Egaitsu, H 1998
[794] Burgess, J 1998, p. 57
[795] Ibid. p. 60
[796] Ibid. p. 57
[797] Kaufman, G 1998
[798] Discogs 2019ddd

wanted someone I grew up on, so I insisted on having Kool G Rap on the record. And I think he'll admit I was right".[799]

Also appearing alongside Kool G Rap on *Guns Blazing* were two of Shadow's Solesides labelmates Latyrx, aka Lateef The Truth Speaker, and Lyrics Born, who provided additional vocals.[800]

The U.N.K.L.E. 77 character returns throughout the song as their story continues and *Guns Blazing* ends with Mission Control announcing they have lost contact with 77 before we hear 77 calling on their radio asking "is anybody out there." During this sequence there are several samples from someone *Galaxian,* a videogame produced by Namco in 1979[801] which is similar to *Space Invaders,* and went on to spawn the popular sequel *Galaga*.[802]

Ahead of its release a white label promo was distributed in the US as Shadow hoped that a white label would allow America DJs to become intrigued by the track without any preconceived prejudices they otherwise might have. As Shadow tells it though, "nobody played it anyway...[It was] Too hardcore for rock dudes, too out there for rap dudes. At the time, anyway."[803] The promo contained the uncensored street vocal alongside the album version and an acapella and instrumental.[804]

A video was also created for *Guns Blazing*, initially as part of the *NME Brats Review* program in 1999, and also toured across the USA and Tokyo as part of the ResFest 1999 film festival.[805] [806] The film was created by Shynola, a group of artists which included Gideon Baws, Jason Groves, Chris Harding, and Richard

---

[799] Cigarettes, J 1998, p. 15
[800] Discogs 2019zz
[801] WhoSampled 2019r
[802] Arcade Classics 2019
[803] DJShadow.com n.d. f
[804] Discogs 2019ddd
[805] ResFest 1999b
[806] ResFest 1999a

Kenworthy.[807] The group had read about UNKLE in a magazine and wrote to James Lavelle offering to make a video for him which became *Guns Blazing,* and was made using Adobe Photoshop and Adobe Premiere, combing elements of Ben Drury and Futura's UNKLE artwork.[808]

Lavelle next put the group in charge of another video for Mo' Wax, Quannum's *I Changed my Mind* released in 2000,[809] and later in 2001 Shynola created the *Eye For An Eye* video for UNKLE.[810]

---

[807] ResFest 1999b
[808] Ibid.
[809] Neil, 2010
[810] Onedotzero 2004, p. 161

"UNKLE Main Title Theme"

Recorded at DJ Shadow's home studio in late April 1998,[811] the *UNKLE Main Title Theme* begins with samples from the end of the previous *Guns Blazing (Drums of Death, Pt. 1)*'s "there, there, there," from the UNKLE 77 character asking "is anybody out there?"

While the track is short, running under four minutes, there are more than fifteen samples throughout the *UNKLE Main Title Theme*.[812] "Put aside the everyday world, and come with us into the world of imagination. The middle ground between light and shadow" is the first of many vocal samples, this one from an advertisement for an episode of *The Twilight Zone*. The voice belongs to James Franciscus as Lieutenant Mueller in the 1959 episode *Judgment Night* from the *The Twilight Zone's* first season.[813] This is followed by "ladies and gentlemen tonight," sampled from Bass Dominators feat. M.C.C.'s *Go Head, Go Head (Yo! Yo!)* released in 1986,[814] and the Beastie Boys' Mike D spelling out "U.N.K.L.E."

Mike D's vocals are sampled from *The Knock (Drums of Death Pt. 2)* which appears later on *Psyence Fiction*, and they reappear across the *UNKLE Main Title Theme* cut up and with various effects over them as well.

Mike D is followed by the voice of Hubert J. Bernhard, sampled from his 1967 album *The Planetarium Lecture Series: No. 3: The UFO's*, discussing whether professional astronomers report the existence of UFO's.[815] After a flurry of quick hip hop samples, the albums second *Star Wars* sample is featured, again from the 1976 teaser which was used in *Guns Blazing (Drums of Death, Pt. 1)*.[816] Directly after the "Somewhere in space, this may all be happening right

---

[811] McLean, C 1998, p. 69
[812] WhoSampled 2019n
[813] WhoSampled 2019jj
[814] WhoSampled 2019ee
[815] WhoSampled 2019gg
[816] De Lange, S 2015

now" used in *Guns Blazing,* the trailer announced "20th Century Fox and George Lucas, the man who brought you *American Graffiti*, now bring you an adventure unlike anything on your planet: *Star Wars*," and it was the end of that line which is used in *UNKLE Main Title Theme*, now referencing the album you are listening to.

Following George Lucas' *Star Wars*, Shadow and Lavelle sample *Hearts of Darkness: A Filmmaker's Apocalypse*, the 1991 documentary about the makings of Francis Ford Coppola's 1979 war film *Apocalypse Now*.[817] Lavelle had watched the film during the making of Psyence Fiction and it is said to have resonated with him, as he felt the madness that Coppola was going through was similar to what he and Shadow were going through with the creation of their album.[818] The sample of Coppola stating "there were too many of us, we had access to, too many…too much money, and little by little we went insane" was often brought up by the press,[819] with *Q Magazine* referring to it as a "dark in-joke about ambition."[820]

The next vocal sample comes from Ridley Scott's 1982 film *Blade Runner*, where the character Roy Batty played by Rutger Hauer says "Fiery the angels fell; deep thunder rolled around their shores; burning with the fires of Orc,"[821] while Shadow and Lavelle removed the "deep thunder rolled around their shores." The final vocal sample, "a ticket to nothingness" is from the 1997 film *Event Horizon,* directed by Paul W.S. Anderson.[822]

The instruments which feature beneath these samples are made up from a handful of recordings, with the guitar sampled from *A Pilgram's Path* by Rage which appeared on their 1988 album *Noise*.[823] This simple loop is repeated throughout *UNKLE Main Title Theme* alongside drums from Matthew Cang and Eddie Chin's *Slow*

---

[817] WhoSampled 2019ff
[818] Grundy, G 1998, p. 80
[819] Burgess, J 1998, p. 57
[820] Wright, R 2017
[821] WhoSampled 2020e
[822] The Sample Source Wiki 2019
[823] WhoSampled 2019hh

Glide, released on 1983's *Surprise Package*, and more drums from Joy Unlimited's *Rudiment* off their 1971 album *Schmetterlinge*.[824] In the last section of *UNKLE Main Title Theme* during the scratching, a new guitar sample begins which was taken from The Luv Bandits' 1967 song *Mizzer-Bahd*.[825]

Many reviews of *Psyence Fiction* enjoyed *UNKLE Main Title Theme*, and the track was variously described as "a pileup of turntable scratching and tortured violins,"[826] "a blend of percussive beats, plangent guitar and sci-fi sounds,"[827] and "a liquid mix of gauzy guitar, psychotic violin and Shadow's own furious scratching."[828] *The Times* were particularly impressed with how *UNKLE Main Title Theme* segued from *Guns Blazing (Drums of Death, Pt. 1)*, and suggested the "implication is that UNKLE are leaving the mundane bluster of gangsta to forge fresh ground."[829]

---

[824] WhoSampled 2019n
[825] WhoSampled 2019ii
[826] Gundersen, E 1998
[827] Ludovic, H-T 1998
[828] Lorraine, A 1998
[829] Pattenden, M 1998

"Bloodstain" feat Alice Temple

Bloodstain was one of the earliest tracks demoed for *Psyence Fiction*, and was recorded around the same time as *Lonely Soul* in 1996.[830] But *Bloodstain* is also reminiscent of an earlier unreleased UNKLE demo called *Dissatisfied* from before DJ Shadow had become a member of the group, and which was created by Tim Goldsworthy and James Lavelle.[831]

What makes *Dissatisfied* similar to *Bloodstain* is the fact they both contain a very similarly utilised sample from the song *Alone* by BeBe K'Roche, with the vocal "I'm alone and dissatisfied." This suggests Lavelle had wanted to use it with UNKLE for some time, as *Dissatisfied* was likely recorded around 1994 or 1995 if it was one of Lavelle and Goldsworthy's earliest tracks[832] seeing as *The Time Has Come* was released in 1994.[833]

Bloodstain, apart from using the same sample, is otherwise completely different and features a vocal performance by Alice Temple. Temple recorded her demo in November 1996 at The Strongroom, East London, before returning in August 1997 to record the final vocals at Metropolis studios, Chiswick.[834]

Before she became a singer, Alice Temple was originally a BMX racer and in 1982 at the age of 15 was already winning competitions,[835] becoming the first person to win the Girls Number 1 plate two years in a row in the UK, as well as picking up a Number 3 in Europe.[836] With such a successful career at an early age she would surprise everyone by announcing at the end of 1983 that she

---

[830] Cigarettes, J 1998, p. 14
[831] Lavelle, J 2018a, 00:35:35
[832] Cooper, D 2018
[833] Discogs 2019rr
[834] McClean, C 1998, p. 66, 68
[835] UKBMXHistory 2017
[836] Poole, Gary 1985, p. 60

was retiring from the sport.[837] Speaking to a reporter in *BMX Racer + Freestyle* for their September 1984 issue, the 17 year old Temple told the reporter she was retiring from competing as her mother wanted her to focus on her education.[838]

In 1985 Temple became part of the Blitz Kid scene[839] which would herald the New Romantic music genre, as Temple became a regular at the Blitz club-night in Covent Garden, London, spending time with Boy George.[840]

Temple next moved in to modelling, telling a reporter "it was a good excuse to travel,"[841] appearing on the cover on *I-D Magazine* in May 1986 photographed by Nick Night,[842] and that same year appeared in the Culture Club video for *Move Away*.[843] Temple is believed to be the subject of Boy George's 1988 song *A Boy Called Alice*, where she provides the backing vocals "My name's Alice and I'm not a boy."[844]

In 1990 Temple furthered her move into music when she teamed with Eg White,[845] real name Francis White,[846] previously of British boy band Brother Beyond.[847] The pair recorded the album *24 Years of Hunger* in their kitchen,[848] and in 1991 it was released under the band name Eg & Alice. *Q Magazine* were fans, describing it as one the best albums of the 20th Century,[849] and *The Times* enjoyed the album's sound, describing Eg & Alice as "a British Steely Dan."[850]

---

[837] BMX Racer & Freestyle 1984, p. 8
[838] Ibid.
[839] Teen Machine 1985
[840] Berke, C 2018
[841] Gaitney, S 1999, p. 21
[842] Magazine Canteen 2020
[843] Thomas, B 2017
[844] Berke, C 2018
[845] Eaton, A 2009
[846] McKormick, N 2009
[847] The Irish Times, 2009
[848] Jenkins, L 2013
[849] Swihart, S 2019a
[850] The Times 1992

While the press were on their side, the pair didn't tour the album[851] which resulted in sales of only 8,000 copies, unfortunately missing the charts,[852] and by 1992 Temple had left the group to pursue other things.[853] While she may have left music behind for the time, she continued to gain recognition for her work, with *The New Yorker* describing her in 1995 as an "English punk-rock musician."[854]

Back in England, *24 Years of Hunger* took on a bit of a cult following,[855] and when James Lavelle heard a tape of her singing it impressed him enough to want to bring Temple in to record with UNKLE.[856] He explained:

> I just fell in love with her. I wanted to sign her to Mo' Wax. She represented a lot of things from the environment I'd grown up in. She was a BMX champion as a kid and very left of centre. I didn't know how to fit Alice into the album but then I went round to the flat Josh was working out of and he played me this track and I was like 'that's Alice Temple'.[857]

Alice for her part enjoyed the collaboration telling NME in 1998:

> I was really nervous going into that studio environment...They'd given me a beat and a backing track, and I'm not really used to writing songs like that. I thought what I'd done was so crap. and I didn't know Josh, so I didn't know whether it was what they wanted. But we gritted our teeth and when we eventually got a finished version I was really dead chuffed with it[858]

---

[851] Swihart, S 2019b
[852] The Irish Times, 2009
[853] Ibid.
[854] Als, H 1995, p. 37
[855] The Irish Times, 2009
[856] UNKLE 1998, 00:18:00
[857] Burgess, J 1998, p. 57
[858] Cigarettes, J 1998, p. 16

But while she enjoyed *Bloodstain*, she initially wasn't impressed with the rest of the album telling *Out Magazine* in 1999, "I thought it was all a load of crap at first. But I have to say I'm very proud to be on it now."[859]

Bloodstain contains several samples throughout the song, beginning at around 25 seconds in when a drumbeat is heard, sampled from Head West's *Attention* off the 1970 album *Disques Vogue*, accompanied by a guitar sample which remains unknown,[860] before Alice Temple's lyrics follow. Temple recorded her vocals in August 1997[861] over a beat provided by Shadow,[862] while her lyrics are reportedly about heroin abuse.[863] Lavelle later commented on the song, "She wasn't in a good state. There were a lot of drugs going on at the time…You only need to listen to the song to hear what she was going through."[864]

Lavelle also revealed that when they tried to clear the sample from BeBe K'Roche's *Alone,* the record label refused to clear it unless they could prove Alice Temple was a lesbian.[865] The label in question was Olivia Records, a record label which focused on women's music, and has now become a successful lesbian cruise ship business.[866] Lavelle was able to get the sample cleared, and it appears at the end of the song.[867]

Following the "Are you satisfied" vocal sample from BeBe K'Roche's *Alone, Bloodstain* then ends with a guitar solo sampled from The Grodeck Whipperjenny's 1979 song *Evidence for the Existence of the Unconscious*,[868] and dialogue from the *Star Wars*

---

[859] Gaitney, S 1999, p. 21
[860] WhoSampled 2019a
[861] Burgess, J 1998, p. 57
[862] Cigarettes, J 1998, p. 16
[863] Pattenden, M 1998
[864] Spencer, R 2012, p. 15
[865] Ibid.
[866] Riese 2016
[867] Spencer, R 2012, p. 15
[868] WhoSampled 2019o

Holiday Special ("You Are Alone?"), which leads directly in to the next track.

The Star Wars Holiday Special was a TV special produced in 1978 that has become infamous for how bad it is, with *Star Wars* creator George Lucas apparently so embarrassed by it that he tried to find and destroy every copy in existence.[869] Regardless of the truth surrounding that rumour, copies have been made and it is now easy to find online thanks to YouTube and other video sharing websites.[870]

The most notable segment is one which featured the first appearance of fan-favourite Boba Fett, the bounty hunter who would appear in *Star Wars* sequels *The Empire Strikes Back*, and *Return of The Jedi*. The two samples which appear on *Psyence Fiction*, "You Are Alone?" on *Bloodstain*, and "Maybe I Can Help You" on *Unreal*, are dialogue spoken by the Boba Fett character. In the short animated segment, known as "The Faithful Wookiee", Fett meets Luke Skywalker and offers to help him while actually planning to betray Skywalker and his friends to their enemy Darth Vader.[871]

The animation was produced by Nelvana Ltd. in Toronto, Canada, who would go on to produce the *Droids*, and *Ewoks* animated *Star Wars* series' in the mid-1980's. Boba Fett was voiced by Don Francks in *The Holiday Special* and reprised the character for Boba Fett's appearance in an episode of *Droids* entitled *A Race to the Finish* which aired in 1985. Of interest, the actor also appeared in a 1966 episode of the television series *Man From U.N.C.L.E.*, entitled *The Round Table Affair*.[872]

Outside of its appearance on *Psyence Fiction*, a one-track promo of *Bloodstain* was released in 1998 by London Records[873] and in

---

[869] Warren, RB 2014
[870] Ibid.
[871] The Star Wars Holiday Special 2018
[872] IMDB 2020a
[873] Discogs 2019xx

2015 the song was released in remixed form as *Blood Stain (UNKLE Reconstruction)* for the Mo' Wax Future Past collection.[874] The *Blood Stain* release was in collaboration with the Japanese Fashion Label Hysteric Glamour, and featured a 12" record limited to 50 copies, as well as a series of Mo' Wax x Hysteric Glamour t-shirts[875] and jacket.[876] The remix was also featured on Lavelle's *Naples* mix for Global Underground released that same year.[877]

---

[874] Cooper, D 2017a
[875] Goodhood n.d. c
[876] Goodhood n.d. b
[877] Discogs 2019t

"Unreal"

Opening with the second half of the sample that ends *Bloodstain*, "Maybe I Can Help You?", *Unreal* then begins with a large string and bell sample from the opening Leroy Vinnegar's 1974 song *Reservation*, and drums from The Other Brothers 1968 song *No Class*, slightly slowed down.[878]

The guitar and bell samples that start around the one-minute mark are from The Jules Blattner Group's *Birth*, sampled from their 1971 album *Call Me Man!*[879] The *Birth* sample featured so heavily that Jules Blattner is credited as a co-writer of the track in the album credits,[880] and Shadow has commented that Blattner was one of the few artists who has been happy to be sampled by him.[881]

The song title *Unreal* comes from the source of the "How do you feel?" vocal sample that appears after the four-minute mark. The sample is from The Eclectic Mouse's *Pre-Dawn Retrospective Chant*, taken from their 1969 album *Everything I've Got*,[882] and the full vocal goes "How should you feel when you've felt everything you can feel, and you still feel unreal. Oh, you're unreal. How do you feel?"

Unreal would later be re-released as the non-album track *Be There* and feature vocals by Ian Brown of The Stone Roses, with later editions of the album containing both tracks, and *Be There* becoming the final track on the album. Lavelle had sent the track to Brown prior to the release of *Psyence Fiction*, but Brown sent it back and told Lavelle "You're crazy, leave it alone, it doesn't need a vocal."[883]

---

[878] WhoSampled 2020f
[879] WhoSampled 2019ll
[880] Discogs 2019zz
[881] Raz, G 2012
[882] WhoSampled 2019kk
[883] Mixmag 2003, p. 39

"Lonely Soul" feat Richard Ashcroft

In 1996 after discussing the UNKLE project with Richard Ashcroft, James Lavelle brought him in to the studio in September to record a demo which would become *Lonely Soul*,[884] with DJ Shadow telling *The Quietus*, "James Lavelle and I were huge fans of the Verve album *A Northern Soul*, so James really wanted to have Richard Ashcroft come down and sing. He came down and did a guide vocal and we built a track around it."[885]

For *Lonely Soul* Shadow upgraded from the MPC 60 MK II sampler he had used for his solo album to the newer MPC 3000 model. He explained the benefits to *The Quietus*, "It was a very different way of working and suddenly I had a whole new arsenal, so to speak, and much more sample time, but it was a lot more complicated to work with. That song represented me getting my head around the new MPC."[886]

Will Malone created the string arrangement for *Lonely Soul* after Lavelle explained he wanted something similar to *Adagio For Strings*,[887] an orchestral piece composed by Samuel Barber in 1936, arranged for a string orchestra and which originated as a movement from his *String Quartet, Op. 11*.[888]

Lavelle had enjoyed Malone's work on Massive Attack's *Unfinished Sympathy*, and played him the original demo of *Lonely Soul* shortly after Ashcroft had recorded his vocals, Lavelle explained "He was into the track so we asked him to do the strings for it, to write an end piece and also write, as a featured artist, his own piece which is '*Celestial Annihilation*'."[889] The strings for *Lonely Soul* were recorded in September 1997, one year after Ashcroft had recorded

---

[884] Burgess, J 1998, p. 60
[885] Tuffrey, L 2012
[886] Ibid.
[887] Harcourt, N 1998, 00:44:00
[888] Keller, J 2010
[889] Burgess, J 1998, p. 57

his vocals over Shadow's original demo,[890] and the recording of *Lonely Soul* took almost two years.[891] This took its toll on Shadow who described recording the song as a painful experience, telling *CMJ* in 1998:

> I don't like to get dramatic, but recording '*Lonely Soul*' was difficult...There was the demo, Richard Ashcroft's guide vocal, the strings, filling in the gaps, making it cohesive. After mixing it for the third day, I went home and went to sleep. When I woke up I couldn't walk, I couldn't get out of bed. I had slipped a disc in my back due to all of the stress. That wasn't good. And it changed my life. I think about it everyday. I feel I am much more in tunes (sic) with my body now.[892]

The drum beat used on *Lonely Soul* was sampled from Lionel Morton's *Fearless Fred's Amazing Animal Band,* a novelty record which produced by the BBC in 1972.[893] The strange rocket noises after the four minute mark were sampled from the *Apocalypse Now Soundtrack*, namely *Do Lung Bridge* written by Carmine Coppola and released in 1979.[894] The sitar samples are from Shanti's 1971 song *Innocence,*[895] with the bass guitar sounds throughout taken from Renaissance's *Bullet* released in 1969.[896]

In 2012, DJ Shadow released a Greatest Hits compilation entitled *Reconstructed*, which featured songs from the various eras of his career, including a shortened edit of *Lonely Soul*. In an interview focused around the compilation Shadow discussed the track with *The Quietus*:

---

[890] Burgess, J 1998, p. 60
[891] Dummy, 2013
[892] Micallef, K 1998, p. 14
[893] WhoSampled 2019v
[894] WhoSampled 2019u
[895] WhoSampled 2019x
[896] WhoSampled 2019w

> 'Lonely Soul' is definitely one of my finest achievements during this twenty-year period and in the process of going back through a lot of DAT tape during the course of putting together the greatest hits, I found this radio edit that I had forgotten about and was never released and I liked the way it felt. I remember when we did it in the studio thinking "wow, I wonder if this will be the version we end up with on the album?" I really liked the way it ended and felt like it was a complete vision without being a sort of butchered version of the album version.[897]

The song was performed live twice by Richard Ashcroft with members of UNKLE, first in 2000 during a show where Ashcroft was supporting Madonna and he brought out Lavelle and Rich File (the current UNKLE line-up at the time) to perform. Then in 2003 Ashcroft would join Shadow on stage for his Live at ICA set to perform *Lonely Soul*, with both performances recorded and circulating among fans online.

While UNKLE had planned to use *Lonely Soul* as a single to promote the album, Mo' Wax had to first seek permission from Ashcroft's label who refused to grant it.[898] [899]

Regardless of whether it could be a single or not, Lavelle contacted film director Stanley Kubrick about making a video for *Lonely Soul*, and Kubrick's publicist told him that while Kubrick was interested in the idea he was currently filming *Eyes Wide Shut*, and suggested Lavelle get back in contact after the film was complete.[900] Unfortunately, Kubrick died soon after, prior to the release of *Eyes Wide Shut* in 1999. The video would later be made as a film entitled *The Corridor* for Lavelle's 2016 exhibition *Daydreaming With... Stanley Kubrick*, a collaboration between Lavelle and the Stanley Kubrick estate.[901] The film starred Joanna Lumley and Aiden Gillen

---

[897] Tuffrey, L 2012
[898] Farsides, T 1998
[899] Cigarettes, J 1998, p. 16
[900] BFI 2014, 00:02:00
[901] Brewer, J 2016

and was written and directed by filmmaker Toby Dye. The film, or art installation as it has been described, features the actors within four simultaneous, interweaving narratives on a continuous loop.[902]

---

[902] Dye, T 2019

"Getting Ahead in the Lucrative Field of Artist Management"

A short interlude, *Getting Ahead in the Lucrative Field of Artist Management* was a jab at the management shared by Richard Ashcroft and Badly Drawn Boy. Mo' Wax had intended on releasing *Lonely Soul* and *Nursery Rhyme* as singles to promote *Psyence Fiction*, but their shared management refused to let them. [903]

Notably the song is directly in the middle of tracks featuring both artists, and on the Japanese edition of *Psyence Fiction* this song is subtitled in the credits with the quote "As the record industry falls down around our ears, let's raise a glass to the ambulance chasers...",[904] with an ambulance chaser being slang for a lawyer.[905] Lavelle explained their frustration:

> All these people are trying to get involved, and you're trying to explain what you're trying to do to all these management and record companies. But it reached the point where me and Josh were saying, 'Who the fuck are all these people? These artists are on our record, who the fuck are these idiots? What right have they to say anything about it, they're not on the record'.[906]

The skit is short and allows for a tonal change between the haunting *Lonely Soul* and the punk rock-esque *Nursery Rhyme* which comes next. But it equally serves as reminder to the listener regarding the mindset of the UNKLE duo whilst recording the album. Lavelle explained, "That track was a reflection of how bonkers we were getting...There were times when I looked at Josh and he looked at me and we said 'Fuck it, I give up… It's not worth the grief'."[907]

---

[903] Spencer, R 2012, p. 15
[904] Discogs 2019rrr
[905] Cambridge Dictionary 2019
[906] Cigarettes, J 1998, p. 16
[907] Ibid.

The game itself, which was indeed named *Ball Busters*, is described as an abstract strategy game and was released in 1975 by Mego, designed by John McNett. Board Game Geek providing the following further description regarding the gameplay:

> Players move around groups of playing pieces set up similarly to checkers. Each piece consists of a plastic ball mounted on a long springy stem which is mounted on a peg which fits into holes in the board. Players can attack an opponents piece by pulling back on one of their own adjacent pieces and releasing it, causing the plastic balls to collide.[908]

Mego was famous for its action figure range which included the 1974 *Planet of the Apes* figures,[909] as well as figures based of the original *Star Trek* TV series.[910] In 1976 Mego refused the license for a new film entitled *Star Wars*, with the license eventually going to rival Kenner. This windfall led to sales at Kenner jumping from $100 million in 1975, to $200 million in 1978, largely credited to their *Star Wars* line as the film was a success.[911] Meanwhile Mego struggled to regain market share and by 1981 were reporting losses of over $40 million, leading to the company filing for bankruptcy in 1982.[912]

---

[908] Board Game Geek 2019
[909] Scott, S 2009, p. 3
[910] Mego Collector 2014
[911] Barnhill, J 2009, p. 345
[912] The New York Times 1982

"Nursery Rhyme / Breather" feat Badly Drawn Boy

In November 1997 Damon Gough, aka Badly Drawn Boy, released his first EP, a five track vinyl only release called *EP 1*,[913] and made his live debut on stage to a small crowd a few weeks after.[914]

James Lavelle had wanted a new, undiscovered, "northern voice" on the UNKLE album and after he heard some of Gough's work they met up at the Mo' Wax Christmas lunch, held the day before Christmas Day in 1997.[915] Lavelle would later explain further in 1998:

> I was desperate to get a central character and I'd heard his 7" and really liked it. We met up and presented him with the ideas and at the time thought he'd become involved in a lot more tracks. Josh was working on a hardcore track for somebody and it felt right for him. If Damon's kind of lo-fi in the way he records himself then '*Nursery Rhyme*' is the most fucked up sounding so the two work well together.[916]

The collaboration was first teased in an issue of *Melody Maker*, reporting it as a rumour in January 1998,[917] with Gough's vocals recorded the next month in February[918] featuring lyrics written from the point of view of a foetus, Gough would explain:

> I'd just been to the Electric Ballroom in Camden to see the Beta Band...I had this idea of a baby being inside its mother and her dancing and smooching, getting really fresh with some guy who wasn't its dad. I imagined the baby getting

---

[913] Bainbridge, L 2015
[914] Scanlon, A 2000
[915] UNKLE 1998, 00:19:00
[916] Burgess, J 1998, p. 57
[917] Naylor, T 1998
[918] Burgess, J 1998, p. 57

angry, so I thought of the line, 'It's Electric Ballroom love/It's Electric Ballroom love' and of the baby repeating the phrase, 'Won't you sing me a nursery rhyme to keep me quiet while you're on fire', as though it was going to tell the father that she was snogging some other bloke. I liked the idea of a baby inside the womb rebelling and of these electric impulses being sent to it through the mother's feelings of false love for this character.[919]

Gough had only released one EP at the time of recording, with his follow up *EP 2* released in April 1998, so he was understandably apprehensive about taking part in UNKLE's star studded album. He explained:

> I heard the Thom Yorke track and thought. 'Fuck me, how do I follow that?' I really don't do 'mood' music very well, so I wanted to do something 'In yer face'. Trouble was James sent me three instrumental tracks and none of them felt right. But then he sent "*Nursery Rhyme*" and I immediately went for it.
>
> I was mega intimidated in the studio because it was such a big project, totally under the microscope. They initially wanted me for three tracks, and '*Nursery Rhyme*' as a single. But the other two ended up as instrumentals. I'm dead proud to be on the record in general, though. James had the vision to get an unknown like me on it, and it was worth the trouble because I think it's an album that people will still listen to in 30 years' time.[920]

The instrumental for *Nursery Rhyme* was created from multiple different samples but with the intention of sounding like a live band had recorded the song, as Shadow explained in 1998:

---

[919] Scanlon, A 2000
[920] Cigarettes, J 1998, p. 16

> As rock bands try to sound more sampled, I've wanted to make songs that are 100% sampled and feel live...I had to go through about 30 records to find the stick clicks. It could have been worse if I hadn't known to look for them in punk records. That was a fun song. It was a milestone for me on the record. It came together faster than anything else.[921]

He further discussed his satisfaction with *Spine Magazine*:

> ...even though I know what I did, it still feels like a live band - like a 'live punk band' kind of thing. That's what I'm always trying to achieve. Not always, but it's really nice when you can do that. And there's just little touches like if a drummer is going to be doing a two-handed roll, he couldn't possibly be playing the hi-hat (at the same time), so you've got to take that out. Just paying attention to little details like that makes things feel more live, like not having the same snare played over. If you're gonna take a snare, why not take five snares and play them in different orders all the time?[922]

Gough would later comment on the song, telling *Dazed & Confused* "I'm very proud of it, mainly just because it's so different from everything else I've ever done."[923]

The song ends with a second section called *Breather*. The interlude takes its name from the fact the breathing sound is reportedly of James Lavelle after Shadow had him run around the studio and then recorded him breathing heavily into a microphone.[924] *Breather* earned Lavelle his only performance credit on the album, and the song ends with a short sample from L.A. Dream Team's *Calling on the Dream Team* which also features some breathing, this time sampled from Kraftwerk's *Tour De France*.[925]

---

[921] Stenman, E 1998, p. 17
[922] Spine Magazine n.d. b
[923] Gough, D 2000, p. 46
[924] Werde, B 2002 p. 37
[925] WhoSampled 2019b

Samples in *Nursery Rhyme* include a section of The New Dave Pike Set's *Ritmos Do Bahia* from their 1973 album *Salomão*, but while it's acknowledged the entire song is made from samples[926] none of the others have been found and reported as yet.[927] Shadow spoke about the samples with *Tape Op* where he acknowledges it is always a possibility the samples used across his work will one day be discovered. He explained:

> I grew up on sample-based music. Breakbeats are the foundation of what I do. I like the fact that, even though it doesn't always sound the greatest, someone could go out and find the beats. They are out there. Everything I use can be found somewhere else if you look hard enough. I think that makes it very interesting. I love finding other people's samples. It's great to not only find the sample but then to also see how it was used. It's great when people aren't lazy and take the sample as a whole. I like it when people chop up stuff and flip it around.[928]

---

[926] Future Music 1998
[927] WhoSampled 2019g
[928] Stenman, E 1998, p. 17

"Celestial Annihilation"

Celestial Annihilation was originally intended as a cover of Fleetwood Mac's 1977 single *Dreams,* from their album *Rumours*.[929]

Two singers were considered for the song, with the first being Lavelle's friend Richard File (better known as Rich File). I was able to interview Rich File in 2018 and he explained his early involvement in these sessions.[930] At the time File had released some music on Mo' Wax with Will Bankhead as Forme, with one of their tracks appearing on the *Headz 2A* compilation album in 1996,[931] but he was not a singer. He had previously auditioned for UNKLE at Shadow's home studio, but he told me "nothing great came out of it." Lavelle believed in him though and invited him to audition again at Metropolis Studio in Chisic, this time on the cover of *Dreams*. Rich File explained:

> The instrumental [*Celestial Annihilation*] which you may or may not be aware, it has the chords for *Dreams* by Fleetwood Mac, and I sung, or attempted to sing *Dreams* by Fleetwood Mac on top of that song which would have been great, well it could have been, but it's completely in the wrong key. So it was way too low for me and I was trying to sing notes that I couldn't sing 'cause they were really way too low so I didn't stand a chance and it was before the days of now in Pro Tools you can just take a song up as many semitones as you like and it generally sounds just as good as it originally did but that was way before those days and everything that Shadow made was on the MPC and just didn't have those capabilities and even if you did, and it was never suggested.

---

[929] Aubrey, E 2017c
[930] Rich File 2018, personal conversation November 6
[931] Discogs 2020i

I just remember coming out of there so deflated, just sitting outside thinking 'Fuck. What a nightmare. This is not happening and I am gutted!' But I realised, I looked on the brightside, thankfully the brightside appeared of 'this has been an experience', two weeks ago, or three months ago or whatever it was I hadn't even considered that I could sing on top of making records. Suddenly it's like 'there's this other area, this other potentially that I want to explore' and it didn't finish me. It was super disappointing I wasn't going to be on *Psyence Fiction* but those experiences had made me hungry, and made me excited to write songs and learn to play instruments so I could write songs. And have a guitar, so that's what I did. That experience led me to wanting to do this at some point. It wasn't happening this time but it gave me enough, it made it utterly clear that singing and songwriting was something I wanted to do.[932]

While Rich File's take on *Dreams* didn't work out, Lavelle and Shadow tried one more time to record the cover, this time with Badly Drawn Boy's Damon Gough invited to contribute vocals.[933] But the night before he was due to fly from England to the studio in California where Shadow and Lavelle were recording, Gough won his local pub quiz and stayed out celebrating leading to him missing his flight.[934] Lavelle had originally hoped to feature Gough across four tracks on the album so *Psyence Fiction* would have a central voice, or character. But after the missed flight Gough's sole contribution was *Nursery Rhyme*,[935] and the *Dreams* cover became the instrumental *Celestial Annihilation* instead.

Lavelle later discussed his appreciation for Fleetwood Mac to *The Quietus* in 2017, revealing that part of *Psyence Fiction* was recorded in the same studio as *Rumours*. He explained further:

---

[932] Rich File 2018, personal conversation November 6
[933] Aubrey, E 2017c
[934] Scanlon, A 2000
[935] Mixmag 2003, pp. 38-39

I didn't engage with rock and pop as a kid: I was very much about hip-hop, electro house, and everything being very modern. Then I discovered a lot of these records. It wasn't that I hadn't heard these records because everybody did – you just heard them, because they were such monumental records. But I didn't engage with them in the way that I did now until later. I'm talking about when I was an early teenager and you start discovering the power of songs, what songs mean, the history of things, and I think there was a lot of stuff with that record and the process of how it was made that I kind of found intriguing. It was one of those records that I just fell in love with. We were going to do a cover version from it actually…but we didn't do it in the end sadly.

Celestial Annihilation begins with a drum sample from Byron Davis and the Fresh Krew's 1988 song *Now Dance*,[936] combined with samples of Will Malone's *Concerto for Strings and Beats*,[937] a song especially created for UNKLE.[938] The bass and drums with synths that are heard next come from Newcleus' *Lets Jam* off their 1985 album *Space Is The Place*[939] and then we are introduced to several vocal samples.

The high-pitched "We Came Here To Rock" vocal is from Toddy Tee feat. Mix Master Spade's 1988 song *Do You Wanna Go to the Liquor Store*, the "Annihilating" vocal sample is from the Grace Jones 1985 song *Operattack* while the "B-Boy B-Girl" vocal is from RunDMC's 1985 song *Rock The House*, and "321 Fire" is from Began Began's 1982 song *Computer Wars*.[940]

The song was another stand out for many reviewers who were looking for instrumentals, with *Select* called it "a lovely instrumental

---

[936] WhoSampled 2019cc
[937] Wu'Matt 2008
[938] Burgess, J 1998, p. 57
[939] WhoSampled 2019dd
[940] WhoSampled 2019k

hybrid of strings and electro,"[941] and *The New York Times* were impressed by how "a full string orchestra squares off beautifully against a rush of electronic percussion and sound effects."[942] While most were positive, Rob Young writing for *The Wire* was not a fan. In his overall negative review of *Psyence Fiction* he stated, "giving a piece of limp-dick Electro a title like "*Celestial Annihilation*" makes about as much sense as pointing a flintlock at the Doomsday asteroid."[943]

---

[941] Grundy, G 1998, p. 80
[942] Hermes, W 1998
[943] Young, R 1998, p. 69

"The Knock (Drums of Death, Pt. 2)" feat Mike D

James Lavelle had been a fan of the Beastie Boys for a long time, DJing on their 1994 tour of England and pushing a collaboration between his record label and Mike D's Grand Royal Records.[944]

Lavelle and Mike D, aka Michael Diamond, had bonded when Lavelle initially tried to sign Lucious Jackson who were signed to Grand Royal,[945] and the pair also shared an admiration for keyboardist Money Mark, with Grand Royal issuing his debut album in the US while Mo' Wax released it in the UK.[946] Mike D had also originally been planned as a collaborator during the 1995 recording sessions in LA, but schedules at the time didn't align.[947]

Likewise, during the recording of *Psyence Fiction* the Beastie Boys were in the middle of completing their next album *Hello Nasty*, which released in June 1998, and Mike D's vocals weren't recorded until March 1998,[948] making it one of the last song completed for the album.[949] [950] Shadow and Lavelle had sent Mike D a beat for him to record to at his home, telling him the track would be called *Drums of Death* as a homage to the 1990 hip hop song *Drums of Death* by K-Solo.[951] These were the only vocals recorded for *Psyence Fiction* without Shadow in the studio as they arrived on a DAT via post,[952] [953] with Mike D sending them over with a note attached apologising for the delay.[954]

---

[944] Aubrey, E 2017a
[945] Ibid.
[946] Discogs 2020b
[947] McLean, C 1995a, p.104
[948] Burgess, J 1998, p. 57
[949] Cigarettes, J 1998, p. 16
[950] Mclean, C 1998, p. 69
[951] Ibid.
[952] Bradshaw, P 2014b
[953] Mclean, C 1998, p. 69
[954] Lavelle, J 2014

Regarding the collaboration Lavelle said, "He's a friend of mine who's always really supported Mo' Wax. He really influenced me as a kid so it was like working with a childhood hero but I've never had that strange relationship with him where I've been made to feel like that. For somebody in his position he was one of the easiest people to deal with."[955] He later continued, explaining his excitement at the collaboration, "It was unreal to get that support from Mike D on *Psyence Fiction*. It was unheard of at the time to get the Beasties on another record; they were killing it at the time, and they were at the top of their game. To have that support when I was so young was amazing."[956]

While Kool G Rap on *Guns Blazing (Drums of Death Part 1)* had represented Shadow's idea of hip hop, on *The Knock (Drums of Death Part 2)*, Mike D represented American hip hop for Lavelle.[957] In fact both *Drums of Death* parts had been intended as one large track, with both Kool G Rap and Mike D together on the same track. But this didn't work out and instead they were split and placed at apposing ends of the album.[958]

Another collaborator for the track was Jason Newstead from Metallica, who contributed bass guitar and Theremin, recording in February 1998[959] after Shadow had spent six months struggling to find a bass sample that fit the beat and guitar he had put together for the song.[960] Lavelle explained the idea behind Newstead's involvement, showing his ability to get things done:

> Shadow needed a bass player to play on the Mike D track because he couldn't find a bass-line to sample that was right. We were in the Bay Area of San Francisco and we said, "We need to find a bass player'. I said, 'Why don't we

---

[955] Burgess, J 1998, p. 59
[956] Aubrey, E 2017a
[957] Ibid.
[958] Adventures in Psyence Fiction 2019, 00:15:30
[959] Burgess, J 1998, p. 59
[960] Stenman, E 1998, p. 17

get Metallica,' and Shadow said, 'Yeah, that'd be great'. It was a really fun session. Jason really wanted to meet Shadow because he was really into what he'd done with Metallica loops on *Endtroducing*. I wanted to include some of Shadow's history in an alternative sense so that's why it seemed like the right thing to do.[961]

The samples used on *The Knock (Drums of Death Part 2)* are similar to those found on *Guns Blazing (Drums of Death Part 1)*, with Frank Zappa's *Apostrophe*, and *Buffalo Station/Get on Down to Memphis* by Wizzard featuring on both versions of Drums of Death.[962] [963] While Part 2 also features Billy Squier's *The Big Beat*, from 1980's *The Tale of the Tape*, Troy the Wonderboy & Electric 1000 featuring Boo Boo B's 1985 song *Boo Boo's Break*, and *Modus Operandi* by the British band Nirvana from their 1971 album *Local Anaesthetic* providing the opening drum beat.[964] While the "Whew! that was hot, now dig this" is Michael Holman on the *Graffiti Rock* TV show.[965] The bass at the end is often misattributed to Manfred Mann's *Snakeskin Garter*,[966] but this is played by Jason Newstead from Metallica.

While many reviews for *Psyence Fiction* weren't enthused by *The Knock*,[967] [968] [969] [970] *The Guardian* were fans, exclaiming "Mike D's wonderful *The Knock* trumps even the best of the Beasties' recent output."[971]

---

[961] Burgess, J 1998, p. 59
[962] WhoSampled 2019m
[963] WhoSampled 2019e
[964] WhoSampled 2019m
[965] Wu'Matt 2008
[966] Genius 2019b
[967] Bresnark, R 1998, p. 37
[968] Casimir, J 1998
[969] Lewis, S 1998, p. 83
[970] Higgins, M 1998
[971] Bennun, D 1998

"Chaos" feat Atlantique Khan

Chaos is primarily a solo song written by singer Atlantique Khan, with DJ Shadow only receiving a co-producer credit. This is one of the only songs on the album not to include sampled instruments, though it does still contain a collection of samples. The song opens with short sound bites from unknown sources talking about order and chaos in society, while later at around the three minute mark there are a series of street sounds heard, and an ambulance drives by playing UNKLE's *Lonely Soul*.[972] At one point Shadow and James Lavelle added several beats to the track, but removed them again as they realised it didn't work, instead preferring to leave the song with a more atmospheric feel to it.[973]

When Atlantique Khan originally showed the song *Chaos* to Shadow and Lavelle they liked it as they felt the theme of chaos fit their idea for the UNKLE album.[974] [975] Part of that chaos was also the act of recording which was not only spread across several years, but between studios in England and America, as Shadow told *NME*, "We were constantly in different time zones, we recorded in a million different studios. So it was like every day was a new adventure and every day had a different cast."[976]

Khanh recorded her vocals in August 1997,[977] but Lavelle had met her much earlier having worked with her previously on some UNKLE demos such as the unreleased *Dissatisfied* during the groups early period,[978] with Lavelle explaining, "Her's were the first demos me and Tim ever worked on."[979] Lavelle and Khanh became good friends afterwards and he invited her back for *Psyence Fiction*

---

[972] McLean, C 1998, p. 67
[973] Spencer, R 2012, p. 16
[974] Cigarettes, J 1998, p. 16
[975] Micallef, K 1998, p. 14
[976] NME, 1998e
[977] Burgess, J 1998, p. 59
[978] Lavelle, J 2018a, 00:35:35
[979] Burgess, J 1998, p. 59

explaining, "I asked her to write in English and she wrote *'Chaos'*. I wasn't comfortable with her singing French."[980] For her part, Khanh had spent two years learning to write songs in English, telling the NME "Since I learnt to sing and write in English...I like it much better than French, so I will sing in English from now on."[981] This became the first song Khanh released in English as for her previously released music she had sung exclusively in her native language, French.[982]

Khanh, who now goes by Atlantique Ascoli after marrying Source Records boss Philippe Ascoli,[983] released her first single in 1987, *Je N'Aime Personne*, and after two more singles she released her debut album, 1991's *Trampolino* which was followed by 1994's self titled *Atlantique*.[984] Her husband Philippe Ascoli and James Lavelle were also old friends, with Source Records being the sole distributer of Mo' Wax in France,[985] and Mo' Wax releasing Source Records group Air's first single in England.[986] The two labels also partnered on the *Source Lab Vs. Mo' Wax* compilation promo in 1995.[987]

During the *Psyence Fiction* sessions, Lavelle brought another collaborator in for *Chaos* alongside Atlantique Khan, Mark Hollis of the band Talk Talk.[988] Talk Talk were formed in 1981 by Mark Hollis, Lee Harris, Simon Brenner, and Paul Webb.[989] Their first album, *The Party's Over*, was released in 1982 and was followed by four more albums until the group disbanded following the release of 1991's *Laughing Stock*. Their second-last album, 1988's *Spirit of Eden*, had seen a shift in the band's sound to a more experimental influence which relied on long improvised instrumental pieces being edited down into songs. While the album was well received by the

---

[980] Ibid.
[981] Cigarettes, J 1998, p. 16
[982] Burgess, J 1998, p. 59
[983] VOGUE Paris 2017, p. 178
[984] Discogs 2020a
[985] Philster 1997
[986] Discogs 2019a
[987] Discogs 2019III
[988] NME 1998f
[989] Ankeny, J 2020

press, it did not chart as well as its predecessors likely due to the band deciding not to tour it.[990]

While the experimental nature of Talk Talk's last two albums didn't appeal to everyone, James Lavelle was a fan and he had been trying to release something by Hollis on Mo' Wax.[991] But although Hollis was recording a solo album in 1997 it was tied up in a contract signed to Polydor Records. Originally Talk Talk had signed an agreement to release two albums with Polydor after leaving their previous label EMI, but when Talk Talk disbanded they had only given Polydor one of these albums so Hollis' solo album fulfilled the contract instead.[992]

Lavelle discussed his admiration for Hollis when speaking with *Jockey Slut* in 1998:

> *Spirit of Eden* was one record I really got into because I don't like conventionally structured records. I like records that create soundscapes as well as being emotional, that journey through sound. He was uneasy with the idea of contributing vocals but was keen to collaborate. All the music on his last album was recorded live so he didn't want to do anything too programmed. Originally we thought he was going to play guitar but he came back and said he loved the track and wanted to play piano.[993]

Mark Hollis completed his work on UNKLE's *Chaos*, recording his piano contribution in September 1997[994] but he would cause some drama afterwards initially requesting his name be taken off the album, before going back and forth until Lavelle persuaded him to allow them to re-record the track without his contribution, before Hollis finally agreed to allow Lavelle to leave him on the album.[995]

---

[990] Feemster, S 2020
[991] Burgess, J 1998, p. 59
[992] in't Veld, H & Weber, H 1998
[993] Ibid.
[994] Burgess, J 1998, p. 59
[995] Cigarettes, J 1998, p. 16

"Rabbit in Your Headlights" feat Thom Yorke

UNKLE and Radiohead first crossed paths in 1995, when UNKLE were invited to contribute a remix of *Planet Telex* from *The Bends*, Radiohead's second album which had released in March of that year. The remix, *Planet Telex (Karma Sunra Mix)*, was released in August 1995 on the single for *Just*,[996] and was created by Masayuki Kudo and Tim Goldsworthy.[997] Prior to this, James Lavelle hadn't followed Radiohead's career outside of knowing their debut single *Creep*, but after completing the *Planet Telex* remix Lavelle listened to *The Bends* and soon met with Thom Yorke and the rest of the band in Oxford.[998]

DJ Shadow had also met with Thom Yorke in 1996 at the Tibetan Freedom Festival in New York held in May,[999] and again in London on October 9, when Lavelle and Shadow both DJed at Nokia Dazed Live, a concert held by *Dazed & Confused Magazine* which featured a performance by Yorke with Radiohead bandmate Johnny Greenwood.[1000] Radiohead had heard Shadow's album *Endtroducing* and took inspiration while recording their next album, specifically on the drumming for tracks *Airbag*[1001] and *Paranoid Android*, both of which appeared on 1997's *OK Computer*.[1002]

In June 1997, while promoting *OK Computer* in America, Yorke told radio station *KCRW* that he had met with Shadow and they had discussed plans to work with one another, explaining that the collaboration would likely be through Lavelle's UNKLE project.[1003] He explained the idea further to *Vox*:

---

[996] Discogs 2019gg
[997] UNKLE 1998, 00:16:00
[998] Ibid.
[999] NME 1998e
[1000] Dazed & Confused 1996
[1001] Sutherland, M 1997
[1002] NME 1997
[1003] Douridas, C 1998

> I don't know exactly what's going to happen, there's absolutely no plan. We're gonna turn up on the day and sit in a very large room in this cinematic studio with big screens behind us. He's going to set up his decks and his mixer and sampler and I'm going to set up a microphone in the middle of this huge empty room, heh heh! We're just gonna sit around and confuse each other.[1004]

Finding time to record became a problem as Radiohead began a world tour in May 1997 which would continue through until April 1998. Their album *OK Computer* had blown up, reaching the #1 spot in the UK Album Charts,[1005] and peaked at #21 in America[1006] where it eventually sold over two and half million copies,[1007] almost one million more than in the UK.[1008]

Shadow recalled the difficulty of finding time to record the track, "You had to catch people when they were around...That was the nature of this record: 'OK, stop that track, cos Thom Yorke's got a two-day window in San Francisco, and we gotta make sure that demo's ready.'"[1009]

On July 27 1997, Radiohead were performing at The Warfield Theater in San Francisco, with their next gig planned for July 31 in Vancouver, Canada.[1010] This short period between dates allowed Thom Yorke to meet with Shadow and Lavelle to record what would become *Rabbit In Your Headlights*.[1011]

Shadow drove Yorke to the studio, The Site, located in San Rafael, Marin County, California, outside of San Francisco.[1012] As they

---

[1004] Dalton, S 1997, p. 60
[1005] Official UK Charts Company 2020
[1006] Billboard 2020
[1007] RIAA 2020
[1008] BPI 2020
[1009] Higgins, M 1998
[1010] Green Plastic Trees n.d.a
[1011] Higgins, M 1998
[1012] Discogs 2019ll

drove Shadow described the local flora and fauna to Yorke, as detailed in a feature article published by *The Face*:

> "What's that really sweet smell?" asks Yorke.
> "Oh that's Baby's Breath," replies Shadow. "It's a flower with little white puffs."
> Up at the studio, Yorke sings of being "a rabbit in your headlights" and "sweet baby's breath…". [1013]

While the baby's breath lyric ended up being removed by Yorke, the final lyrics still feature a chorus around a rabbit in your headlights.

Shadow constructed the music from a wide range of samples, with the piano originating from Supersister's *Pudding en Gisteren - Music for Ballet*,[1014] a 1972 song which took up the whole second side of their *Pudding en Gisteren album*, and was reportedly originally written for use in a ballet.[1015] Of note, Shadow had previously sampled from the album for the extended version of *Organ Donor*.[1016]

The first drums which appear in *Rabbit In Your Headlights* are provided by Talk Talk's *New Grass* from their 1991 album *Laughing Stock*, while the heavier ones which enter near the end are from *Essa Menina Tá Ficando Moça* off Dom & Ravel's 1971 album Terra Boa. This Dom & Ravel sample was often thought to be from David Axelrod's *Holy Thursday* until recently.[1017]

The vocal sample "If you're frightened of dying and you're holding on, you'll see devils tearing your life away. But…if you've made your peace then the devils are really angels freeing you from the earth," is Danny Aiello as Louis Denardo in the 1990 film *Jacob's Ladder*

[1013] McLean, C 1998, p. 69
[1014] WhoSampled 2019h
[1015] Lemmens, P n.d.
[1016] WhoSampled 2020b
[1017] WhoSampled 2019aa

directed by Adrian Lyne.[1018] *Rabbit In Your Headlights* ends with whooshing sounds which close the track and are taken from the 1997 film *Contact* starring Jodie Foster and directed by Robert Zemeckis.[1019]

Lavelle explained the origins of the collaboration between Thom Yorke:

> This was discussed before Richard because I'd been inspired by their music a lot longer than the Verve's. I really liked the drums on *The Bends* and the emotions in the songs and sounds. I told Josh to check their stuff out. Originally I was going to collaborate with the band as a whole but I think he wanted to step away from what he was doing, it was an opportunity for him to do something completely different. It took him longer to get on board because they were always touring or recording. Thom had got acceptance through OK Computer, that massive reaction from press and fans, so he then was able to slightly dissociate himself from what he needed to attain with Radiohead. We developed a far stronger relationship over a long period of time and he really wanted to work with Josh so finally last year we managed to hook up for two days.[1020]

With Yorke completing his vocal in one take, he spent the rest of the time jamming with DJ Shadow,[1021] tuning pianos, and recording extra bass parts for the song, making full use of the two days they had booked in the studio.[1022] Shadow referred to the track as the most rewarding of the album, and described the last minute of the song as feeling like "your hair is being blown back...It's really emotional and it was really special working with him. There's no histrionics, it's just right."[1023]

[1018] WhoSampled 2019z
[1019] WhoSampled 2019y
[1020] Burgess, J 1998, p. 60
[1021] *The Man from Mo' Wax* 2018, 00:36:00
[1022] NME, 1998e
[1023] Kaufman, G 1998

Rabbit In Your Headlights was chosen as the last song on the album as it was thought they'd never have anything more intense,[1024] with Shadow explaining that anything placed after it would seem "flaccid".[1025]

In October 1998, *Rabbit In Your Headlights* was released as a single featuring remixes by Massive Attack's 3D[1026] and David Axelrod.[1027] Back in 1997 when Lavelle and Shadow had been given a tour of the Skywalker studios, Lavelle met a staff member who had previously worked at Capital Records in the 1960's and was still friends with David Axelrod. She set up a meeting between Lavelle and Axelrod and they became friends which led to further collaborations between the pair.[1028]

Radio One in the UK refused to play *Rabbit In Your Headlights* citing it as too alternative,[1029] and the song became further enveloped in controversy when the video directed by Jonathan Glazer was released and initially banned.[1030]

Originally Lavelle had hoped to make more than one video for the album, with a trilogy planned which would have included *Nursery Rhyme*, *Lonely Soul*, and *Rabbit In Your Headlights*, with all three of the videos linked, all containing the same character. Unfortunately, Badly Drawn Boy and Richard Ashcroft's shared management refused to allow their songs to be released as singles, so the idea was scrapped.[1031] Lavelle explained the idea further:

> So '*Rabbit In Your Headlights*' was one part of a journey that this guy was going through. There was that, then when he

---

[1024] Roberts, M 1998
[1025] Kaufman, G 1998
[1026] Prasad, A 1998
[1027] Thompson, B 2001
[1028] Benstead, B 2014, 01:38:00
[1029] Harcourt, N 1998, 00:28:00
[1030] Bradshaw, P 2014b
[1031] Ibid.

woke up a car explodes, and he wakes up in the council estate with monkeys running around. It's like Stanley Kubrick for *'Lonely Soul,'* and then he opens a door and walks in to a club and the people have no eyes, no ears, like precursors to the whole Alexander McQueen look that he did. It was this amazing film.[1032]

Once it was decided that *Rabbit In Your Headlights* would receive a video, Lavelle and Jonathon Glazer began discussing ideas, with an initial concept being of a man being hit by several objects that would remain unseen by the viewer and instead the camera would focus on the man's reactions. One of the objects was to be a car and this idea evolved into the final video which is of a man walking down a road inside a tunnel as cars drive by and hit him. Glazer then digitally removed all of the cars so the man was being hit by nothing, but Lavelle felt it looked strange and took away from the emotion so they were placed back in to the video again.[1033]

Because of the violence featured in the *Rabbit In Your Headlights* video MTV initially banned it as they felt it was too realistic and they were worried it conveyed a negative image.[1034] They would later show it after 9PM, and an edited version was also created, though apparently never shown.[1035] [1036] Lavelle commented on the video:

> When you see something that's so realistic people really freak out, so I suppose in many ways maybe that's why they banned it...[On] MTV you can have your kind of glitzy fantasy type environments, whether they're moralistically right or not it's kind of OK because it's fantasy, it doesn't really happen. But because this is something that could happen people are like 'No, no, no, you don't want to show that. You don't want to show the reality of life."[1037]

[1032] Bradshaw, P 2014b
[1033] James Lavelle Interview 2005
[1034] Ibid.
[1035] Bradshaw, P 2014b
[1036] Roeder, M 1998
[1037] James Lavelle Interview 2005

Glazer explained his take on the video:

> I think what's interesting is that when he gets hit by cars there's something kind of odd going on in it. When he first gets knocked down and you look at him lying there he looks like he could be dead, which would normally be the case. But then he takes a breath and gets up. Each time he gets hit, it almost gets easier for him to get up. So it's working opposite to what would happen because normally, every time you'd get hit, it would take more minutes to get up. When the ending comes, it's inevitable, but you didn't guess it. Then the last time he gets up he becomes superhuman.[1038]

The video features a cameo from James Lavelle as the passenger in a car that slows down to try and talk to the man, and future UNKLE collaborator Rich File is seen in the back seat, with actor Craig Kelly driving, and French actor Denis Lavant appearing as the man walking on the road.[1039]

Jonathon Glazer had met Lavant when he cast him for a Stella Artois commercial and during the filming Glazer asked Lavant if he would be interested in working on the *Rabbit In Your Headlights* video, which he agreed to. During the filming of the *Rabbit In Your Headlights* video Lavant couldn't speak English so he was given a Walkman to wear underneath his parker which played English words and phrases for Lavant to quote and repeat through the video.[1040]

The *Rabbit In Your Headlights'* video would go on to be nominated for the Breakthrough Video category in 1999 MTV Video Music

---

[1038] Epstein, DR 2005
[1039] IMDB 2019b
[1040] Denis Lavant Interview 2005

Awards,[1041] and won MVPA's International Video of The Year in 1999.[1042]

[1041] Hay, C 1999a, p. 73
[1042] Hay, C 1999b, p. 76

"Outro (Mandatory)"

Outro opens with a vocal sample of Whitley Strieber,[1043] an author who wrote about being visited by "non-humans."[1044] Strieber occasionally appeared as a guest on Art Bell's *Coast to Coast AM*, a late-night radio talk show which focuses on topics related to the paranormal or conspiracy theories. At one point Strieber hosted the weekend edition of another of Art Bell's programmes called *Dreamland*[1045] and so the sample used by UNKLE is often associated to "Whitley Strieber, the host of the weekend edition of Art Bell's Coast to Coast nightly radio talk show."[1046] In the sample he appears to be describing his personal experience with the paranormal and says,

> Uh, I feel that this has given me the most incredible and wonderful thing that I have ever been given, and also, the worst. It's a mixed bag. Uh, I have been taken to the, absolutely, to the depths of extreme terror by this. I've had my whole soul undermined by it, on the one hand. On the other hand, uh, in one sense, my experience has been about finding joy.

The word joy is then repeated over and over, getting faster and faster until the song suddenly ends. Meanwhile beneath the voice of Whitley Strieber there has been a slow fade in of strings and beeps, repeating the sample of Alan Hawkshaw's *Countdown* which was also used at the beginning of *Guns Blazing (Drums of Death Pt. 1)*.[1047] The sample of *Countdown* was also used in an episode of Blake's 7 titled *Duel*[1048] from 1978, and fans initially thought that was the source of the music.[1049]

[1043] Genius 2019a
[1044] Speigel, L 2011
[1045] Wikipedia 2019
[1046] Genius 2019a
[1047] WhoSampled 2019c
[1048] Blakes 7 2014, 00:03:30
[1049] shivo 2004

For fans who had purchased the Australian or Japanese editions of *Psyence Fiction* in 1998 they would have an extra minute of silence before being greeted with two bonus instrumental tracks, *Guns Blazing (Instrumental)*, and *The Knock (Drums Of Death Pt. 2) (Instrumental)*.[1050] [1051]

[1050] Discogs 2019rrr
[1051] Discogs 2019aaa

"Be There" feat. Ian Brown

While not originally part of the album sequence, *Be There* has appeared on some subsequent editions of *Psyence Fiction*[1052] and was released as a single itself in February 1999.[1053]

Ian Brown is primarily known as a member of the Stone Roses, a band of which he is lead singer. The group released their debut self-titled album in 1989 and followed it with *Second Coming* in 1994 before splitting in 1996. Brown released his debut solo album, *Unfinished Monkey Business*, in February 1998, and that same month made headlines when Brown was accused of harassing an airline stewardess and captain on a flight from Paris.[1054]

James Lavelle had met Brown through their girlfriends who were good friends,[1055] and Lavelle asked Brown to appear on the UNKLE album, but in July 1997 he called Lavelle to say no.[1056] Brown later changed his mind though and in 1998 Lavelle sent him a DAT with the instrumental track *Unreal* from the album, and in October 1998 Brown recorded vocals by himself in his home studio.[1057]

Brown sent them back to Lavelle before he was sentenced to prison for four months after being found guilty of harassing airline staff in February.[1058] Brown was later bailed after four days[1059] before returning to jail again due to having his appeal denied,[1060] but was officially released December 24 1998.[1061] Brown's jail time forced him to cancel a solo tour which was scheduled for November 1998, and was initially rescheduled for February 1999 until it became clear

---

[1052] Discogs 2020f
[1053] Discogs 2020g
[1054] NME 1998b
[1055] McLean, C 1998, p. 69
[1056] Ibid. p. 67
[1057] NME 1998a
[1058] BBC 1998a
[1059] BBC 1998c
[1060] NME, 1998d
[1061] MTV News 1999

no one had asked Brown if he was actually available, leading to the rescheduled tour to be cancelled as well.[1062]

At the time DJ Shadow was out of the country but he gave his blessing for Lavelle to work on the track with someone else,[1063] and so Rich File stepped in, marking the first time he would appear on an UNKLE release. For *Be There* File took on a co-production role sharing duties with Lavelle. File discussed his involvement on *Be There* with me in 2018:

> The vocals had been recorded, I wasn't involved with that. [*Be There*] was my first involvement in the studio, it was kind of some additional production really, Shadow and James had made the music for the original, for *Unreal*, and then Ian had sung on *Unreal*. And in the session I was involved in, we added the mellotron [and] we found a couple of samples to put in the middle eight.
>
> We were basically just finishing it. It was just some additional production. And then the mix with Spike Stent, it was Mike Stent, but I do think he goes under the name Spike Stent. So, my involvement was just in the additional production of keyboards and samples and then just, the mix which, to be honest was all mostly all down to Spike anyway as that's his thing. We were there just to go "fucking hell sounds awesome." Turn up when all the works done, because that's how Spike generally works "leave it with me, and I'll give you a shout when I want you to come in and have some feedback" and generally [we'd later] go in and go "sounds amazing, should we go up the pub?"[1064]

Be There was released as a single in February 1999 with remixes by Underdog, and KZA & Kent.[1065] When Lavelle was asked if he

---

[1062] NME, 1998c
[1063] Bradshaw, P 2014b
[1064] Rich File 2018, personal conversation November 6
[1065] Discogs 2020g

wished *Be There* would have been on the album instead of *Unreal* he said, "No, I think on the album there was a need for instrumental tracks and I like the fact it's different and it makes it unique and takes the project into another area."[1066]

Outside of Ian Brown's vocals and the new mellotron the song also features one extra sample which didn't appear on *Unreal*, Terry Callier's *Dancing Girl* from the 1972 album *What Color Is Love*. The vocal sample "here am I, and there you are" from *Dancing Girl* is used in the middle of *Be There* as a break before Brown's vocals return.[1067] *Dancing Girl* also made an appearance on *Intro (Optional),* as one of the collection of samples which play on this secret bonus track.[1068]

Be There ends with another sample, though this one is yet to be identified. In the sample a voice narrates the following "Corrupt, a plea for free will. An irresponsible horrorshow. It has been suggested that this contradictory..." and at that point the song ends.

A music video was released for *Be There* starring Emma Griffiths Malin walking around the Mornington Crescent tube station,[1069] with a short cameo from James Lavelle and Rich File at the beginning. The video was directed by Jake Scott, son of *Alien* and *Blade Runner* director Ridley Scott,[1070] and features Malin sitting on a train alone, falling asleep and being approached by a dark figure. At the end of the video, presumably set the following morning, a cleaner wakes up the sleeping girl only for it to be revealed that she has turned in to an old lady. The video ends abruptly and no explanation is given.

[1066] Beeb 1999
[1067] WhoSampled 2020d
[1068] Snaporaz100 2010
[1069] Mubi 2019
[1070] Ibid.

Unreleased and Unrecorded

Prior to Tim Goldsworthy and Masayuki Kudo leaving UNKLE, Lavelle also spoke about the album including Deborah Anderson but this never eventuated. Likewise, Terry Callier was meant to be on the album but was busy.[1071] At the time he was releasing music on Giles Paterson's Talking Loud label and working with Beth Orton.[1072] Finally, Massive Attack's 3D was also intended as a guest artist but nothing ever came of it.[1073]

While the cover version of Fleetwood Mac's *Dreams* featuring Badly Drawn Boy or Rich File never happened, there are at least two songs that were recorded during the *Psyence Fiction* sessions which received a later release in some form or another.

Untitled Heavy Beat (Part 1 & 2)

Originally recorded in 1996, this was part of the original demo sessions that also featured *Lonely Soul*, *Unreal* and *Bloodstain*. When compiling a shortlist of tracks to use for *Psyence Fiction*, this song didn't make the list, though Lavelle remained a fan of it. When the soundtrack producer working on Wim Wenders *The End Of Violence* requested an exclusive track from DJ Shadow this song was available, with the soundtrack releasing September 1997.[1074]

Untitled Heavy Beat (Part 1 & 2) starts with a double bass sample before a guitar stab and drumbeats come in, occasionally fading or abruptly cutting out and back in again. Soon a keyboard fills out the song with some flutes and other sound snippets building the track up until it abruptly ends.

War Is Hell

[1071] Lavelle, J 2018b, 00:54:00
[1072] Discogs 2019jj
[1073] Manning, T 2003, p. 34
[1074] DJShadow.com n.d. e

Another unused UNKLE track that later appeared on Shadow's *Diminishing Returns* release in 2003, and the Vexille Soundtrack in 2007. It is unclear when it was recorded.[1075]

War Is Hell begins with a slow acoustic guitar sample looping beneath a choir before a beat stutters in and the track is soon filled with synthy sounds which build up to a heavy electric guitar taking over. Once the song is built up it stops and starts again, this time with similar but different sounding samples, and near the end the original choir and acoustic guitar return for the ending.

Rich File Demos

Rich File, who almost appeared on *Psyence Fiction* as part of *Celestial Annihilation*, and would provide additional production for *Be There*, was also part of some other early recordings which remained unreleased. Rich File spoke about these sessions when I interviewed him in 2018:

> I auditioned for *Psyence Fiction*. What led up to that was James and I went out one night, cause we used to go partying together, and we were in a cab and I was singing to Oasis in the cab on the way back, just because I was drunk and singing along, and he goes 'You should sing. You can sing!' and I think I sobered up at that moment and was like 'Really? Um Ok' I was up for anything and I used to sing when I was a kid and I've always loved signing but never thought I could sing professionally, for lack of a better word. The next thing I was in San Francisco, in Davis where Shadow lived, at Shadow's house. He put a couple of beats together, but I was so green. I was literally... sobered up out of this cab singing to Oasis, the next thing I'm in Josh's bedroom and it's just like...It was an amazing experience to be there, totally surreal, but nothing great came out of it on that particular occasion.

[1075] DJShadow.com n.d. g

Josh only gave me a beat, there was no music attached to it and I couldn't play an instrument yet, so I was trying to sing melodies over no music, over just a beat and you won't be surprised to hear nothing of any substance came out of it. But that was the first writing session. Back in the UK a few months later I auditioned again. Audition is probably the wrong word, I did a session again on a track...and I sung or attempted to sing *Dreams* by Fleetwood Mac.

Oh, there was another part. I forgot. I was songwriting with Kudo as well downstairs when Mo' Wax was in Caledonia Road, so I did some demos with Kudo as well. I think that was…after the Davis session if you can call it that. In the basement of Mo' Wax, where Kudo had a studio, I did some demos with him and there was one of those I really liked actually but that didn't happen.

Then there was also another recording session with James and I and Johnny Dollar, who produced *Blue Lines*, and that was amazing. Johnny, James and I wrote a song on top of a Shadow beat and a sample which I can't remember. Johnny heard the song, he heard a melody, he sung the melody to us, and we liked it and then we wrote the lyrics together and I sung it and it was fucking awesome! We all really loved it. It didn't make it on to the album, but it was awesome. And it was the first time I'd sung a finished vocal with a producer. It was the first finished song that I'd ever sung on. We finished it on that day. It was done on a day, and it was really exciting. It never made it on to the album, but it does exist still, and I spoke to James recently and he's heard it recently and he really loves it, and he's really excited to have rediscovered it and I'd love to think that it would be released one day...I'd be proud of it if it got released today.[1076]

[1076] Rich File 2018, personal conversation November 6

In July 2016 James Lavelle announced on his Facebook page that he had found the song recorded with Johnny Dollar and Rich File and suggested it would be released as part of the *Psyence Fiction Director's Cut*.[1077]

[1077] Lavelle, J 2016

Finalising Psyence

While working on *Psyence Fiction* DJ Shadow was spending twenty hours a day in the studio, and during the completion of *Lonely Soul* he slipped a disc, telling *Filter* "It was the first time in my life where I realized I better slow down a little bit, that I'm not invincible."[1078] For Shadow the album had begun in August 1996 with the initial *Lonely Soul* demos,[1079] and after a slight pause, had begun in earnest once more in May 1997, continuing in to 1998.[1080] Shadow explained his frustrations with the drawn out process in 1998:

> You have relationships you need to maintain. You can't be living in hotels all the time. Then there were all these problems. We didn't have the Mike D vocal in, time was ticking and I was getting sick of it. There was a crunch point where I thought, 'I have nothing left to give'. Even at the end of '96 I didn't want anything more to do with it. But, as in every case, you listen to the music and you think, 'I'm gonna regret it forever if I don't see this through'.[1081]

In March 1998 Shadow told Lavelle he'd had enough, "I finally had to sit James down and say, 'It's time for this to end.' I mean I had to turn everything down for a year and a half. So now, there's a ton of things I need to get out of my system. I'm very happy with the record we made and I'd do it again in a heartbeat. Absolutely. But it was draining."[1082]

On June 2nd the pair began sequencing the album, a process of choosing the final tracklist and running order, featuring everything they had recorded between August 1996 - March 1998. While both Lavelle and Shadow agreed it was time to release the album, they

---

[1078] Friedman, K 2013
[1079] Mclean, C 1998, p. 66
[1080] Cigarettes, J 1998, p. 14
[1081] NME 1998e
[1082] URB 1998

also would each later discuss some regrets on what the album could have been,[1083] with Shadow in particular discussing this at length in 2006:

> I'm so hard on myself in the studio because I don't want to confront failure. Although I have had to deal with it, like on the UNKLE album ... When we were mastering it, I knew in my heart that it was missing a song or two. I was really conflicted about the nominal segues between the songs because I thought they were just a waste and not helping the album. But you never know that until you get to sequencing. That's the day of reckoning. With *Endtroducing...*, sequencing was really effortless. With the UNKLE record, I think there are great songs there, some among my best work. But as an album, it doesn't really hold together.[1084]

These feelings aside, the album was handed in as complete and promotion began shortly afterwards in June 1998 with photoshoots in Japan, and *Lonely Soul* receiving its radio debut.[1085] The album's title and release date were revealed on the *NME* website on June 16th 1998, announcing to the world that Psyence Fiction would be released August 24th of that year.[1086]

Regarding the album's title, *Psyence Fiction*, Lavelle explained that it represented his and Shadow's common reference point of science fiction films, such as Stanley Kubrick's *2001*. But Lavelle didn't want to spell the album title as *Science Fiction*, afraid that it would be taken too literally and that he would be mocked. Instead Lavelle felt that *Psyence Fiction* was a better fit, as he saw the album as being a very psychological record, with the *Psy* in *Psyence* referring to psychology.[1087]

[1083] Graphotism 2000
[1084] Sterling, S 2006
[1085] Mclean, C 1998, pp. 67-69
[1086] NME 1998b
[1087] UNKLE 1998, 00:21:00

Further, Lavelle felt that films such as *2001* used psychology to look forward and imagine something new yet familiar, and he wanted to achieve the same thing with UNKLE's music.[1088] He explained, "This album is not trying to be *Independence Day*, it's trying to be *2001*. It's not a big flashy spaceship-type adventure, it's a psychological look at what can be done when you combine the past, the present and the future."[1089]

Adding to the futuristic sci-fi look of the album, was the album artwork. While the Futura and DJ Spooky's UNKLE comic that was begun during the LA sessions in 1995 never saw the light of day, Futura was still involved with UNKLE for *Psyence Fiction*. Lavelle explained his ongoing appreciation with Futura and his work in 1998:

> I've been into him since I was a kid, he's always inspired me. He's a living legend, almost a mythical character. I really wanted him to create an image that would not involve our faces. He's just created that UNKLE world. We wanted a universe of characters that I want people to see and instantly think of UNKLE. He's also based the toys on these characters.[1090]

The 'pointmen', as the UNKLE characters became known, had represented Lavelle's UNKLE project since 1994's *The Time Has Come EP*, and the band helped popularise the characters, with Futura telling an interviewer, "Without the UNKLE experience, I don't think anyone would have ever heard of the Pointman."[1091] But the characters themselves had existed prior to UNKLE, with Lavelle initially seeing them in some artwork during a visit to Futura's studio before using them on *The Time Has Come EP*.[1092] They had originally been inspired by H.R. Giger's work for Ridley Scott's *Alien* film that had released in 1979, with Futura explaining he "started

---

[1088] Ibid.
[1089] Adams, C 1998
[1090] Burgess, J 1998, p. 60
[1091] Adesanya, J 2018
[1092] Donners, B 2018

scribbling them a few years later."¹⁰⁹³ He has also noted that the name pointmen, or pointman, was not a name he had given the characters, and was something created by "those in the public space", presumably Mo' Wax.¹⁰⁹⁴

The pointmen themselves have a larger story outside of the UNKLE project that tells of how the characters are part of "the Robotronic regime from the planet Extron,"¹⁰⁹⁵ but within UNKLE they are used purely as representing the groups members.¹⁰⁹⁶ Lavelle explained their intentions in a 2000 interview with *Graphotism*:

> We wanted to utilise characters and that was always going to be the identity of the band. So when he came over we just did loads and loads of stuff with characters...we kind of had a bit of a pact where the characters were going to be kept much more for Mo' Wax and the identity for UNKLE, and he's kind of always respected that. The good thing with Futura is he understands that relationship that is key to an artist. That is, if you have a definitive style – which he does – and its spread thinly over different peoples work, then it will lose its appeal. And he's kept to that. The only people he's been working with is me and Japan, really. It's been good because as soon as I did this stuff with him, everyone came out of the woodwork and wanted to do loads of things but he's been very honourable on that level, which I'm really happy about because it's allowed us to retain an identity.¹⁰⁹⁷

Lavelle had always been hands on when it came to the direction and concepts of the cover art for Mo' Wax's releases, and *Psyence Fiction* was no different.¹⁰⁹⁸ The design of the cover of *Psyence Fiction* was completed by Ben Drury, adapting Futura's artwork, while Will Bankhead took the photographs of most of the artists

---

¹⁰⁹³ futuradosmil 2018
¹⁰⁹⁴ Ibid.
¹⁰⁹⁵ Spence, S 2001
¹⁰⁹⁶ Higgins, M 1998
¹⁰⁹⁷ Graphotism 2000
¹⁰⁹⁸ Butler, A 2014

which are featured within the sleeve.[1099] For the Japanese release Nigo[1100] and Sk8thing[1101] created new artwork which featured a unique design, different from Drury's version.[1102] A striking cover has always been part of Mo' Wax, and as Lavelle said in 1998, "You don't remember the day a record was released, all you remember is what you've got in your hand. If it looks special then you will value it for more."[1103]

The initial vinyl release of *Psyence Fiction* featured a foldout gatefold cover, with the album cover split so that it opened from the middle to reveal two booklets of photographs of the guest artists.[1104] This design idea had previously been attempted by Mo' Wax that same year for a promo of Money Mark's *Push The Button* album.[1105] But while the gatefold design didn't make it to the final edition of *Push The Button,* it was featured on initial copies of *Psyence Fiction* on CD[1106] and vinyl pressed by Mo' Wax in England,[1107] and the initial CD pressing in Japan.[1108] Other editions such as the US vinyl pressing featured a more standard gatefold design, with the gatefold opening at the edge rather than from the middle of the cover.[1109]

Looking back in 2000, Lavelle noted that the cover wasn't quite what he wanted at the time, talking about the album and commenting "I wish it had been... more. In retrospect, the sleeve isn't how I really want it to be but it was such an intense period of time, and there are a lot of times I look back and want to change things."[1110]

[1099] Discogs 2019zz
[1100] Toy's Factory 2000b
[1101] Lavelle, J 2014
[1102] Discogs 2019rrr
[1103] Sturges, F 1998, p. 15
[1104] Discogs 2019bbb
[1105] Discogs 2019cc
[1106] Discogs 2019yy
[1107] Discogs 2019bbb
[1108] Discogs 2019rrr
[1109] Discogs 2019ccc
[1110] Graphotism 2000

Release

Promotion for *Psyence Fiction* begun in June 1998, with *Lonely Souls* premiering on BBC Radio 1 June 22nd,[1111] marking the first time any of the new UNKLE songs had been played publicly outside of James Lavelle and DJ Shadow's DJ sets. While Lavelle and Shadow sat listening to the premiere they realised that the song had been edited to make it shorter, with Lavelle especially annoyed and announcing that he would write a letter to the BBC to complain.[1112]

June also saw Shadow and Lavelle take part in interviews and promotional photoshoots in Japan, with the photoshoots reportedly taking over eight hours in themselves. The photoshoots also caused a few disagreements, with a photographer requesting Shadow use some guns as props, which Shadow refused alongside requests for him to wear certain clothing, with Shadow preferring to wear his own clothes.[1113] This was repeated at another photoshoot in America where UNKE's American record label London announced they had secured a four page spread in a major music magazine, which would have a stylist and lots of "cool clothes".[1114] Shadow explained he preferred to wear his own clothes and believed they had understood him, but then London drove him to the photoshoot and tried to guilt him in to taking part. Shadow refused and later explained the consequences were that *Psyence Fiction* "got moved from the lead review to the back of the magazine, with a star and a half taken off."[1115]

In July 1998 early promo copies of the album began being sent out,[1116] and the album was played in its entirety at listening parties

---

[1111] McLean, C 1998, p. 65
[1112] Ibid. p. 69
[1113] Ibid.
[1114] Werde, B 2002, p. 37
[1115] Ibid.
[1116] Endersby, R <rob@idlemedia.co.uk> 1998

in New York[1117] and Los Angeles.[1118] The album was first released in Japan on August 21st,[1119] with the official album release parties for Japan scheduled for later in September.[1120]

For the launch in England, Shadow and Lavelle spent the night of the August 23rd at HMV on Oxford Street, London with hundreds of fans who lined up to buy the album.[1121] Both Shadow and Lavelle DJed until midnight when the album was officially made for sale at 12am August 24th. The pair were accompanied by Futura who created a live painting during the event,[1122] while Lavelle and Shadow stayed a further 3 hours after the launch signing copies of the album.[1123]

Shadow and Lavelle next returned to Japan for a series of three release parties in September in Osaka, Sapporo, and Tokyo.[1124] The party in Tokyo was billed as "Hearts of Darkness" and James Lavelle played a DJ set which featured Kan Takagi giving a live performance of *Last Orgy 3*, while Shadow performed a live reconstruction of *Psyence Fiction*.[1125]

As part of the American launch, Shadow and Lavelle took part in a five-stop promotional tour across the USA, featuring a screening of the *Rabbit In Your Headlights* music video, a DJ Shadow DJ set, a Q&A session with Lavelle, and finally both Shadow and Lavelle signing copies of the album. The first date was held at Virgin Records in Los Angeles on September 28, the day before the albums American launch, with Shadow's DJ set being particularly well received by fans as he would throw the records he was playing in to the crowd once he was finished with them.[1126]

[1117] Banez, C <cbanez@hotmail.com> 1998
[1118] Bennun, D 1998
[1119] Discogs 2019rrr
[1120] Discogs 2019sss
[1121] Freeman, M 1998
[1122] Fiona 1998
[1123] Freeman, M 1998
[1124] Ele-king 1998, p. 2
[1125] Toy's Factory 1998
[1126] Reid, T <t-bird@salata.com> 1999

The tour then went on to San Francisco on the 29th for the official American release date of *Psyence Fiction*. They then travelled to Chicago and New York City, before completing the tour with a show in Austin, Texas.[1127] The two last shows, in New York and Austin, were recorded and later released by Shadow as *The UNKLE In Stores*.[1128]

While there were rumours at the time surrounding the possibility of a special show featuring all of the guest artists performing their parts, at Albert Hall in England[1129] or somewhere in New York City,[1130] these never materialised.

Meanwhile the album began to enter the charts in England with sales starting at almost 35,000,[1131] allowing the album to enter the charts on the 5th of September 1998 at #4 where it peaked and spent a total of 14 weeks in the Top 100 Albums Chart, dropping in and out across the new year until finally exiting in March 1999.[1132] In America it didn't fare as well, spending only two weeks in the Billboard Top 200 and peaking at #107 on October 17 1998.[1133]

According to London Records, UNKLE's American label at the time, this was to be expected, with Guy Higgins their international marketing manager telling *MTV*, "It will be hard to break in America, but it's always a challenge to get Americans excited for something slightly unconventional."[1134] Even Lavelle admitted he wasn't expecting the album to break any records, speaking at the American launch he said, "I don't expect it to be a huge commercial record...I don't think it's going to be a big record like the Beastie

---

[1127] BAO <tunde@arches.uga.edu> 1998
[1128] Discogs 2019j
[1129] Burgess, J 1998, p. 60
[1130] Jazzbo, 1998
[1131] Music Week 1998c
[1132] Official UK Charts Company 2019j
[1133] Billboard, 2019
[1134] Kaufman, G 1998

Boys'. But then I think it's a lot more dangerous than the Beastie Boys record, to be honest."[1135]

While at the time Lavelle and the label didn't openly discuss their disappointment surrounding the albums lack of sales in America, Shadow for one was unimpressed. Following the short tour of America, Shadow took two weeks off and was surprised to hear how poorly the album was selling in America. He explained his disappointment to *CMJ*:

> I was on a ferry from Galveston, Texas...just sitting and feeling the wind. The record had been out for three days and I was totally away, didn't have a cell phone, nothing. I was thinking, I did everything I could do.' I didn't shirk on promoting or anything. And I had these fantasies-'I wonder if things were just going crazy right now?' I broke my own rule, and four days before the end of the trip. I called this woman at London and she says, 'Oh yeah, things are great! You're number one on [Billboard chart] Heatseekers.' And I go, 'What does that mean?' She says, That's when you're not in the top 100, but you're almost there.' I just thought to myself. This album didn't even crack the top 100?' I think I had a small little breakdown at that point. I mean, hey, many people do records that don't break the top 100. But I just thought, of anything I'll ever do, this would be it.[1136]

While Shadow was initially frustrated at how *Psyence Fiction* was being received,[1137] he decided to get back to work and began recording songs for the *Quannum Spectrum* album,[1138] a compilation featuring Shadow along with Latryx, Lyrics Born, Blackalicious, and Jurassic 5 released in 1999 on Mo' Wax and

---

[1135] Cigarettes, J 1998, p. 16
[1136] Werde, B 2002 p. 37
[1137] Ibid.
[1138] Carroll, J 1999

Quannum Projects,[1139] the new record label started by Shadow and his friends after their Solesides label closed.[1140]

Meanwhile, reviews for *Psyence Fiction* were mixed, with many focusing on Lavelle having likened the album to *Hearts of Darkness*, the documentary detailing the makings of the movie *Apocalypse Now*. The press took this analogy as a reference to how overblown and bloated the album was, yet Lavelle explained he had meant it more in the sense that the album had been a struggle to complete, and that during the recording of *Psyence Fiction* Lavelle had watched *Hearts of Darkness* and it had resonated with him.[1141] He explained to *NME*:

> It's not that we've made the musical equivalent of *Apocalypse Now* – that's like saying you're trying to write *Lord Of The Fucking Rings* – it's just that it felt like the making of that film. The logisitics of it all, the relationship splitting up, and the abuse, going from being into drugs and then going into some other fucking lifestyle, you know, then made times with girlfriends coming and going and having kids, moving around the world, record companies falling apart and managers getting involved and bands blowing up, and the stress of trying to see your vision through to reality when the whole world seemed to be conspiring against you.[1142]

In England the album received 2/5 stars from *Muzik*, who praised some of the production but accused it of being "too obviously cool to actually be cool."[1143] Likewise *NME* gave the album 6/10, describing it as a "grandiose, bloated, egotistical folly,"[1144] and Lavelle has continually referred to the original *NME* review by John

---

[1139] Discogs 2019kkk
[1140] Roeder, M 1999
[1141] Grundy, G 1998, p. 80
[1142] Cigarettes, J 1998, p. 14
[1143] Bonner, M 1998, p. 65
[1144] Mulvey, J 1998

Mulvey as particularly horrific[1145] as it focused most of its antagonism at Lavelle, with Mulvey stating:

> If 'Psyence Fiction' is a failure, one suspects that fault lies squarely with Lavelle rather than the patently gifted men and women employed to flesh out his nebulous concepts, that full-on creativity has been stifled by the adolescent-dream-come-true of forming a supergroup.[1146]

Lavelle had spoken out against the NME on an episode of Jo Wiley's self titled chat show on Channel 4 in early September 1998,[1147] where he expressed his opinion that music journalism was suffering due to publications such as NME putting pop stars on their covers which boosted their sales, but led to a change in focus for the publications as they now had to maintain the sales they'd gained from featuring people like Robbie Williams on their cover. Lavelle felt that his comments led to the poor review in the NME for Psyence Fiction,[1148] though they would later list Psyence Fiction at #38 on NME's Top 100 Albums of 1998 calling it "breathlessly eclectic."[1149]

America meanwhile was far kinder, Spin awarded the album 8/10,[1150] Rolling Stone 3.5/5,[1151] and Time Magazine described it as like seeing the film Pulp Fiction for the first time and concluded, "The album also surveys the sounds of trip-hop, hip-hop and indie rock. Despite its disparate parts, a sustained mood is achieved."[1152]

Fans at the time took to the internet to share their own reviews, with a consensus that if you were able to look past the hype you might actually enjoy the album.[1153] One fan commented at the time:

[1145] Pollard, A 2018
[1146] Mulvey, J 1998
[1147] Jordon, R 1998, p. 20
[1148] Pollard, A 2018
[1149] NME 1999a
[1150] Walters, B 1998, p. 135
[1151] Lorraine, A 1998
[1152] Farley, C J 1998
[1153] Gaderlund, E <erikg@macconnect.com> 1998

> I agree, there was too much hype and I did get sucked into it but it is overall a very good CD. I could do without the first track but the tracks that have that "classic" UNKLE sound (soundtracks, weird sound effects, heavy scratching) are dope. I don't like the Verve but Richard Ashcroft sounds great on "Lonely Soul".[1154]

Ex-UNKLE member Tim Goldsworthy was also asked his thoughts on the album when it launched, and he wasn't impressed, telling NME:

> It doesn't sound like there's much excitement going on. It's a bit too clinical for me. A bit of a chin-scratcher, and a bit of a boys' bedroom record. I prefer something to get pissed and throw yourself around the room to. It's well put together, but I don't think it's as complete and flowing as 'Endtroducing...'. I think it sounds a bit too much like a compilation.[1155]

The album was considered a flop by many, and the fact that *Psyence Fiction* featured Thom Yorke and Richard Ashcroft, who had recently had their biggest hits with their respective bands, was seen as a cash grab by many reviewers who either weren't aware the songs had been recorded years earlier, or didn't care. Lavelle commented on the blessing and curse of this coincidence:

> When we started working with Richard and Thom, *Urban Hymns* and *OK Computer* hadn't come out yet, so they weren't these uber stars that they became. Right in the moment that we're trying to get them into a studio, lo and behold, the Verve sells whatever ridiculous amount of records it was, and *OK Computer* comes out to become what many think is the best British record ever made. So suddenly we went from these quite relaxed conversations

---

[1154] L R <lr68@hotmail.com> 1998
[1155] Cigarettes, J 1998, p. 16

> about being in the studio with people to dealing with managers. And from beginning to end that was a two-year process.[1156]

Equally polarising to many reviewers was how the album mixed electronica, hip hop, and rock together, which at the time was rarely done, and had never been done on such a scale.[1157] Albums which featured various genres and multiple guests from across those genres were also uncommon at the time, though several would pop up over the coming years, with Dan The Automator and Prince Paul releasing their Handsome Boy Modelling School project in 1999, an album which featured DJ Shadow, Mike D, Money Mark, and Del Tha Funkee Homosapien. Automator and Del then teamed up with Blur's Damon Albarn to release *Clint Eastwood* from the Gorillaz's self titled album in 2001, with Gorillaz now seen as one of the most successful groups to blend multiple genres and guest artists,[1158] and which bandleader Albarn once described to Lavelle in jest as "the ultimate Unkle rip off."[1159]

Shadow later recalled many of the tracks from *Psyence Fiction* with fondness, commenting:

> When I listen back to my favorite tracks off that record, like "*Lonely Soul*" or "*Rabbit In Your Headlights*," what I like about them is that they seem really audacious—there were no rules or restrictions. We weren't trying to make pop music. We combined elements of the rock world and the electronic/hip-hop world, and that really wasn't done at that time. Since then, of course, it's become almost a cliché, but back then, they were completely different universes. James and I thought it was fun and groundbreaking at the time, to mix up those waters.[1160]

[1156] Bradshaw, P 2014b
[1157] Ibid.
[1158] Mitchum, R 2011
[1159] Wright, R 2017
[1160] Fader, L 2012

While the music had its fans, one other piece of contention raised in reviews was the question of what did James Lavelle actually do on the album?

Lavelle has never made it a secret that he didn't play instruments or make any of the music from the early UNKLE releases,[1161] and that his contributions were with ideas.[1162] Initially he had Tim Goldsworthy, and then Masayuki Kudo, to help him realise his ideas, and when Shadow took over production of the UNKLE album Lavelle continued collaborating in this nature, with Lavelle discussing and describing ideas and bringing in records to sample, collecting ideas for himself and Shadow to work on between studios in America and England throughout.[1163] Lavelle described these early sessions, and the collaborative process between Shadow and himself, when he spoke to *Westworld* about the album in 1998:

> It was quite naive in the beginning...I came up with the vision for everything, and then me and Shadow would have these huge conversations about music, film and all kinds of reference points--just the emotions we were trying to portray, the reactions for and against music at the time--past, present and trying to look into the future a bit. And then Shadow would try to make audio sense of these conversations. Like, 'Let's go do a hardcore track. Yeah-yeah-yeah.' Or 'We want this to sound organic. Yeah-yeah-yeah.' A lot of it stemmed from technical talk between the two of us; we'd talk about gating this or adding that, and then something would come out of it. It was conceptual in that way.[1164]

Lavelle explained further in an interview in the *NME* from 1998:

[1161] Cole, B 1998, p.154
[1162] Adams, C 1998
[1163] Harris, L 2011
[1164] Roberts, M 1998

I wanted to make a record where I was personally involved, lived through it, came up with the idea and developed the whole thing from scratch. Sure, I didn't write the record. I brought in Shadow, because it was my concept, my thing and I wanted it to be the best it could be, because in five years' time people aren't going to remember the review or the day it came out, they'll remember the music. People are going to say, 'Oh he's so egotistical because he's done nothing', but in a way I've shattered any ego thing by letting everyone have their creative freedom in it…I have a very definite feeling of how things should be but I'll never be, 'It's my way or the highway'. You've got to have that confidence in people to let go and trust their way sometimes or there's no point. I've surrounded myself with people who are great at what they do, and sometimes they need challenging or channelling but you can't take over because that's why they come to you – to have their freedom. I don't want a bunch of fucking Yes men around me, I want them to give me as much as I give them.[1165]

But while he may have contributed, at the end of the day the album credits don't feature J. Lavelle, instead most writing credits feature J. Davis, aka DJ Shadow. Lavelle explained, "There are millions of samples in the record that I put in there, just not the main musical progression. And when it came down to defining who wrote it and who didn't, it felt a bit awkward saying I wrote it."[1166] This awkwardness was further frustrated as Lavelle initially believed he *was* going to receive writing credits split between Shadow and Lavelle, but Shadow insisted "you're not touching my writer credits," not realising the issue would become controversial.[1167] Lavelle was obviously frustrated as he felt he had contributed through bringing in ideas and samples, but he backed down, describing it as "a very strange scenario to be in."[1168]

[1165] Cigarettes, J 1998, pp. 14-15
[1166] Braddock, K 1998, p. 42
[1167] *The Man from Mo' Wax* 2018, 00:39:00
[1168] Slow 1999

Shadow explained further in 1998:

> It's a conceptual collaboration...At one point, we were arguing and I was like, 'Look James, this isn't a musical collaboration.' James has always been a delegator. He can't make a beat, so he gets Kudo. He can't sing, so he gets Richard Ashcroft. The music was my domain, the same way the artwork was [graffiti artist] Futura's domain...for whatever reason, I'm able to translate his chaotic thinking. He'll say something like, 'For this song, you know that sense of loneliness in *2001* or *The Abyss*?' And I'll be like, 'James, don't say any more. I'll play it for you when it's ready.'[1169]

Lavelle has held up Massive Attack and their *Blue Lines* debut as the benchmark of what he wanted to achieve with UNKLE's album,[1170] and it is an apt comparison as during the early Massive Attack sessions the group would also be questioned about what they actually had done[1171] as they reportedly didn't play instruments.[1172] Instead, while recording *Blue Lines* and *Protection* Massive Attack would put together their albums from collections of samples they had which would be sent out to other producers to embellish.[1173]

Both Lavelle and Shadow had different ideas of their role, and Lavelle at times wanted to be more hands on, admitting to the *NME* that there were screaming fits when he wanted to hear tracks Shadow hadn't completed. He explained that "eventually I'd agree to waiting to a certain point in its creation, and through that we'd learn to discuss things without having a fight…"[1174] There were also problems outside of the Shadow/Lavelle collaboration, either from outsiders or guest's managers as referenced in the Ball Busters

---

[1169] Jazzbo 1998
[1170] NME 1998e
[1171] Johnson, P 1997, p. 102
[1172] Ibid. p. 97
[1173] Ibid.
[1174] Cigarettes, J 1998, p. 15

sampling *Getting Ahead in the Lucrative Field of Artist Management* skit. Lavelle, in explaining the frustration admitted it sometimes worked out:

> There were some tracks that were very hard to do. Sometimes the problem was that the music wasn't going the way we wanted it to, and sometimes it was other people's faults, because they needed to find themselves or they were going through their own problems. But in retrospect, those problems can give a song a buzz. It can be very painful, but if you win, it's a fucking great feeling.[1175]

Lavelle has repeatedly described his role on *Psyence Fiction* as like that of a film director,[1176] and one that fits in with director Stanley Kubrick's description of what he considered the director's role, "A director is a kind of idea and taste machine; a movie is a series of creative and technical decisions, and it's the director's job to make the right decisions as frequently as possible."[1177] But it has been an argument Lavelle has had to have repeatedly, with Ben Drury describing the problem:

> It's his vision…I think some people are uncomfortable with that. That they're servicing the vision of this other dude. People think 'why are we doing this for this guy, when we could be doing it for ourselves?' And they underestimate what he brings. The fact that some people can't see it has been quite damaging for him.[1178]

In 1998 Lavelle seemed to be tired of arguing though, telling an interviewer at the time, "I put the whole thing together, it wouldn't exist without me. It wasn't Josh's idea, and he wouldn't have made this record."[1179] Which Shadow agreed with somewhat, explaining: "The record couldn't have been done without James…James was a

---

[1175] Roberts, M 1998
[1176] Braddock, K 1998, p. 42
[1177] Gelmis, J 1969
[1178] Williams, E 2017
[1179] Braddock, K 1998, p. 42

very hands-on A&R role and a very hands-on executive producer role. I know what I did musically and he knows what he didn't do. He didn't do the music. There has never been a battle."[1180]

While their opinions of their collaboration and each other tend to change depending on the tone of the interview, Lavelle and Shadow did work on the album together, and while Lavelle continued working as UNKLE, Shadow's work with the group ended with *Psyence Fiction's* release in 1998 and he moved on to other projects.

[1180] Ibid.

Touring with the NME / Be There

With the American promo tour over, Shadow elected to stay in America and work with his Quannum crew,[1181] while Lavelle went back to the UK to return to work at Mo' Wax and plan for the next year.[1182]

In November of 1998 Lavelle met with the Scratch Perverts DJ team to discuss an UNKLE tour that would feature both Lavelle and the Scratch Perverts together on stage performing the album as a DJ set.[1183] The idea was picked up by *NME* who invited Lavelle to tour as part of their NME National Tour,[1184] with dates arranged to begin in January 1999 across the UK.

The Scratch Perverts at the time were made up of Prime Cuts and Tony Vegas, a turntable duo who were World DMC team champions in both 1999 and 2001. Tony Vegas had previously worked with Lavelle, providing scratches on UNKLE's *Last Orgy 3* and *Ape Shall Never Kill Ape*, as well as Lavelle's 1997 remix of The Verve's *Bitter Sweet Symphony*.[1185]

In Japan Nigo was preparing his *Worldwide Bape Tour 1998*, and Lavelle asked if he could join the tour with the Scratch Perverts as a means to warm up before the UK shows.[1186] Nigo agreed on the condition that Kan Takagi would appear with them,[1187] which Lavelle agreed to leading to the only known recorded live performance of UNKLE's *Last Orgy 3*. For their *Worldwide Bape Tour* performance the stage featured two separate sets of turntables on either side of the stage with the Scratch Perverts together on one side and Lavelle alone on the other. Their set was

---

[1181] Werde, J 2002, pp. 37-39
[1182] Harcourt, N 1998, 00:43:34
[1183] Fuller, J 1998
[1184] Slow 1999
[1185] Discogs 2020e
[1186] Worldwide BAPE Heads Show 1998, 00:08:09
[1187] Ibid. 00:08:55

recorded and was screened in Japan as part of a *Worldwide Bape Tour 1998* TV special which featured interviews with Nigo and the many groups who appeared on the tour.[1188] Lavelle looks quite lost during the performance, no doubt regretting the decision to be placed so far away from the Scratch Perverts, and by the time of the NME Tour all three of them would appear standing next to each other sharing six Turntables.[1189]

Speaking to *Straight No Chaser*, Prime Cuts explained the concept of performing *Psyence Fiction* live, "We broke the whole thing down into parts, much like a band. I might have a bassline record or a drum loop record, Tony could have the accapella and James could have some backing record. We'd splice the whole thing together on three sets of decks with James usually playing the backing track and laying sound effects over the top. We must have had 25 records pressed up of each part of each song in the live show."[1190]

Starting January 10 in Glasgow, Scotland, UNKLE were joined on the tour by Llama Farmers, Delakota, and Idlewild, with UNKLE serving as the headliners.[1191] The tour travelled across England and Scotland and was made up of twelve dates which ended on January 24 at The Astoria in London.

Reviews for the shows were positive, with only a few disappointed that DJ Shadow wasn't there.[1192] [1193] *The Independent* called their Glasgow show "Damn funky",[1194] while *Muzik* referred to the Oxford show as "a brilliantly executed, inventive and possibly revolutionary performance".[1195] Their Liverpool show was described by *NME* as "amazing",[1196] with Lavelle throwing his records in to the crowd at

---

[1188] Worldwide BAPE Heads Show 1998
[1189] Horan, T 1999
[1190] Rayner, A 1999, p. 24
[1191] Music Week 1998a
[1192] Horan, T 1999
[1193] Braddock, K 1999, p. 129
[1194] James, M 1999
[1195] Braddock, K 1999, p. 129
[1196] Empire, K 1999

the end of their set where they were eagerly snatched up by fans.[1197] The *NME* summarised the event by writing, "It's hard to account for the awe that's inspired tonight by grown men destroying vinyl."[1198]

The live show featured visuals projected behind the performance which were provided by The Light Surgeons who described their work as "a multi screen visual production using video, slide and 16mm film projection."[1199] The video work featured elements of Shynola's *Guns Blazing* video[1200] intercut with film clips, slogans, and a live feed showing close ups of scratching and other turntable tricks picked up by mini cameras placed nearby.[1201]

Their final show at The Astoria also featured Ian Brown in his first live performance since being released from jail at the end of 1998. He performed *Be There* which was soon after released as a single by UNKLE, and on February 20th, 1999 entered the UK Singles Charts at #8 where it peaked. It would spend six weeks in the Top 100 before exiting again.[1202] During this period *Psyence Fiction* re-entered the UK Album Top 100, after disappearing at the end of January. After returning in the first week of February, *Psyence Fiction* remained in the Top 100 for five weeks, or fourteen in total since its release in August 1998.[1203]

The BBC's Jo Tyler witnessed Ian Brown's performance at The Astoria, later commenting, "He sang surprisingly sweetly for just the one song, and left suddenly without saying anything."[1204] While the *NME* describe Brown's appearance as "a great rock and roll moment, the equivalent of a fireworks display."[1205]

[1197] Ibid.
[1198] Ibid.
[1199] The Light Surgeons 2019
[1200] Ibid.
[1201] Horan, T 1999
[1202] Official UK Charts Company 2019m
[1203] Official UK Charts Company 2019j
[1204] NME 1999b
[1205] Ibid.

The Scratch Perverts again teamed with Lavelle as a trio for a session on the BBC Radio 1's *The Breezeblock* on the 1st of February 1999, billed as UNKLE vs. Scratch Perverts.[1206] The group would then perform in Ireland on February 4th as part of a Mo' Wax night at the fifth Heineken Weekender in Galway,[1207] and DJ Shadow was also present and made a quick cameo appearance during the set.[1208]

On the 19th of February, DJ Shadow returned to England to reunite with Lavelle and perform *Be There* with Ian Brown on BBC's *Top Of The Pops*. Other guests on the show were Whitney Houston, Cher, Boyzone, the Corrs, Blur, and Next of Kin. UNKLE performed live and featured Lavelle on the Mellotron playing the introduction to the track before sitting back and watching the performance as Shadow scratched records and Ian Brown sang. Lavelle would later describe the performance as degrading as he had wanted to DJ alongside Shadow, but Shadow refused.[1209]

[1206] MixesDB 2019
[1207] The Sun 1998
[1208] Beeb 1999
[1209] *The Man from Mo' Wax* 2018, 00:43:00

Downfall of Mo' Wax / Never Never Land

While *Psyence Fiction* was being prepared for release James Lavelle's other project Mo' Wax Records, the record label he started at 18 in 1992, was in trouble.

In the August 8th 1998 issue of *Music Week* it was revealed that Mo' Wax and A&M's three year deal was set to expire soon.[1210] While Lavelle had enjoyed a good relationship with A&M and became good friends with Osman Eralp, the Managing Director of A&M in the UK, things changed when in May 1998 Eralp announced he was leaving the company.[1211] At the time A&M had been considering restructuring themselves due to worries over the increasing cost of doing business in the UK, but Eralp's leaving "precipitated" these plans.[1212]

Many of the problems Lavelle had regarding *Psyence Fiction* were linked with Eralp's departure, as he had always been supportive of Mo' Wax and Lavelle's vision. But in the week that *Psyence Fiction* was handed in to A&M Eralp announced he was leaving, and Lavelle's grand plan for a three-part UNKLE music video series directed by Jonathan Glazer were instantly cancelled.[1213]

In June 1998 it was announced that A&M would be closing down due to the imminent merger of A&M's owner PolyGram with Universal Music Group.[1214] A&M announced their current artists would be moving to one of their other labels Polydor, Mercury or Island Records. UNKLE were one of the affected acts with *Psyence*

[1210] Farsides, T 1998
[1211] Music Week 1998b
[1212] Snell, T 1998c
[1213] Bradshaw, P 2014b
[1214] Snell, T 1998c

Fiction released by Island Records as negotiations over Mo' Wax continued.[1215]

By the end of 1998 fans on the internet began reporting that Mo' Wax was closing down,[1216] [1217] and even Lavelle's own staff seemed to have already lost faith in the label as early as 1997, as when Lavelle tried to sign the band Air to Mo' Wax they were warned off by Lavelle's assistant who told them Mo' Wax was bankrupt and they shouldn't sign with the label.[1218] The band listened and signed to Virgin Records who released Air's album *Moon Safari* in the UK in January 1998 where it would reach number 6 in the charts and remain in the Top 100 for 110 weeks.[1219]

While Mo' Wax wasn't churning out chart-topping hits, and very few of their releases made money outside of DJ Shadow's *Endtroducing* album,[1220] there was still interest in the label, with many releases gaining good press. In 1998 Lavelle described Mo' Wax as "the label with the fattest concepts...It's the vibe rather than the sales."[1221]

The closing of A&M was seen by the British Press as a sign of the death of the UK music industry, but John Kennedy, PolyGram's UK Chairman/CEO at the time, was not someone who shared the view, "The industry's going through a tough time. It may be that we didn't address some of the problems early on and had our head in the sand...But the industry is not dying."[1222]

In December 1998 Seagrams, then owner of Universal Music Group, acquired PolyGram for $10.4 billion, and A&M was merged

---

[1215] Farsides, T 1998
[1216] KidCaL <calvin@hklink.net> 1998
[1217] Keefe, M < MARKEEFE@aol.com > 1998
[1218] Wines, B 2016
[1219] Official UK Charts Company 2019a
[1220] Penn, A 2014
[1221] Raygun, 1998,
[1222] Snell, T 1998b

into Universal Music Group with Mo' Wax artists such as DJ Shadow transitioned to Universal.[1223]

With their contract now expired Mo' Wax were free to move elsewhere, with Virgin Records reported as interested, and Polygram/A&M were more than aware of it. John Kennedy at the time commented "James Lavelle was close to Osman and ever since he left they have been considering what they're going to do in the future."[1224]

Problematic for Lavelle was the realisation that his deal with A&M meant that while he owned the name Mo' Wax, A&M owned all of the artists he had signed including UNKLE.[1225] Undeterred, in 1999 Lavelle signed a deal with the record label XL, part of Beggars Banquet, which gave Mo' Wax a new home, and without any of the artists from A&M he had no option but to start again.[1226] He appeared optimistic at the time, explaining to the *BBC*:

> We are now working with Beggars Banquet, which is really exciting for me because we are independent and it allows me to have the full creative control I couldn't have when working with Polygram. I am trying to find a way of working with the old artists and also building a new rosta (sic) of future talent. My dream is to make my Mo'Wax the company I always wanted it to be and I think with this new label it's quite possible.[1227]

Lavelle's old artists who had signed to Mo' Wax now found themselves signed to Polygram and Universal[1228] and were understandably upset. It was reported in *Muzik* that some of the artists had begun to rebel, with rumours DJ Shadow and Money Mark might refuse to release anything as a sign of allegiance with

---

[1223] Pfenninger, L 2019
[1224] Snell, T 1998c
[1225] Williams, E 2017
[1226] Snell, T 1998a
[1227] Beeb 1999
[1228] Snell, T 1998a

Lavelle.¹²²⁹ Shadow would comment in 2002, "I could have held my breath for ten years and not done a record (for Universal), but that's not for me...I realized, 'Okay, this is the situation; let's make the best of it,"¹²³⁰ as he explained further to Zane Lowe, Shadow didn't want to be "one of those artists who doesn't record for ten years just to spite their label."¹²³¹ He would go on to release *The Private Press* in 2002 with some editions featuring the Mo' Wax logo.¹²³²

Initial Mo' Wax releases after the XL deal featured albums from Nigo, Blackalicious, Malcom Catto, South, David Axelrod, skateboarder Tommy Guerrero, and Quannum. But by 2002 Lavelle realised he needed a break, later explaining to *The Independent* in 2014:

> When you're young, you're caught up in the energy and the madness of it. There's the money and the drugs and the massive ego that comes with that. Mo'Wax felt like a band in which I was the lead singer. But there's a point where you have to go 'OK, we're done'. The whole thing had lost its momentum and I was pretty burnt out...My life had crashed. My relationship was over and I had a young child. It was quite a strange time for me. Luckily, I was young when Mo'Wax started and pretty young when it finished so I was able to start a whole other chapter. I toured with UNKLE and the DJing just took off. I would take my daughter to school on a Monday morning and the other parents would be talking about their weekends picnicking on Primrose Hill. They'd ask what I'd been up to and I'd say 'Playing records on a beach in the Black Sea'.¹²³³

In 2019 he would express regret at closing the label, "I wish somebody had said, "Take six months off." But it's hard to take six months off when you're 27, 28, and you're DJing every club in the

---

¹²²⁹ Muzik 1999, p. 10
¹²³⁰ Hermes, W 2002, p. 97
¹²³¹ Lowe, Z 2002
¹²³² Discogs 2019i
¹²³³ Sturges, F 2014

world and you have a seven-year-old child and you're trying to deal and you don't really have the knowledge. The snowball goes out of control. There was nobody there just to say, "Stop. Let's just stop for six months. It will be OK." It was literally like, "It's over. Goodbye.""[1234]

With Mo' Wax no more, other projects fell apart such as *Headz 3*,[1235] the planned follow up to 1996's *Headz 2* compilation that would have featured a broader range of musical styles than before.[1236] Artists such as The Neptunes were planned as contributors[1237] and Mo' Wax contacted their label, requesting some instrumental music for the compilation.[1238] *Headz 3* was first teased in 1997,[1239] and in late 2000 was still being advertised as coming soon in the August issue of *Jockey Slut*.[1240] Other planned releases which never eventuated were a Sun Ra remix album, a re-release of the *Wild Style* soundtrack, and the *Grand Royal VS Mo' Wax* mixtape which was intended as a collaboration between Lavelle and the Beastie Boys' Mike D.[1241] This mix had been mentioned for most of Mo' Wax's life and even had a release date of August 1998 at one point appearing on Grand Royal's website,[1242] but it never eventuated. Artist Futura also spoke about releasing an album on Mo' Wax which never released,[1243] as did The Dust Brothers.[1244] While the long promised debut album from The Psychonauts[1245] eventually was released in 2003, but not on Mo' Wax.[1246]

[1234] Sherburne, P 2019
[1235] Mo'Wax Bulletin Board 2000
[1236] AVdeck 2000?
[1237] Cooper, D 2013c
[1238] The Fashion Post, 2013
[1239] Mo' Wax Discography 2011e
[1240] dusted 2012
[1241] Lavelle, J 2014
[1242] Bodnarchuk, B 1998
[1243] Meadley, P 1996
[1244] Smart, CK 1996
[1245] Raygun 1998
[1246] Burgess, J 2004

Other plans for the label had included a magazine, a range of clothing, a Mo' Wax Museum,[1247] and collaborations with brands such as Vans and Lego.[1248] Ambitious ideas like these are why many see Mo' Wax's partnership with XL as having proved financially disastrous, as during this period Lavelle set up Mo' Wax Arts,[1249] which produced toys, clothing, and books, many of which didn't sell, though they have since become collector items.[1250] For XL there was at least one positive financial gain to their time with Mo' Wax as Lavelle had hired Nick Huggett, who moved to XL in 2002 and signed Adele, MIA and Dizzee Rascal.[1251] While Lavelle "officially walked away" from Mo' Wax in 2002,[1252] there were still a small handful of releases which came out through 2003 including albums by Parsley Sound and Tommy Guerrero.[1253]

One of Mo' Wax's final releases was UNKLE's follow up to *Psyence Fiction*, 2003's *Never Never Land*. In 2001 Lavelle announced to *NME* that he was working on the next UNKLE album, and that it wouldn't feature DJ Shadow.[1254] UNKLE at the time were now James Lavelle and Rich File, who had previously produced *Be There*, and the new album was produced by UNKLE and Antony Genn, aka Ant, an ex-member of the British band Pulp. After his experience on *Psyence Fiction* Lavelle hoped to try something different and go back to what had made UNKLE fun originally. He explained in 2001:

> The difficult thing with UNKLE was that there was such a jump from when it was this mad little group of people making fucked-up records to this massive kind of DJ Shadow,

---

[1247] Darby, A 2013
[1248] Wilson, R 2014
[1249] Williams, E 2017
[1250] Wilson, R 2014
[1251] Music Business Worldwide 2018
[1252] Mo'Wax Official 2020
[1253] Discogs 2019dd
[1254] NME 2001

> James Lavelle, Richard Ashcroft… you ran before walking, you know? I'd like to learn how to walk again.[1255]

Prior to *Never Never Land*, Lavelle's partnership with XL had come to an end so the album was released by Island, the label owned by Polygram/Universal and the label DJ Shadow had ended up on after Mo' Wax moved to XL. The two final Mo' Wax releases of this period were *Never Never Land* and DJ Shadow's second album *The Private Press*[1256] which Lavelle worked on as A&R and received a thank you in the credits.[1257]

Psyence Fiction for its part has continued to be a large part of both James Lavelle's and DJ Shadow's legacies, featuring within their live shows as both artists are obviously still admirers of their work as much as their own fans are today.

In 2020 as UNKLE release their latest album, fans are eagerly awaiting the release of *Psyence Fiction Director's Cut*, a promised expanded edition of the album which Lavelle described in 2019:

> I always envisaged this album as a cinematic experience, so in keeping with legendary director's cuts from the past, this has been a chance for me to re-visit the material and create the record I always had in mind. There was plenty of material left on the cutting room floor, and it has been really amazing re-discovering a lot of work that I thought had been lost forever, which has taken me four years of endless searching to find and compile.[1258]

While fans are eager to hear more of the LA sessions from 1995 and to imagine what could have been had Tim Goldsworthy and Masayuki Kudo remained in UNKLE, Lavelle himself discussed his reasoning for moving away from his early "trip hop" sound in 1998,

---

[1255] Ibid.
[1256] Bradshaw, P 2014b
[1257] Discogs 2019i
[1258] Lavelle cited in Timo Fett 2019

telling *I-D*, "If I'd made a record with Tim and Kudo, I think that would have been very much a record everyone would have expected. A trip hop record. And that wasn't something I was prepared to do."[1259]

As we near the release of the *Director's Cut* we can be assured that this story is not over yet, and there will be more to learn as Lavelle reveals further details found in his extensive archives.

[1259] Cole, B 1998.

Where Are They Now

Alice Temple
Following the release of *Psyence Fiction*, Alice Temple reteamed with her Eg & Alice collaborator Eg White to record an album entitled *Hang Over*, which was released as a promo only in 1999. Temple would again work with UNKLE when she appeared on *Mistress*, a bonus track from UNKLE's 2007 album *War Stories*. She has continued to work as an artist and model, and in 2018 released her debut solo album *The End*.

Atlantique Khan
Following *Psyence Fiction* Atlantique hasn't released any music, though is credited with Art Direction on Carla Bruni's 2007 album *No Promises*. In 2013 she opened her eponymous fashion line under her married name Atlantique Ascoli. The clothing has been praised for its effortless minimalism.

Badly Drawn Boy
Damon Gough released his third EP, *EP 3*, at the end of 1998 on XL Recordings which was followed by his debut album *The Hour of Bewilderbeast* released in 2000. The album was well received by critics and Gough won the 2000 Mercury Music Prize and would go on to score the Hugh Grant film *About A Boy*, based on the Nick Hornby novel of the same name. His most recent album was *Being Flynn*, released in 2012 by Lakeshore Records.

Ben Drury
Following the closure of Mo' Wax, Ben Drury became a freelance artist but continued working with James Lavelle as part of Lavelle's Surrender clothing label which Lavelle founded with Earn Chen in 2003. Drury has created designs for labels such as Source, XL, and ATP Recordings, and he has worked with artists such as Dizzee Rascal, Elliott Power, and Roots Manuva. Drury last worked with UNKLE on their *Only The Lonely* EP in 2011, but

also created the Urban Archaeology logo for James Lavelle's Mo' Wax 21st Anniversary book printed by Rizzoli in 2014.

DJ Shadow
Following his work on UNKLE's *Psyence Fiction*, Shadow contributed to the *Quannum Spectrum* album, and released his next solo album *The Private Press* in 2002. Since 2006's *The Outsider* each album by DJ Shadow has seen him experimenting with and embracing new sounds. Shadow has continued to release chart topping albums as well as DJ widely, and has released several highly successful mix albums with fellow DJ Cut Chemist following their 1999 *Brainfreeze* mix. His most recent album was 2019's *Our Pathetic Age*, his first in three years.

Futura 2000
Futura has continued to be involved in Mo' Wax and UNKLE related releases through James Lavelle's use of his pointman characters and associated designs. Futura himself has collaborated with everyone from Nike, Converse, Bape, Uniqlo, and Medicom Toys, and in 2015 Futura designed artwork for The Rammellzee's *How's My Girlfriends?*, a posthumous musical release by musician and artist Rammellzee. Futura continues to exhibit his artwork worldwide and in 2019 relaunched his clothing brand Futura Laboratories.

Ian Brown
Following the release of *Be There* in 1999, Brown released his second solo album, *Golden Greats*, and has continued to release new albums regularly. In 2002 UNKLE remixed Brown's song *F.E.A.R.* for his remix album *Remixes Of The Spheres*, and in 2003 Brown appeared on *Reign* from UNKLE's *Never, Never, Land* album. All of UNKLE and Ian Brown's collaborations were later featured on the 2CD edition of the compilation *The Greatest*, a 2005 release career retrospective by Ian Brown. In 2019 Brown released his latest album *Ripples*.

James Lavelle

Outside of UNKLE James Lavelle has collaborated with several brands such as Bape, Nike, and Medicom, to create Mo' Wax and UNKLE related merchandise. These have included t-shirts, shoes, toys and even a fragrance created in partnership with Azzi Glasser. Following the closure of Mo' Wax, Lavelle set up Surrender All, which released all UNKLE albums from 2006-2014. This was followed by Songs For The Def which has been UNKLE's label since Surrender All's closure. Lavelle was the subject of 2014's Meltdown Festival held at the Southbank Centre in England. The festival included a curated Mo' Wax exhibition as well as live performances from acts handpicked by Lavelle. This included a set by DJ Shadow, and saw Lavelle and Shadow together for the first time since their performance on *Top of The Pops* in 1999. In 2018 Lavelle featured in *The Man From Mo' Wax*, a documentary on Lavelle which charted his career from Mo' Wax to Meltdown.

Jason Newstead
The Knock (Drums of Death, Part 2) is the only time Jason Newstead has worked with either James Lavelle or DJ Shadow, and he is best known as the bassist for the group Metallica, which he joined in 1986 and worked with until 2001 when Newstead left. Following his departure Newstead worked with Ozzy Ozbourne, the supergroup WhoCares, and in 2016 he announced his new group Jason Newstead and the Chophouse Band. Outside of music Jason Newstead also paints, and he began exhibiting his work in 2010.

Jim Abbiss
Abbiss continued his work with James Lavelle after mixing *Psyence Fiction*, with Abbiss working as engineer for the James Lavelle remix of The Verve's *Bitter Sweet Symphony* in 1997, and UNKLE's 2003 single *Eye For An Eye*. Abbiss also worked alongside Lavelle on South's *From Here On In* album, and provided additional production Money Mark's *All The People*. DJ Shadow also continued to work with Abbiss after *Psyence Fiction*, with Abbiss providing mixing or engineering for Shadow's next three albums, *The Private Press*, *The Outsider*, and *The Less You Know, The*

Better. Jim Abbiss continues to work in production, most recently contributing to releases by Ladytron, Placebo, and Stereophonics.

Jonathan Glazer

Following his work with UNKLE for the *Rabbit In Your Headlights* video, Jonathan Glazer next created a video for Richard Ashcroft's solo single *A Song for the Lovers* in 2000. Also in 2000, Glazer released his debut feature film *Sexy Beast* which featured a soundtrack compiled by James Lavelle. This was followed by *Birth* in 2003, and *Under The Skin* in 2013, though he continued to create commercials in between films, and has worked with companies such as Stella Artois, Sony, and Nike. Glazer is currently working on his fourth feature film which is in pre-production as on 2019.

Kan Takagi

Following his work with UNKLE on *Last Orgy 3*, Kan Takagi continued working with Mo' Wax collaborators Masayuki Kudo and Money Mark for his 1999 solo album *Hello* and has since appeared on several albums released by Nigo. In 2004 Kan Takagi and Kudo produced a remix of UNKLE's *Panic Attack* entitled *Panic Attack (Ape Sounds Mix),* and in 2006 Takagi and Kudo again teamed up for the *Projection* album, released under their J.O.Y. alias on Ape Sounds. Most recently Kan Takagi appeared on 2018's Major Force Productions' *Top Secret Man* 12" which featured Nakanishi Toshio and Hajime Tachibana, and a remix by Kan Takagi and Kudo.

Kool G Rap

After working with UNKLE in 1998, Kool G Rap released his second solo album *Roots of Evil*. His most recent solo release was 2017's *Return Of The Don*, which was followed in 2018 with the album *Son Of G Rap* recorded with his son 38 Spesh.

Latryx

Lateef the Truth Speaker and Lyrics Born, aka Lateef Daumont and Tsutomu "Tom" Shimura, both appeared on UNKLE's *Guns*

Blazing alongside Kool G Rap, while Lateef also appeared on DJ Shadow's *The Private Press, The Outsider, and Our Pathetic Age* albums. Lateef the Truth Speaker and Lyrics Born continued to work together as Latryx releasing *The Album* in 1997 on both Solesides and Mo' Wax, which was followed by 2013's *The Second Album*. Lateef The Truth Speaker's most recent solo album was 2011's *Firewire*, while Lyrics Born has continued to release solo albums with the most recent being 2018's *Quite A Life*.

Light Surgeons
Since creating visuals for UNKLE's 1999 tour, The Light Surgeons have continued to work across multiple platforms, from installation, album artwork, typeface creation, and live cinema shows. They have also continued creating tour visuals for artists, working with groups as varied as U2, Rolling Stones, and Cornershop.

Mario Caldato Jr.
Following the UNKLE sessions in 1995, Mario C continued producing the Beastie Boys work until *Start!*, from 1999's *Alive* single. He continued working with Money Mark, and remixed Nigo's *Dream Unit* in 2001 for *Ape Sounds Remix*. Blackalicious recorded their 2002 album *Blazing Arrow* at Mario C's studio, with the album also featuring contributions from DJ Shadow and Money Mark.

Masayuki Kudo
Following 1995's UNKLE sessions in LA Kudo appears to have left the group and focused on projects such as Major Force West which released the *93-97* compilation, and Nigo's *Ape Sounds* album. Both Tim Goldsworthy and Kudo are credited with production for The Verve's *Bitter Sweet Symphony (James Lavelle Remix)* which released in 1997, and this appears to be the final time the three original members of UNKLE are credited together. Following the closure of Mo' Wax, Kudo has contributed to albums and EP's by Fujiwara Hiroshi, Tycoon To$h, and Money Mark. In 2018 Major Force celebrated their 30th anniversary and Kudo, Takagi Tsuyoshi,

Yashiki Yashikata, Fujiwara Hiroshi, and more teamed up for a live performances and DJ sets.

Massive Attack
In April 1998 Massive Attack released their third album *Mezzanine*, featuring the singles *Angel*, and *Teardrop*. The album was an incredible success but was the last featuring original members 3D, Daddy G, and Mushroom together, with Mushroom leaving the group soon after the album's release. Their most recent album was *Heligoland* released in 2009, though they have continued to release EP's. 3D has continued collaborating with UNKLE, contributing artwork and vocals across several albums, while UNKLE have also remixed Massive Attack with their most recent contribution being 2006's *False Flags (UNKLE Surrender Sounds Session #2)*.

Max Burgos
Money Mark's manager, and occasional Beastie Boys collaborator, left his position of A&R at London / Polygram Records to become VP of Breaking Records, the record label run by Hootie and the Blowfish. Following this he joined The Collective as a talent manager for their comedy acts and is now currently co-head of the Comedy department of Agency For The Performing Arts (APA).

Mike D
Mike D contributed his vocals for *Psyence Fiction* while completing the Beastie Boys' *Hello Nasty* album which released in 1998. Following *Hello Nasty* and the release of 1999's *Anthology* compilation the Beastie Boys released three more albums until the untimely passing of member Adam Yauch, aka MCA. Outside of the Beastie Boys Mike D has contributed to vocal duties to projects by Handsome Boy Modelling School, De La Soul, and Cassius, as well as remixes for Moby, Fatboy Slim, Lykke Li, Wapaint and Yoko Ono. Since 2016 Mike D has been presenting the radio show *The Echo Chamber* on Beats 1.

Money Mark

Following his work with UNKLE in 1995, Money Mark continued collaborating with the Beastie Boys, as well as releasing his own albums. In 1999 he appeared on Nigo's *Ape Sounds* album, as well as Kan Takagi's *Hello* album, with both albums also featuring Kudo. Mark's most recent solo album was 2001's *Songs From Studio D*, and more recently he has been working with the group Mangchi who released their *Nega Mola* album in 2015.

Mo' Wax

While Mo' Wax officially closed in 2003 after the release of UNKLE's *Never Never Land*, the label was revived somewhat in 2006 for Mo Wax Classics, a series of re-releases which was cancelled prior to going on sale, with only a few copies pressed and later found by fans. In 2016 Lavelle revived Mo' Wax again for Elliott Power's *Once Smitten* album in partnership with Marathon Artists, and in 2018 the soundtrack for *The Man From Mo' Wax* documentary film was also released on Mo' Wax and Island, with the tracklisting made up of Mo' Wax related tracks.

Nakanishi Toshio

Following his work with UNKLE, Toshi worked with Masayuki Kudo, Howie B, and Mat Ducasse on two Skylab albums, and continued to work with Kudo on albums such as 2000's *Year Of Dragon 2000* under the Tycoon To$h & Terminator Troops alias. Toshi was very prolific, working with his early bands Plastics and Melon, as well as spin-off groups Plasticsex and Water Melon, new projects such as 2003's Blair Witch And Bush Of Ghost Project, and the *Children Of The Radiation* EP released in 2017 under his Tycoon To$h monica. This was one of his final releases as Toshi died in 2017.

Nigo

Following the release of 1999's *Ape Sounds* album, Nigo continued releasing music and collaborated with Biz Markie, Rakim, and GZA on 2000's *Shadow Of The Ape Sounds*. During the early 2000's he contributed Nigo's General Seminar to *Relax* magazine and continued with his successful clothing brand Bape until selling the company in 2011. He has continued to work in fashion through his position at Japanese clothing brand Uniqlo, as well as music as part of the group Teriyaki Boyz, who released their 2005 album *Beef or Chicken* in 2005 which featured collaborations with DJ Shadow, Adrock, and Dan The Automator.

Rammellzee
Following his work with UNKLE on *Rock On* in 1995, Rammellzee continued to create visual art and music, releasing his debut album *This Is What You Made Me* in 2003. In 2010 Rammellzee died at the age of 49, leaving behind an album of music entitled *Cosmic Flush* which was later released in 2017, after singles from the album were released across 2015. These releases were accompanied by an exhibition featuring artwork from the singles by Futura 2000 and others. In 2014 Mo' Wax released a 12" record of an interview recorded in 1995 while Rammellzee was in London for the *Rock On* recording sessions. A transcript of the interview was also provided in the Mo' Wax 21 book, though the interview is incomplete as part of the recording was lost.

Richard Ashcroft
Prior to the release of *Psyence Fiction*, Ashcroft reformed his band The Verve and released the album *Urban Hymns* in 1997 before breaking up and reforming to release their fourth album, *Fourth*, in 2008 before breaking up again. In between albums by The Verve Ashcroft has released several solo albums as well as contributing vocals on *The Test* from The Chemical Brothers 2002 album *Come With Us*. In 2002 Ashcroft told reporters he planned to have DJ Shadow contribute to his next album, though the collaboration never eventuated as Shadow was said to be too busy at the time.

Richard File
Following the release of *Psyence Fiction*, File began working with UNKLE on the single *Be There*, and continued as a member for several years, touring with James Lavelle as UNKLE Sounds, and releasing the UNKLE Sounds mixes *Do Androids Dream Of Essential Beats* and *Edit Music For A Film*. File left UNKLE during

the recording of 2007's *War Stories* and partnered with Wendy Rae Fowler to release 2009's *We Fell To Earth* album. He has continued to produce music both for himself and others, and in 2018 released his latest solo album titled *Rich File*.

Scratch Perverts
Prime Cuts and Tony Vegas (aka The Scratch Perverts) followed the UNKLE tour with James Lavelle in 1999 with a residency alongside Lavelle at Fabric in London. The pair were joined by DJ's Mr Thing and First Rate when they won the DMC World Championships in 1999 and were later joined by DJ's Craze and Infamous in 2001 when they again won as the Perverted Allies. They later added fellow DJ Plus One as a member and contributed to the *DJ Hero* videogame series starting in 2009. Prime Cuts and Tony Vegas are the current sole members of the group and continue to tour worldwide.

Shynola
Shynola have continued creating award winning music videos for artists such as Blur, Radiohead, Queens of the Stone Age, and Beck. They have also created visuals for films such as *The Hitchhiker's Guide To The Galaxy*, and television programs such as *The IT Crowd*. In 2013 Shynola created the short film *Dr. Easy* for Warp Films and are currently developing their first feature length film.

South
South were a rock band featuring members Brett Shaw, Jamie McDonald, and Joel Cadbury. The debut album, *From Here On In*, was released by Mo' Wax in 2000 and featured production from James Lavelle. UNKLE remixed several of their tracks, and the two groups collaborated on the soundtrack for *Sexy Beast*, which featured UNKLE versions of many of South's songs. All of South's members contributed to UNKLE remixes for various artists over the next few years, and the band continued to release albums until 2008's *You Are Here*. South are mostly remembered now for when their single *Paint The Silence* featured on an episode of the

television program *The O.C.* and included on its soundtrack in 2004.

Swifty
Following his departure from Mo' Wax Swifty continued working with *Straight No Chaser* magazine and began working with the record label Far Out Recordings. In 2017 GAMMA released a career spanning book dedicated to Swifty with highlights from his work with That's How It Is, Mo' Wax, and *Straight No Chaser*. In 2019 Swifty released a new book of work and he continues to design flyers for Gilles Peterson's and Patrick Forge's Dingwalls sessions.

Thom Yorke
Following the release of Radiohead's 1997 album *OK Computer* the band experimented more with an electronic sound on 2000's *Kid A*. Yorke explored these sounds and themes further on his debut solo album *The Eraser*, and in collaborations with Modeselektor, Flying Lotus, and Björk. In 2012 he debuted his new group Atoms For Peace who released their album *Amok* the following year. The band was made up of Joey Waronker, Mauro Refosco, Michael Balzary, Nigel Godrich, and Yorke. Meanwhile Radiohead have continued to release albums with 2016's *A Moon Shaped Pool* being their most recent, while Yorke has also continued to release solo work, and in 2018 he scored the soundtrack to the film *Suspiria*.

Tim Goldsworthy
After leaving Mo' Wax and UNKLE, Tim Goldsworthy partnered initially with David Holmes before moving to New York City and setting up DFA with James Murphy in 2001. Since then he has contributed to albums by Goldfrapp, Massive Attack, Cut Copy and Hot Chip. In 1999 Domino Records signed Goldsworthy and Kudo as Flacco, but outside of some remixes nothing else was released. Similarly, in 2016 the record label Island Of The Gods announced an album from Tim Goldsworthy was forthcoming, but it too never eventuated.

UNKLE

UNKLE continue to release albums, with their most recent *The Road Part II: Lost Highway* released in 2019. Following DJ Shadow's departure on completing *Psyence Fiction*, Rich File joined the band until 2008 when he was replaced fulltime by The Psychonauts' Pablo Clements, who in turn left in 2014. Each UNKLE album has explored different sounds from electronica to rock, and their albums have continued to feature contributions from various guest artists such as Brian Eno, Josh Homme, 3D, Ian Astbury, Gavin Clark, Carl Craig, Dhani Harrison, Elliott Power, Will Malone, and Lavelle's childhood friend Matthew Puffet.

Wil Malone

Wil Malone contributed strings to The Verve's *Bitter Sweet Symphony* after first working with the group on their 1995 song *History*, and continued working with Richard Ashcroft on several of Ashcroft's solo albums. His collaboration with James Lavelle and UNKLE also continued post *Psyence Fiction*, and includes 2003's *Reign,* 2017's *The Road: Part I* and 2019's *The Road Part II*. In 1998 Malone contributed string arrangements for Andrea Parker's *Kiss My Arp* which was released by Mo' Wax.

Will Bankhead

After Mo' Wax closed, Will Bankhead continued working in design for labels such as Honest Jon's Records (a record label set up by the record store Honest Jon's in partnership with Damon Albarn), Source, Swamp 81, and his own label The Trilogy Tapes which began as a blog in 2008. Bankhead also DJ's regularly and more recently in 2019 he DJed as support for UNKLE at their UNKLE:AI show celebrating Fabric's 20th Birthday.

Zoe Bedeaux

Following her unreleased contribution to the abandoned UNKLE sessions in 1995, Bedeaux worked with the group The Baby Namboos who released only one album in 1999. Since then Bedeaux has worked as a model, visual artist, stylist for Grace

Jones, and recently curated the *Gossamer* show for the Carl Freedman Gallery in 2019.

Select UNKLE Discography

Albums
1998 – Psyence Fiction
2003 – Never, Never Land
2007 – War Stories
2010 – Where Did The Night Fall
2017 – The Road Part I
2019 – The Road Part II – Lost Highway

EPs & Singles (1994 – 2003)
1994 – The Time Has Come
1996 – Berry Meditation
1997 – Rock On
1997 – Ape Shall Never Kill Ape
1998 – Last Orgy 3 Remixes
1998 – Rabbit In Your Headlights
1998 – Guns Blazing (promo)
1998 – Celestial Anhiliation (promo)
2002 – Eye For An Eye
2003 – In A State

Notable Appearences (1994 – 2003)
1994 – Headz
1995 – 110 Below :: Trip To The cHIP sHOP Vol. 2
1996 – Headz 2A
1996 – Header #1
1997 – A Bathing Ape Vs Mo'Wax
2001 – Sexy Beast (Original Soundtrack)

Remixes (1992 – 2003)

No Date - Ronnie Jordan - Get to Grips (unreleased)
1992 - Men From U.N.K.L.E. Featuring Marden Hill Come On (2010 Version)

1992 - United Future Origanization - Moondance (Moon Chant: Hip Sensibility Mutates...)
1993- Mondo Grosso - Vibe P.M. (Stranger Things Have Happened - Brazil On A Jimmy Hill Mix)
1995 - Karmacoma (U.N.K.L.E. Situation) (as U.N.K.L.E.)
1995 - John Spencer Blues Explosion - Bellbottoms (Old Rascal Mix)
1995 - Geisha Girls - Shounen (U.N.K.L.E.'s Remix)
1995 - Radiohead - Planet Telex (Karma Sunra Mix
1996 - Tortoise - Djed (Bruise Blood Mix)
1996 - Folk Implosion – Natural One
1996 - Butthole Surfers - Pepper (Short Shot Remix)
1996 - Beck - Where It's At (Remix By U.N.K.L.E.)
1997 - Agent Provocateur – Agent Dan (UNKLE remix)
1997 - Buffalo Daughter - Li303ve (Suzuki Dekard San)
1997 - Can - Vitamin C (U.N.K.L.E. Mix)
1997 - Liquid Liquid - New Walk (U.N.K.L.E. Remix)
1997 - The Verve - Bitter Sweet Symphony (James Lavelle Remix)
1998 - Stina Nordenstam – People Are Strange (UNKLE remix)
1998 - Cornelius - Free Fall (U.N.K.L.E. Remix)
1998 - Placebo - Without You I'm Nothing (UNKLE Remix)
1999 - Garbage - The World Is Not Enough (U.N.K.L.E. Remix)
1999 - Blur - Battle (UNKLE Remix)
1999 - Breakbeat Era – Bullitproof (UNKLE Remix)
1999 - Ian Brown – Dolphins Were Monkeys (UNKLE Remix)
1999 - Furslide - Over My Head (UNKLE Mix)
1999 - Emperors New Clothes Leaders And Believers (U.N.K.L.E. Remix)
2000 - South - Overused (UNKLE Remix)
2000 – South – Paint The Silence (U.N.K.L.E. Variation)
2000 - Mr.Children - Nishi-E-Higashi-E West (Remixed By UNKLE)
2001 – Howie B. - Hey Jack (UNKLE Metamorphosis Mix)
2001 – Slam - Narco Tourists (Unkle Mix)
2001 – Sunna - I'm Not Trading (UNKLE - In Utero)
2002 - Queens Of The Stone Age - No One Knows (UNKLE Reconstruction)

2002 - Ian Brown – Fear (U.N.K.L.E. Mix)
2002 – DJ Shadow - GDMFSOB (Unkle Uncensored)
2003 – South - Colours In Waves (Unkle Reconstruction)
2003 – Metallica - Frantic (U.N.K.L.E. Remix)

References

Aaron, C 1994, 'Singles', *Spin*, December, vol. 10, no. 9, p. 110.

Ace Records 2019, *BGP*, Ace Records, viewed 29 July 2019, <https://acerecords.co.uk/bgp-label>.

Acid Jazz 2018, *Eddie Piller*, Acid Jazz, viewed 29 July 2019, <http://www.acidjazz.co.uk/portfolio-item/mar-morriss-3-2/>.

Adams, C 1998, 'Men From UNKLE', *Herald Sun*, 20 August, viewed 26 July, ProQuest Database.

Adesanya, J 2018, '15 Of The Most Important Vinyl Toys That Are Not "Toys"', *The Block*, viewed 15 July 2019, <https://everpress.com/blog/15-important-vinyl-toys-not-toys/>.

Adventures in Psyence Fiction 2019, *The Man from Mo' Wax*, Vimeo, BFI, London, viewed 31 January 2020, <https://vimeo.com/ondemand/themowaxvaults/297278562>.

Allen, R 2018, *Ross Allen & James Lavelle*, radio program, NTS Radio, London, 15th November, viewed 9 May 2019, <https://www.mixcloud.com/NTSRadio/ross-allen-james-lavelle-15th-november-2018>.

AllMusic.com 2019a, *Sleeping with the Enemy - Paris*, All Music, viewed 12 July 2019, <https://www.allmusic.com/album/flower-to-the-sun-mw0001471204>.

AllMusic.com 2019b, *The Federation - Flower to the Sun*, All Music, viewed 25 June 2019, <https://www.allmusic.com/album/sleeping-with-the-enemy-mw0000093210>.

Als, H 1995, 'A Model Affair', *The New Yorker*, 27 March, p. 37

Anderson, J 2008, *Slaves to the rhythm*, CBC, viewed 25 June 2019, <https://www.cbc.ca/news/entertainment/slaves-to-the-rhythm-1.771508>.

Ankeny, J 2020, *Talk Talk Biography*, All Music, viewed 25 February 2020, <https://www.allmusic.com/artist/talk-talk-mn0000790814/biography>.

Arcade Classics 2019, 'Galaxian Vs Galaga Vs Space Invaders', *Arcade Classics*, 19 November, viewed 26 February 2020,

<https://www.arcadeclassics.net/blog/galaxian-vs-galaga-vs-space-invaders>.

Artnet, 2019, *Futura*, Artnet, viewed 12 July 2019, <http://www.artnet.com/artists/futura-2000-lenny-mcgurr/biography>.

Artnet, 2019, *Untitled (The sky is the limit) by Jean-Michel Basquiat*, viewed 12 December 2019, <http://www.artnet.com/artists/jean-michel-basquiat/untitled-the-sky-is-the-limit-pBitYvDp9ia7ssCwIkU6Dg2>.

Aubrey, E 2017a, *Irrepressible Discoveries: James Lavelle Of UNKLE's 13 Favourite Albums - Beastie Boys - Check Your Head*, The Quietus, viewed 14 June 2019, <https://thequietus.com/articles/23215-james-lavelle-unkle-interview-favourite-albums-bakers-dozen?page=7>.

Aubrey, E 2017b, *Irrepressible Discoveries: James Lavelle Of UNKLE's 13 Favourite Albums – DJ Shadow - Entroducing*, The Quietus, viewed 14 June 2019, <https://thequietus.com/articles/23215-james-lavelle-unkle-interview-favourite-albums-bakers-dozen?page=10>.

Aubrey, E 2017c, *Irrepressible Discoveries: James Lavelle Of UNKLE's 13 Favourite Albums - Fleetwood Mac - Rumours*, The Quietus, viewed 14 June 2019, <https://thequietus.com/articles/23215-james-lavelle-unkle-interview-favourite-albums-bakers-dozen?page=3>.

Aubrey, E 2017d, *Irrepressible Discoveries: James Lavelle Of UNKLE's 13 Favourite Albums - Massive Attack - Blue Lines*, The Quietus, viewed 14 June 2019, <https://thequietus.com/articles/23215-james-lavelle-unkle-interview-favourite-albums-bakers-dozen?page=6>.

Aubrey, E 2017e, *Irrepressible Discoveries: James Lavelle Of UNKLE's 13 Favourite Albums - Vangelis - Blade Runner OST*, The Quietus, viewed 14 June 2019, <https://thequietus.com/articles/23215-james-lavelle-unkle-interview-favourite-albums-bakers-dozen?page=12>.

Aubrey, E 2017f, *Irrepressible Discoveries: James Lavelle Of UNKLE's 13 Favourite Albums - Young Disciples - Road To Freedom*, The Quietus, viewed 14 June 2019, <https://thequietus.com/articles/23215-james-lavelle-unkle-interview-favourite-albums-bakers-dozen?page=14>.

AVdeck 2000?, *An Interview With James Lavelle*, Build and Destroy, viewed 26 July 2019, <https://web.archive.org/web/20021221210042/http://homepage.ntlworld.com/andrewlochhead/articles/jlinterview.htm>.

Bainbridge, L 2015, 'Badly Drawn Boy: 'Music has saved me in a lot of ways'', *The Guardian*, 12 July, viewed 25 February 2020,

<https://www.theguardian.com/music/2015/jul/12/badly-drawn-boy-interview-hour-of-bewilderbeast-tour-damon-gough>.

Banez, C <cbanez@hotmail.com> 1998, *unkle/on the one's west coast tour for carl craig*, Acid Jazz Archive, 25 July, viewed 26 July 2019, <www.boralv.se/AcidJazz/Backup/1998-Jul/0500.html>.

BAO <tunde@arches.uga.edu> *1998, unkle tour (fwd)*, Acid Jazz Archive, 30 September, viewed 26 July 2019, <http://www.boralv.se/AcidJazz/Backup/1998-Oct/0005.html>.

Barnhill, J 2009, 'Kenner', in Carlisle, R (ed.), *Encyclopedia of Play in Today's Society, Volume 1*, SAGE, Los Angeles, p.345-346.

BBC, n.d. a, *A Quick Guide To Reggae*, BBC, viewed July 8 2019, <https://web.archive.org/web/20040208100025/http://www.bbc.co.uk/music/bluessoulreggae/guide_reggae.shtml>.

BBC, n.d. b, *Story of Reggae: Dub*, BBC, viewed July 8 2019, <https://web.archive.org/web/20040316213351/http://www.bbc.co.uk/music/features/reggae/history_dub.shtml>.

BBC, n.d. c, *Story of Reggae: Sound Systems*, BBC, viewed July 8 2019, <https://web.archive.org/web/20040211220043/http://www.bbc.co.uk/music/features/reggae/history_sound.shtml>.

BBC, n.d. d, *Story of Reggae: Toasting*, BBC, viewed July 8 2019, <https://web.archive.org/web/20040211233201/http://www.bbc.co.uk/music/features/reggae/history_toastingsmc.shtml>.

BBC 1998a, 'Entertainment - Former Stone Roses singer jailed for air rage', *BBC News*, 23 October, viewed 15 July 2019, <http://news.bbc.co.uk/2/hi/entertainment/200016.stm>.

BBC 1998b, 'Profile: The Verve claim their place in pop history', BBC News, viewed 29 July 2019, <http://news.bbc.co.uk/2/hi/uk_news/54225.stm>.

BBC 1998c, 'UK - Ex-Stone Roses star goes back to jail', *BBC News*, 2 November, viewed 15 July 2019, <http://news.bbc.co.uk/2/hi/uk_news/206277.stm>.

BBC 2019, *Bad Meaning Good*, BBC, viewed 29 July 2019, <https://www.bbc.co.uk/programmes/p048j32k>.

Beastiemania, 2009, *Action Figures (Part II),* Beastiemania, viewed 27 July 2019, <http://www.beastiemania.com/qa/actionfigures2.php>.

Beeb 1999, *UNKLE - 18 February 1999*, Beeb, viewed 15 July 2019, <https://web.archive.org/web/20010629160537/http://www.chat.beeb.com:80/chat/transcripts/990218_unkle/index.html>.

Bennun, D 1998, 'Music: The men from UNKLE', *The Guardian*, 14 August, viewed 26 July 2019, ProQuest Database.

Benson, D 2000, 'Baby Namboos - Ancoats 2 Zambia', *Exclaim!,* viewed 12 July 2019, <https://exclaim.ca/music/article/baby_namboos-ancoats_2_zambia>.

Benstead, B 2014, *Mo' Wax: Label Focus*, radio program, BBC Radio 1, viewed 5 February 2020, <https://www.mowaxplease.com/mo-wax-special-benji-b-bbc-radio-1>.

Berke, C 2018, *Lesbian rocker Alice Temple releases a new album*, Out In Jersey, viewed 14 July 2019, <https://outinjersey.net/lesbian-rocker-alice-temple-releases-a-new-album>.

Berry, D 2009a, 'Archive: Andrea Parker interview March 2001', *Consult This Music*, viewed 12 July 19, <https://consultthismusic.wordpress.com/2009/11/15/archive-andrea-parker-interview-march-2001>.

Berry, D 2009b, 'Archive: Attica Blues interview July 2000', *Consult This Music*, viewed 12 July 19, <https://consultthismusic.wordpress.com/2009/09/21/archive-attica-blues-interview-july-2000>.

BFI 2014, *James Lavelle on 2001: A Space Odyssey,* YouTube, 27 November, BFI, viewed 10 January 2020, < https://www.youtube.com/watch?v=4FKkKsJ31kM>.

BFI 2018a, *Bombin' director Q&A; with Goldie and James Lavelle*, BFI, viewed 26 August 2018, <http://www.bfi.org.uk/films-tv-people/4ce2bc2dc7a41>.

BFI 2018b, *In conversation with... James Lavelle on The Man From Mo'Wax,* YouTube, 4 September, BFI, viewed 10 January 2020, <https://www.youtube.com/watch?v=g_pVr8O9rVE>.

Billboard 2015, 'DJ Shadow Expands 'Endtroducing'', *Billboard*, viewed 23 December 2019, <https://www.billboard.com/articles/news/63135/dj-shadow-expands-endtroducing>.

Billboard 2019, *UNKLE – Chart History*, Billboard, viewed 26 July 2018, <https://www.billboard.com/music/Unkle/chart-history/billboard-200/song/174633>.

Billboard 2020, *Radiohead – Chart History*, Billboard, viewed 24 February 2020, <https://www.billboard.com/music/radiohead/chart-history/TLP>.

Birchmeier, J 2019, *Kool G Rap – Biography & History*, All Music, viewed 23 December 2019, <https://www.allmusic.com/artist/kool-g-rap-mn0000110847/biography>.

Bird, G 1996, 'Futura 2000 – Abstract Pioneer', *Graphotism*, vol. 1, no. 8, pp. 6-11, viewed 12 July 2019, <https://issuu.com/illadelstylez/docs/graphotism8>.

Blakes 7 2014, *Blake's 7 - 1x08 – Duel*, YouTube, 20 March, Blakes 7, viewed 10 January 2020, <https://www.youtube.com/watch?v=kUI6IEU6sA0>.

BMX Racer & Freestyle, 1984, 'Alice Temple', *BMX Racer & Freestyle*, September, vol. 1, no. 2, p. 8.

Board Game Geek 2019, *Ball Buster*, Board Game Geek, viewed 14 July 2019, <https://www.boardgamegeek.com/boardgame/33818/ball-buster>.

Bodnarchuk, B 1998, 'Grand Royal vs. Mo Wax in '98', Google Groups, 5 May, *rec.music.hip-hop*, viewed 26 July 2019, <https://groups.google.com/forum/#!search/%22Mo'$20Wax%22/rec.music.hip-hop/_olyINa9yhA/s7GzqEsVH7kJ>.

Bonner, M 1998, 'UNKLE-Psyence Fiction', *Muzik*, September, no. 40, p. 65

BPI 2019a, *BRIT Awards*, BPI, viewed 13 July 2019, <https://www.bpi.co.uk/brit-certified/award-levels>.

BPI 2019b, *BRIT Certified* [Psyence Fiction], BPI, viewed 13 July 2019, <https://www.bpi.co.uk/brit-certified>.

BPI 2020, *BRIT Certified* [OK Computer], BPI, viewed 24 February 2020, <https://www.bpi.co.uk/brit-certified>.

Braddock, K 1998, 'the men from UNKLE', *Muzik*, September, no. 40, pp. 40-42.

Braddock, K 1999, 'UNKLE – Oxford Brookes University', *Muzik*, March, no. 46, p. 129.

Bradshaw, P 2011, *Straight No Chaser: From World Jazz Jive to Interplanetary Sounds : Ancient To Future - 1988 - 2009*, Ancient to Future, viewed 13 June 2019, <https://ancienttofuture.com/straight-no-chaser-3>.

Bradshaw, P 2013, 'James Lavelle', *Jocks&Nerds*, vol. 1, no. 9, pp. 126-131.

Bradshaw, P 2014a, 'Introduction', in Lavelle, J 2014, *Mo'Wax : Urban Archaeology: 21 Years Of Mo'Wax Recordings*, Rizzoli, New York.

Bradshaw, P 2014b, 'James Lavelle in conversation with Josh Davis - Interview by Paul Bradshaw', in Lavelle, J 2014, *Mo'Wax : Urban Archaeology: 21 Years Of Mo'Wax Recordings*, Rizzoli, New York.

Bremser, W 1998, 'Into The Shadow of Hip Hop', *Rolling Stone*, viewed 13 July 2019, <http://www.mtv.com/news/503041/into-the-shadow-of-hip-hop>.

Bresnark, R 1998, 'Sci-Fi All Stars', *Melody Maker*, 22 August, vol. 75, no. 34, p. 37

Brewer, J 2016, *The Corridor is the music video Kubrick never got to make,* It's Nice That, viewed 14 July 2019, <https://www.itsnicethat.com/news/the-corridor-daydreaming-with-stanley-kubrick-050716>.

Bright, M 1995, 'Sampladelic warrior', *Melody Maker*, 22 April, Vol. 72, Iss. 16, p. 37.

British Council, n.d., *The story of the 'Bristol Sound'*, British Council, viewed 25 June 2019, <https://www.britishcouncil.org.il/en/rewind-bristol>.

Burega, G-M 2014, 'Is Sun Ra really from outer space?', *Kind of Pink and Purple*, April 20, viewed 12 July 2019, <http://www.kindofpinkandpurple.com/2014/04/is-sun-ra-really-from-outer-space.html>.

Burgess, J 1996, 'Doing Your Headz In!", *Jockey Slut*, August/September, vol. 2, no. 3, pp. 54-60.

Burgess, J 1998, 'The Horror! The Horror!", *Jockey Slut*, August, vol. 2, no. 15, pp. 57-60.

Burgess, J 2004, *An Audience With... JAMES LAVELLE*, Jockey Slut, viewed 26 May 2019, <https://web.archive.org/web/20041020034256/http://www.jockeyslut.info:80/cover_feature/one/more.php?id=188_0_17_0>.

Bush, C 1994, 'Various Artists – Headz', *Melody Maker*, 19 November, vol. 71, no. 45, p.37

Butler, A 2014, *james lavelle interview – 21 years of mo'wax*, Design Boom, viewed 24 June 2019, <https://www.designboom.com/design/james-lavelle-interview-21-years-of-mowax-06-21-2014>.

C, M 1991, 'Unsigned Hype', *The Source*, June, no. 21, p. 22.

Cambridge Dictionary 2019, *Meaning of ambulance chaser in English*, Cambridge Dictionary, viewed 14 July 2019, <https://dictionary.cambridge.org/dictionary/english/ambulance-chaser>.

Carroll, J 1999, 'Quannum leap In music, like everything else, it's the quiet ones you have to watch. Jim Carroll gets down to it with Josh Davis, the US West Coast genius otherwise known as DJ Shadow', *Irish Times*, 7 August, viewed 12 August 2017, ProQuest database.

Casimir, J 1998, 'Psyence Fiction', *Sydney Morning Herald*, 11 September, viewed 25 February 2020, ProQuest database.

Chang, J 1998, *Blagging and Boasting*, Metro Active, viewed 13 June 2019, <www.metroactive.com/papers/metro/06.18.98/bristol-9824.html>.

Chang, J 2006, 'A Conversation with DJ Shadow', *Believer*, viewed 23 December 2019, <https://believermag.com/a-conversation-with-dj-shadow>.

Chart Magazine 2000, 'Baby Namboos Proliferating The Bristol Sound', *Chart Attack*, viewed 12 December 2019, <https://web.archive.org/web/20000823225718/http://chartattack.com/features/2000/babynamboos/index.html>.

Chennault, S 2005, 'Quannum Mechanics', *SF Weekly*, viewed 23 December 2019, <https://www.sfweekly.com/listen-up/quannum-mechanics>.

Christgau, R 1986, 'Down By Law - Great Dance Records You Can't Buy', *The Village Voice*, March 25, viewed July 8 2019, <https://ddski.com/interview-village-voice>.

Cigarettes, J 1998, 'The Appliance of Psyence', *New Musical Express (NME)*, 29 August, pp. 14-16.

Cole, B 1998, 'The Empire Strikes Wax', *I-D*, September, pp. 150-154.

Companies House 2019, *MO'WAX HEADZ LIMITED - Officers*, Companies House, viewed 9 May 2019, <https://beta.companieshouse.gov.uk/company/03139579/officers>.

Cooke, F 2010, *Hiroshi Fujiwara*, Interview Magazine, viewed 24 June 2019, <https://www.interviewmagazine.com/fashion/hiroshi-fujiwara>.

Cooper, D 2013a, *An Interview With Charlie Dark of Attica Blues*, Mo' Wax Please, viewed 13 June 2019, <https://www.mowaxplease.com/exclusive-an-interview-with-charlie-dark-of-attica-blues>.

Cooper, D 2013b, *Exclusive: An Interview With Swifty*, Mo' Wax Please, viewed 13 June 2019, <https://www.mowaxplease.com/exclusive-an-interview-with-swifty>.

Cooper, D 2013c, *EXCLUSIVE INTERVIEW : JAMES LAVELLE TALKS MO' WAX, UNKLE, STREETWEAR AND MORE…*, Mo' Wax Please, viewed 13 June 2019, <https://www.mowaxplease.com/james-lavelle-talks-mo-wax-unkle-streewear>.

Cooper, D 2014, *21 Years Ago : DJ Shadow's In/Flux, The Second Birth Of Mo' Wax*, Mo' Wax Please, viewed 24 June 2019, <https://www.mowaxplease.com/dj-shadow-in-flux-second-birth-mo-wax>.

Cooper, D 2015, *Mo' Wax And The UK Charts*, Mo' Wax Please, viewed 13 July 2019, <https://www.mowaxplease.com/mo-wax-uk-charts>.

Cooper, D 2017a, *LISTEN : UNKLE REMIXES FROM THE MO' WAX FUTURE PAST SERIES*, Mo' Wax Please, viewed 23 December 2019, <https://www.mowaxplease.com/listen-unkle-remixes-mo-wax-future-past-series>.

Cooper, D 2017b, *THE STORY OF MO' WAX & JAMES LAVELLE – BBC RADIO 1 1996*, Mo' Wax Please, viewed 22 December 2019, <https://www.mowaxplease.com/james-lavelle-story-mo-wax-1996>.

Cooper, D 2018, *UNKLE – DISSATISFIED, AN UNRELEASED PRE-PSYENCE FICTION TRACK*, Mo' Wax Please, viewed 27 March 2020,

<https://www.mowaxplease.com/dissatisfied-unreleased-psyence-fiction-unkle>.

Coultate, A 2015, *Honest Jon's: London is the place for me*, Resident Advisor, viewed 13 June 2019, <https://www.residentadvisor.net/features/2076>.

Crysell, A 1994, 'James Lavelle', *Dazed & Confused*, September 1994, vol. 1, no. 9, p.53

Curtis, N 2017, *My First Designer Toy*, Co Art Magazine, viewed 13 July 2019, <https://coartmag.com/news/editorial/first-designer-toy>.

Dabydeen, D, Gilmore, J, & Jones, C 2007, *The Oxford companion to Black British history*, Oxford University Press, UK, p.549

Dagnini, J 2010, *The Importance of Reggae Music in the Worldwide Cultural Universe*, Études caribéennes, viewed 25 June 2019, <https://journals.openedition.org/etudescaribeennes/4740>.

Dalton, S 1997, 'The Dour & The Glory', *Vox*, September, no. 83, p.54-60

Darby, A 2013, *Mo'Wax 21: An Interview with James Lavelle*, BEINGHUNTED, viewed 24 June 2019, <http://beinghunted1.rssing.com/chan-8044285/all_p1.html?q=nigo+lavelle&site=rssing.com>.

Davis, J 1999, 'Labels Matter', *Business Life*, March, pp. 20-24.

Davis, E 1996, 'Beats Generation', *Spin*, April, vol. 12, no. 1, pp. 72-74.

Dazed & Confused 1996, *Wednesday 9th October*, Dazed & Confused, viewed 28 March 2020, <https://web.archive.org/web/19970704224439fw_/http://www.confused.co.uk/livewire/nokia/9th.html>.

De Lange, S 2015, *Star Wars Trailers Part 1: The Original Trilogy*, Star Wars, viewed 13 July 2019, <https://www.starwars.com/news/star-wars-trailers-part-1-the-original-trilogy>.

Deleon, J 2015, *How Stüssy Became a $50 Million Global Streetwear Brand Without Selling Out*, Business Of Fashion, viewed 24 June 2019, <https://www.businessoffashion.com/articles/intelligence/how-stussy-became-a-50-million-global-streetwear-brand-without-selling-out>.

Denis Lavant Interview 2005, *Director's Series Vol. 5 - Work of Director Jonathan Glazer*, DVD, Palm Pictures, New York.

Diamond, M 1995, 'Re: Mo' Wax vs. Grand Royal 'Battle of the Beats' project', in Lavelle, J 2014, *Mo'Wax : Urban Archaeology: 21 Years Of Mo'Wax Recordings*, Rizzoli, New York.

Diamond, D & Horovitz, A 2018, *Beastie Boys Book*, Faber & Faber Ltd, London. (p305-308)

Didcock, B 1998, 'Fabled Labels', *The Scotsman*, 17 September 1998, p. 19, viewed 17 June 2019, ProQuest database.

Dike, J 2017, *Take a Tour Through James Lavelle's Treasure Chest of OG Supreme and BAPE*, Hypebeast, viewed 24 June 2019, <https://hypebeast.com/2017/5/james-lavelle-bape-supreme-collection>.

Discogs 2019a, *AIR – Modulor Mix (1996, CD)*, Discogs, viewed 11 November 2019, <https://www.discogs.com/AIR-Modulor-Mix/release/3179>.

Discogs 2019b, *Ben Drury*, Discogs, viewed 9 November 2019, <https://www.discogs.com/artist/515232-Ben-Drury?filter_anv=0&subtype=Visual&type=Credits>.

Discogs 2019c, *Death Comet Crew – At The Marble Bar (1985, Vinyl)*, Discogs, viewed 11 November 2019, <https://www.discogs.com/Death-Comet-Crew-At-The-Marble-Bar/release/62685>.

Discogs 2019d, *DJ Krush – Krush (1994, CD)*, Discogs, viewed 9 November 2019, <https://www.discogs.com/DJ-Krush-Krush/release/1113296>.

Discogs 2019e, *DJ Shadow – Endtroducing......*, Discogs, viewed 11 November 2019, <https://www.discogs.com/DJ-Shadow-Endtroducing/master/15313>.

Discogs 2019f, *DJ Shadow – Endtroducing..... (1996, Vinyl)*, Discogs, viewed 11 November 2019, <https://www.discogs.com/DJ-Shadow-Endtroducing/release/5058>

Discogs 2019g, *DJ Shadow – Endtroducing..... (1996, Vinyl)*, Discogs, viewed 11 November 2019, <https://www.discogs.com/DJ-Shadow-Endtroducing/release/59125>.

Discogs 2019h, *DJ Shadow – The 4-Track Era Collection (1990-1992) (2009, CD)*, Discogs, viewed 9 November 2019, <https://www.discogs.com/DJ-Shadow-The-4-Track-Era-Collection-1990-1992/release/1786536>.

Discogs 2019i, *DJ Shadow – The Private Press (2002, CD)*, Discogs, viewed 11 November 2019, <https://www.discogs.com/DJ-Shadow-The-Private-Press/release/433899>.

Discogs 2019j, *DJ Shadow – The UNKLE In-Stores (NYC, October 1st, 1998 - Austin, Texas, October 2nd, 1998) (2009, CD)*, Discogs, viewed 11 November 2019, <https://www.discogs.com/DJ-Shadow-The-UNKLE-In-Stores-NYC-October-1st-1998-Austin-Texas-October-2nd-1998/release/2265952>.

Discogs 2019k, *DJ Shadow – What Does Your Soul Look Like (1994, Vinyl)*, Discogs, viewed 9 November 2019, <https://www.discogs.com/DJ-Shadow-What-Does-Your-Soul-Look-Like/release/3467>.

Discogs 2019l, *DJ Shadow And The Groove Robbers – In/Flux / Hindsight (1993, Vinyl)*, Discogs, viewed 9 November 2019, <https://www.discogs.com/DJ-Shadow-And-The-Groove-Robbers-InFlux-Hindsight/release/17256>.

Discogs 2019m, *DJ Shadow And The Groove Robbers / Asia Born – Entropy / Send Them (1993, Vinyl)*, Discogs, viewed 9 November 2019, <https://www.discogs.com/DJ-Shadow-And-The-Groove-Robbers-Asia-Born-Entropy-Send-Them/release/130152>.

Discogs 2019n, *DJ Shadöw* / DJ Krush – Lost And Found (S.F.L.) / Kemuri (1994, Vinyl)*, Discogs, viewed 9 November 2019, <https://www.discogs.com/DJ-Shadöw-DJ-Krush-Lost-And-Found-SFL-Kemuri/release/5062>.

Discogs 2019o, *Dr. Timothy Leary – Turn On, Tune In, Drop Out (The Original Motion Picture Soundtrack) (1967, Vinyl)*, Discogs, viewed 9 November 2019, <https://www.discogs.com/Dr-Timothy-Leary-Turn-On-Tune-In-Drop-Out-The-Original-Motion-Picture-Soundtrack/release/1740816>.

Discogs 2019p, *Futura 2000*, Discogs, viewed 24 December 2019, <https://www.discogs.com/artist/47366-Futura-2000?filter_anv=0&subtype=Visual&type=Credits>.

Discogs 2019q, *Gettovetts*, Discogs, viewed 11 November 2019, <https://www.discogs.com/artist/185569-Gettovetts>.

Discogs 2019r, *Hurricane #1 – Only The Strongest Will Survive Mixes*, Discogs, viewed 24 December 2019,

<https://www.discogs.com/Hurricane-1-Only-The-Strongest-Will-Survive-Mixes/release/5108694>.

Discogs 2019s, *James* vs. Nigo – A Bathing Ape Vs Mo'Wax*, Discogs, viewed 11 November 2019, <https://www.discogs.com/James-vs-Nigo-A-Bathing-Ape-Vs-MoWax/master/108193>.

Discogs 2019t, *James Lavelle Presents UNKLE Sounds – Naples #GU41 (2015, CD)*, Discogs, viewed 11 November 2019, <https://www.discogs.com/James-Lavelle-Presents-UNKLE-Sounds-Naples-GU41/release/7694796>.

Discogs 2019u, *Josh Davis – Spinning Live At KDVS 1988 (2010, 256kbps, file)*, Discogs, viewed 9 November 2019, <https://www.discogs.com/release/7314668>.

Discogs 2019v, *Lifers Group / Shadow* – Real Deal (Shadow Remix) / Lesson 4 (1991, Vinyl)*, Discogs, viewed 9 November 2019, <https://www.discogs.com/real-deal-shadow-remix-lesson-4/release/1787827>.

Discogs 2019w, *Lisa Haugen*, Discogs, viewed 9 November 2019, <https://www.discogs.com/artist/2529394-Lisa-Haugen>.

Discogs 2019x, *Love T.K.O. – Head Turner (1994, CD)*, Discogs, viewed 9 November 2019, <https://www.discogs.com/Love-TKO-Head-Turner/release/2625566>.

Discogs 2019y, *Major Force West – 93-97 (1999, Vinyl)*, Discogs, viewed 11 November 2019, <https://www.discogs.com/Major-Force-West-93-97/release/31599>.

Discogs 2019z, *Massive Attack – Blue Lines (1991, CD)*, Discogs, viewed 9 November 2019, <https://www.discogs.com/Massive-Attack-Blue-Lines/release/1727736>.

Discogs 2019aa, *Massive Attack – Karmacoma EP (1995, Vinyl)*, Discogs, viewed 11 November 2019, <https://www.discogs.com/Massive-Attack-Karmacoma-EP/release/20679>.

Discogs 2019bb, *Mondo Grosso – Marbley (1993, CD)*, Discogs, viewed 9 November 2019, <https://www.discogs.com/Mondo-Grosso-Marble/release/912075>.

Discogs 2019cc, *Money Mark – Push The Button (1998, Vinyl)*, Discogs, viewed 11 November 2019, <https://www.discogs.com/Money-Mark-Push-The-Button/release/1966043>.

Discogs 2019dd, *Mo Wax Label,* Discogs, viewed 11 November 2019, <https://www.discogs.com/label/111-Mo-Wax?sort=year&sort_order=desc>.

Discogs 2019ee, *Paris (2) – Sleeping With The Enemy (1992, CD)*, Discogs, viewed 9 November 2019, <https://www.discogs.com/Paris-Sleeping-With-The-Enemy/release/242271>.

Discogs 2019ff, *Queen / Shadow* – We Will Rock You / Basic Mega-Mix (1992, Vinyl)*, Discogs, viewed 9 November 2019, <https://www.discogs.com/we-will-rock-you-basic-mega-mix/release/1229308>.

Discogs 2019gg, *Radiohead – Just (1995, Vinyl)*, Discogs, viewed 11 November 2019, <https://www.discogs.com/Radiohead-Just/release/1463625>.

Discogs 2019hh, *Sly & Robbie – Rhythm Killers (1987, Vinyl)*, Discogs, viewed 11 November 2019, <https://www.discogs.com/Sly-Robbie-Rhythm-Killers/release/5441712>.

Discogs 2019ii, *Skylab – Seashell / Next (1994, Vinyl)*, Discogs, viewed 9 November 2019, <https://www.discogs.com/Skylab-Seashell-Next/release/106854>.

Discogs 2019jj, *Terry Callier,* Discogs, viewed 11 November 2019, <https://www.discogs.com/artist/5355-Terry-Callier?filter_anv=0&subtype=Vocals&type=Credits>.

Discogs 2019kk, *The Baby Namboos*, Discogs, viewed 11 November 2019, <https://www.discogs.com/artist/1158877-The-Baby-Namboos>.

Discogs 2019ll, *The Site Label,* Discogs, viewed 11 November 2019, <https://www.discogs.com/label/272875-The-Site>.

Discogs 2019mm, *Tim Goldsworthy,* Discogs, viewed 14 November 2019, <https://www.discogs.com/artist/67374-Tim-Goldsworthy?filter_anv=0&subtype=Management&type=Credits>.

Discogs 2019nn, *Tiny Panx* – Last Orgy (1988, Vinyl)*, Discogs, viewed 9 November 2019, <https://www.discogs.com/Tiny-Panx-Last-Orgy/release/779685>.

Discogs 2019oo, *U.N.K.L.E.* – Berry Meditation (1996, Vinyl)*, Discogs, viewed 11 November 2019, <https://www.discogs.com/UNKLE-Berry-Meditation/release/1089335>.

Discogs 2019pp, *U.N.K.L.E.* – Berry Meditation (1997, Vinyl)*, Discogs, viewed 11 November 2019, <https://www.discogs.com/UNKLE-Berry-Meditation/release/31590>.

Discogs 2019qq, *U.N.K.L.E.* – Rock On (1998, CD)*, Discogs, viewed 11 November 2019, <https://www.discogs.com/UNKLE-Rock-On/release/19014>.

Discogs 2019rr, *U.N.K.L.E.* – The Time Has Come E.P. (1994, Vinyl)*, Discogs, viewed 9 November 2019, <https://www.discogs.com/UNKLE-The-Time-Has-Come-EP/release/942452>.

Discogs 2019ss, *U.N.K.L.E.* – Trilogy Box Set (1998, Vinyl)*, Discogs, viewed 11 November 2019, <https://www.discogs.com/UNKLE-Trilogy-Box-Set/release/1113280>.

Discogs 2019tt, *U.N.K.L.E.* Featuring Nigo & Scratch Perverts – Ape Shall Never Kill Ape (1998, CD)*, Discogs, viewed 11 November 2019, <https://www.discogs.com/UNKLE-Featuring-Nigo-Scratch-Perverts-Ape-Shall-Never-Kill-Ape/release/66557>.

Discogs 2019uu, *U.N.K.L.E.* Featuring Takagi Kan – Last Orgy 3 Special Remixes (1998, CD)*, Discogs, viewed 11 November 2019, <https://www.discogs.com/UNKLE-Featuring-Takagi-Kan-Last-Orgy-3-Special-Remixes/release/1241643>.

Discogs 2019vv, *United Future Organization – Loud Minority (1992, CD)*, Discogs, viewed 9 November 2019, <https://www.discogs.com/United-Future-Organization-Loud-Minority/release/1226809>.

Discogs 2019ww, *United Future Organization – Loud Minority (1993, Vinyl)*, Discogs, viewed 9 November 2019, <https://www.discogs.com/United-Future-Organization-Loud-Minority/release/72649>.

Discogs 2019xx, *UNKLE – Bloodstain (1998, CDr)*, Discogs, viewed 11 November 2019, <https://www.discogs.com/UNKLE-Bloodstain/release/1254866>.

Discogs 2019yy, *UNKLE – Psyence Fiction (1998, CD)*, Discogs, viewed 11 November 2019, <https://www.discogs.com/UNKLE-Psyence-Fiction/release/31601>.

Discogs 2019zz, *UNKLE – Psyence Fiction (1998, CD)*, Discogs, viewed 11 November 2019, <https://www.discogs.com/UNKLE-Psyence-Fiction/release/43468>.

Discogs 2019aaa, *UNKLE – Psyence Fiction (1998, CD)*, Discogs, viewed 11 November 2019, <https://www.discogs.com/UNKLE-Psyence-Fiction/release/66099>.

Discogs 2019bbb, *UNKLE – Psyence Fiction (1998, Vinyl)*, Discogs, viewed 11 November 2019, <https://www.discogs.com/UNKLE-Psyence-Fiction/release/309316>.

Discogs 2019ccc, *UNKLE – Psyence Fiction (1998, Vinyl)*, Discogs, viewed 11 November 2019, <https://www.discogs.com/UNKLE-Psyence-Fiction/release/768202>.

Discogs 2019ddd, *UNKLE With Kool G. Rap* – Guns Blazing (1998, Vinyl)*, Discogs, viewed 11 November 2019, <https://www.discogs.com/UNKLE-With-Kool-G-Rap-Guns-Blazing/release/175205>.

Discogs 2019eee, *Various – 110 Below :: Trip To The cHIP sHOP Vol. 2 (1995, CD)*, Discogs, viewed 9 November 2019, <https://www.discogs.com/Various-110-Below--Trip-To-The-cHIP-sHOP-Vol-2/release/49957>.

Discogs 2019fff, *Various – Acid Jazz (3) Label*, Discogs, viewed 9 November 2019, <https://www.discogs.com/label/770410-Acid-Jazz-3>.

Discogs 2019ggg, *Various – Header#1 (1996, CD)*, Discogs, viewed 11 November 2019, <https://www.discogs.com/Various-Header1/release/107358>.

Discogs 2019hhh, *Various – Headz 2A (1996, Vinyl)*, Discogs, viewed 11 November 2019, <https://www.discogs.com/Various-Headz-2A/release/4463574>.

Discogs 2019iii, *Various – Mo' Wax Record Presents: Mo' Groove Vol.1 (1993, CD)*, Discogs, viewed 9 November 2019, <https://www.discogs.com/Various-Mo-Wax-Presents-Mo-Groove-Vol1/release/50958>.

Discogs 2019jjj, *Various – Mo Wax Vs. Major Force : Time Has Come (1994, Vinyl)*, Discogs, viewed 9 November 2019,

<https://www.discogs.com/Various-Mo-Wax-Vs-Major-Force-Time-Has-Come/release/23665>.

Discogs 2019kkk, *Various – Quannum Spectrum*, Discogs, viewed 11 November 2019, <https://www.discogs.com/Various-Quannum-Spectrum/master/55530>.

Discogs 2019lll, *Various – Source Lab Vs. Mo' Wax (1995, Vinyl)*, Discogs, viewed 11 November 2019, <https://www.discogs.com/Various-Source-Lab-Vs-Mo-Wax/release/79889>.

Discogs 2019mmm, *Various – Street Sounds Electro*, Discogs, viewed 9 November 2019, <https://www.discogs.com/label/785831-Street-Sounds-Electro>.

Discogs 2019nnn, *Various – Street Sounds Electro 1*, Discogs, viewed 9 November 2019, <https://www.discogs.com/Various-Street-Sounds-Electro-1/master/452621>.

Discogs 2019ooo, *Various – Street Sounds Hip Hop 22*, Discogs, viewed 9 November 2019, <https://www.discogs.com/Various-Street-Sounds-Hip-Hop-22/master/162840>.

Discogs 2019ppp, *Various – SubUrbia Original Motion Picture Soundtrack*, Discogs, viewed 9 November 2019, <https://www.discogs.com/Various-SubUrbia-Original-Motion-Picture-Soundtrack/release/279666>.

Discogs 2019qqq, *Zimbabwe Legit – Doin' Damage In My Native Language (1992, Vinyl)*, Discogs, viewed 9 November 2019, <https://www.discogs.com/Zimbabwe-Legit-Doin-Damage-In-My-Native-Language/release/135028>.

Discogs 2019rrr, *アンクル* – サイエンス フィクション (1998, CD)*, Discogs, viewed 11 November 2019, <https://www.discogs.com/アンクル-サイエンス-フィクション-/release/1241486>.

Discogs 2019sss, *アンクル* – サイエンス フィクション (1998, CD)*, Discogs, viewed 11 November 2019, <https://www.discogs.com/アンクル-サイエンス-フィクション/release/205516>.

Discogs 2020a, *Atlantique*, Discogs, viewed 25 February 2020, <https://www.discogs.com/artist/419554-Atlantique-2>.

Discogs 2020b, *Money Mark – Mark's Keyboard Repair (1995, Vinyl)*, Discogs, viewed 16 February 2020, <https://www.discogs.com/Money-Mark-Marks-Keyboard-Repair/release/71674>.

Discogs 2020c, *Nigo – Ape Sounds (1999, Vinyl)*, Discogs, viewed 27 March 2020, <https://www.discogs.com/Nigo-Ape-Sounds/release/897218>.

Discogs 2020d, *Nigo – Ape Sounds (2000, Vinyl)*, Discogs, viewed 27 March 2020, <https://www.discogs.com/Nigo-Ape-Sounds/release/82098>.

Discogs 2020e, *Tony Vegas*, Discogs, viewed 18 February 2020, <https://www.discogs.com/artist/19102-Tony-Vegas?filter_anv=0&subtype=Instruments-Performance&type=Credits>.

Discogs 2020f, *UNKLE – Psyence Fiction*, Discogs, viewed 24 February 2020, <https://www.discogs.com/UNKLE-Psyence-Fiction/release/38782>.

Discogs 2020g, *UNKLE Featuring Ian Brown – Be There*, Discogs, viewed 24 February 2020, <https://www.discogs.com/UNKLE-Featuring-Ian-Brown-Be-There/release/4427>.

Discogs 2020h, *Various – Acid Jazz Vol. 2 (1988, Vinyl)*, Discogs, viewed 16 February 2020, <https://www.discogs.com/Various-Acid-Jazz-Vol-2/release/54367>.

Discogs 2020i, *Various – Headz 2A (1996, Vinyl)*, Discogs, viewed 25 February 2020, <https://www.discogs.com/Various-Headz-2A/release/80035>.

DJ Krush, 2017, *DJ Krush*, MOC, viewed July 8 2019, <https://www.mocmmxw.com/interviews/krush/3/>.

DJShadow.com n.d. a, *DJ Shadow: The 4-Track Era Collection*, DJ Shadow, viewed 25 June 2019, <https://djshadow.com/discography/dj-shadow-the-4-track-era-collection>.

DJShadow.com n.d. b, *High Noon*, DJ Shadow, viewed 23 December 2019, <https://djshadow.com/discography/dj-shadow-high-noon>.

DJShadow.com n.d. c, *Paris: Sleeping With The Enemy*, DJ Shadow, viewed 25 June 2019, <https://djshadow.com/discography/paris-sleeping-with-the-enemy>.

DJShadow.com n.d. d, *Rock On*, DJ Shadow, viewed 12 July 2019, <https://djshadow.com/discography/u-n-k-l-e-rock-on>.

DJShadow.com n.d. e, *The End of Violence*, DJ Shadow, viewed 12 July 2019, <https://djshadow.com/discography/the-end-of-violence-various-artists-soundtrack>.

DJShadow.com n.d. f, *UNKLE (DJ Shadow & James Lavelle) With Kool G. Rap: Guns Blazing*, DJ Shadow, viewed 12 July 2019, <https://djshadow.com/discography/unkle-dj-shadow-james-lavelle-with-kool-g-rap-guns-blazing>.

DJShadow.com n.d. g, *Vexille: The Soundtrack (Various Artists)*, DJ Shadow, viewed 12 July 2019, <https://djshadow.com/discography/vexille-the-soundtrack-various-artists>.

DJShadow.com 2009a, *MPC Receipt*, DJ Shadow, viewed 25 June 2019, <https://djshadow.com/archives/mpc-receipt>.

DJShadow.com 2009b, *Radiohead Tour Set Notes*, DJ Shadow, viewed 25 June 2019, <https://djshadow.com/archives/radiohead-tour-set-notes>.

DJShadow.com 2010, *The 4-Track Era: Best of the Original Productions Vinyl- NOW SHIPPING!*, DJ Shadow, viewed 25 June 2019, <https://djshadow.com/the-4-track-era-best-of-the-original-productions-vinyl-now-shipping>.

DMC 2000?, *An Interview With James Lavelle*, Build And Destroy, viewed 24 July 2019, <https://web.archive.org/web/20021221210807/http://homepage.ntlworld.com:80/andrewlochhead/articles/jlinterviewdmc.htm>.

Donners, B 2018, 'The art of Futura', *Medium*, viewed 12 July 2019, <https://medium.com/@brucedonners/the-art-of-futura-28b4373c73ad>.

Doran, J 2010, *Megadef: DJ Shadow Interviewed*, The Quietus, viewed 13 July 2019, <https://thequietus.com/articles/05112-dj-shadow-interview>.

Double Dee 2017, *Making The Lessons -Tech Notes From Double Dee*, Double Dee and Steinski, viewed July 8 2019, <https://ddski.com/double-dee-making-the-lessons>.

Double Dee & Steinski, 2018, *Lesson 4: The Beat EP*, Double Dee & Steinski, viewed July 8 2019, <https://ddsteinski.bandcamp.com/album/lesson-4-the-beat-ep>.

Douridas, C 1998, *KCRW 'Morning Becomes Eclectic', june 9th 1997*, Citizen Insane, viewed 26 July 2019, <https://citizeninsane.eu/media/usa/radio/03/i01a_1997-06-09_kcrw.htm>.

Doyle, T 2017, 'CLASSIC TRACKS: DJ Shadow 'Midnight In A Perfect World'', *Sound on Sound*, viewed 25 June 2019, <https://www.soundonsound.com/techniques/classic-tracks-dj-shadow-midnight-perfect-world>.

Dubplate To Dubstep, n.d., *1980-89 The Birth of The Bristol Sound*, Dubplate To Dubstep, viewed 25 June 2019, <www.dubplatetodubstep.ujimaradio.com/the-birth-of-the-bristol-sound>.

Dummy, 2013, *The 13 records that defined That's How It Is, according to James Lavelle*, viewed 14 June 2019, < https://www.dummymag.com/10-best/13-records-defined-thats-how-it-is-bar-rumba-according-to-james-lavelle>.

Dummy, 2015, *The 10 best British sound system classics, according to James Lavelle*, viewed 14 June 2019, <https://www.dummymag.com/10-best/the-10-best-british-sound-system-classics-according-to-james-lavelle>.

Drury, B 2001, *The Art & Design of Ben Drury*, We Have A Problem, viewed 12 July 2019, <https://web.archive.org/web/20100309062119/http://www.wehaveaproblem.com/exhibitions/drury/trustmelondon.html>.

dusted 2012, *Check it out. Bottom right hand corner*, U77 Forum, 27 July, viewed 24 Feburary 2020, <http://unkle77.proboards.com/post/118119/thread>.

Duyn, E 1996, *The Mo' Wax Effect*, The Fly, viewed 12 July 2019, <https://web.archive.org/web/20040215074304/http://www.fly.co.uk:80/mowax.htm>.

Dye, T 2019, *The Corridor*, Toby Dye, viewed 14 July 2019, <http://www.tobydye.com/films/the-corridor>.

Eaton, A 2009, 'A very quiet adventure', *The Scotsman*, 30 May, viewed 14 July 2019. ProQuest Database.

Edelson, S 2004, 'Planet of The Bathing Apes', *SINVIN Real Estate*, viewed 16 February 2020, <http://www.sinvin.com/2004/04/planet-of-the-bathing-apes>.

Egaitsu, H 1998, *mo' wax*, Toy's Factory, viewed 26 June 2019, <https://web.archive.org/web/20000612233336fw_/http://www.toysfactory.co.jp/bpm/mo_wax/interview.html>.

Egaitsu, H 2014, *Interview: Toshio Nakanishi on Hip Hop, New Wave, and Punk*, Red Bull Music Academy, viewed 24 June 2019, <https://daily.redbullmusicacademy.com/2014/10/toshio-nakanishi-interview>.

Ekpo, I 2018, 'THE KOOL GENIUS OF RAP TURNS 50: HAPPY BIRTHDAY TO MAFIOSO RAP PIONEER, KOOL G RAP', *The Source*, viewed 13 July 2019, <http://thesource.com/2018/07/20/kool-g-rap-birthday>.

Ele-king, 1998, *UNKLE*, Ele-king, October, vol. 21, p. 2.

Ellis, L 1995, *The Verve*, Detour Magazine, October, Music Saves, viewed 13 July 2019, <http://musicsaves.org/verve/interviews/26.shtml>.

Empire, K 1999, *UNKLE / IDLEWILD / DELAKOTA / LLAMA FARMERS - Liverpool L2*, NME, viewed 15 July 2019, <https://web.archive.org/web/19991114200439/http://www.nme.com:80/reviews/reviews/19990019113341reviews.html>.

Endersby, R <rob@idlemedia.co.uk> 1998, 'UNKLE', *Acid Jazz Archive*, 23 July, viewed 26 July 2019, <www.boralv.se/AcidJazz/Backup/1998-Jul/0445.html>.

Epstein, DR 2005, *Jonathan Glazer - Director's Label DVD*, Suicide Girls, viewed 14 July 2019, <https://web.archive.org/web/20060428075129/http://suicidegirls.com/words/Jonathan+Glazer+-+Director's+Label+DVD>.

Eye Magazine 2017, *A Life In Grafix*, Eye Magazine, viewed 13 June 2019, <http://eyemagazine.com/review/article/a-life-in-grafix>.

Fadele, D n.d., 'MASSIVE - Blue Lines', *NME*, viewed 17 June 2019, <https://web.archive.org/web/20000115091530/http://www.nme.com/reviews/reviews/19980101000006reviews.html>.

Fader, L 2012, *Rewind: DJ Shadow*, XLR8R, viewed 12 July 2019, <https://www.xlr8r.com/features/rewind-dj-shadow>.

Famous Fashion Designers, 2019, *Nigo*, Famous Fashion Designers, viewed 13 July 2019, <https://www.famousfashiondesigners.org/nigo>.

Farley, C J 1998, 'Music: Psyence Fiction', *Time*, 12 October, vol. 115, no. 15, viewed 26 July 2019, EBSCOhost Database.

Farsides, T 1998, 'UNKLE', *Music Week*, 8 August, viewed 26 July 2019, ProQuest Database.

Fearon, R 1981, 'Selector with Fatman Hi-Fi', *NME*, 21 February, viewed July 8 2019, <http://uncarved.org/dub/splash/ribs.html>.

Feemster, S 2020, *Talk Talk – Biography*, Amobea Music, viewed 25 February 2020, <https://www.amoeba.com/talk-talk/artist/144609/bio>.

Fine, J 1997, 'DJ Shadow – Hip Hop Militant', *Option*, March / April, no. 73, pp. 58-73.

Fiona, 1998, *UNKLE Album Release Party @ HMV London Report*, Toy's Factory, viewed 26 July 2019, <https://web.archive.org/web/20000226070257fw_/http://www.toysfactory.co.jp:80/bpm/mo_wax/party/p_980823.html>.

Flynn, Sean <sflynn@pobox.com> 1998, That UNKLE Fseye-insse Psiction Shit..., Google Groups, 1 October, *rec.music.hip-hop*, viewed 27 June 2019, <https://groups.google.com/forum/#!msg/rec.music.hip-hop/bQKGLTniLj8/kqItqVOxIQ8J>.

Freeman, M 1998, 'LP Launched', *Music Week*, 5 December, viewed 26 July 2019, ProQuest Database.

Friedman, K 2013, *FILTER 50: I See A Darkness: The History Of DJ Shadow As Told By Cut Chemist, James Lavelle + More*, Filter, viewed 14 June 2019, <http://filtermagazine.com/index.php/exclusives/entry/filter_50_i_see_a_darkness_the_history_of_dj_shadow_as_told_by_cut_chemist_>.

Foakes, K 2015, *Early Mo Wax designs by Ian 'Swifty' Swift*, DJ Food, viewed 17 June 2019, < http://www.djfood.org/early-mo-wax-designs-by-ian-swifty-swift/>.

Folb, M 1995, *The Verve, Exclaim!, September '95*, Music Saves, viewed 13 July 2019, <http://musicsaves.org/verve/interviews/25.shtml>.

Fox, K 2016, 'Me and the muse: DJ Shadow on his sources of inspiration', *The Guardian*, 26 June, viewed 24 July 2019,

<https://www.theguardian.com/music/2016/jun/26/me-and-the-muse-dj-shadow-inspirations-mountain-will-fall>.

Fuller, J 1998, '7 Days In Dance', *Music Week*, 14 November, viewed 26 July 2019, ProQuest Database.

futuradosmil 2018, *EGRESS*, Instagram, 20 March, viewed 12 January 2020, <https://www.instagram.com/p/Bgi1QWpgc4R>.

Future Music 1998, *The Men From U.N.K.L.E.*, Solesides, viewed 26 July 2019, <http://www.solesides.com/various-the-men-from-unkle-future-music-1098.html>.

Gadelrab, R 2017, 'The man from UNKLE', *Camden New Journal*, viewed 13 July 2019, <camdennewjournal.com/article/the-man-from-unkle>.

Gaderlund, E <erikg@macconnect.com> 1998, 'UNKLE "Psyence Fiction"--I like it', *Acid Jazz Archive*, 5 October, viewed 26 July 2019, < http://www.boralv.se/AcidJazz/Backup/1998-Oct/0062.html>.

Gaitney, S 1999, 'Alice Temple', *Out*, January, vol. 7, no. 7, p.21

Gamble, C 2017, *For the Love of London: What makes London great by the people who make it great*, Hachette, London, ch. James Lavelle

Gaunt, J 2019, 'James Lavelle and His Family of Artists', *Medium*, viewed 12 December 2019, <https://medium.com/@jimmyjrg/james-lavelle-and-his-family-of-artists-2f85ff1ee190>.

Gavin, F 2019, *Rammellzee*, Kaleidoscope, viewed 12 July 2019, <http://kaleidoscope.media/rammellzee>.

Gelmis, J 1969, *An Interview with Stanley Kubrick (1969)*, The Kubrick Site, viewed 15 July 2019, <www.visual-memory.co.uk/amk/doc/0069.html>.

Genius 2019a, *UNKLE – Outro (Mandatory) Lyrics*, Genius, viewed 23 December 2019, <https://genius.com/Unkle-outro-mandatory-lyrics>.

Genius 2019b, *UNKLE – The Knock (Drums of Death, Part 2) Lyrics*, Genius, viewed 23 December 2019, <https://genius.com/Unkle-the-knock-drums-of-death-part-2-lyrics>.

Geoghegan, K 2014, 'Meltdown is 'something joyous' says curator James Lavelle', *BBC*, viewed 17 June 2019, <https://www.bbc.com/news/entertainment-arts-27698391>.

Gill, E 2014, 'MC Rammellzee - Interview by Ed Gill, June 1995 - Introduction', in Lavelle, J 2014, *Mo'Wax : Urban Archaeology: 21 Years Of Mo'Wax Recordings*, Rizzoli, New York.

Girou, B 2018, *James Lavelle and The Man From Mo'Wax*, Inverted Audio, viewed 13 June 2019, <https://inverted-audio.com/feature/james-lavelle-and-the-man-from-mowax>.

Goh, G 2012, KTC: *Fraser Cooke - The Master in Performance Lifestyle Marketing Part 1*, Hypebeast, viewed 17 June 2019, <https://hypebeast.com/2012/6/ktc-fraser-cooke-the-master-in-performance-lifestyle-marketing-part-1>.

Goldberg, M 2000, *Alchemical Opposites*, Metro Active, viewed 13 June 2019, <www.metroactive.com/papers/cruz/02.16.00/namboos-0007.html>.

Goldman, V 1993, 'Electro: U.K.'s Thriving Jazz Groove', *Billboard*, 18 September, col. 105, no. 38, p1 & 74.

Goodhood n.d. a, *Icons – James Lavelle*, Goodhood, viewed 13 June 2019, <https://goodhoodstore.com/mens/news/1759>.

Goodhood n.d. b, *Mo' Wax x Hysteric Glamour Blood Stain Jacket - Black*, Goodhood, viewed 23 December 2019, <https://goodhoodstore.com/store/mo-wax-x-hysteric-glamour-blood-stain-jacket-black-18434>.

Goodhood n.d. c, *Mo' Wax x Hysteric Glamour Blood Stain Vinyl Pack*, Goodhood, viewed 23 December 2019, <https://goodhoodstore.com/store/mo-wax-x-hysteric-glamour-vinyl-pack-blood-stain-18423>.

Gotthardt, A 2018, 'How 1980s Cult Artist Rammellzee Mesmerized Everyone from Basquiat to the Beastie Boys', *Artsy*, viewed 12 July 2019, <https://www.artsy.net/article/artsy-editorial-1980s-cult-artist-rammellzee-mesmerized-basquiat-beastie-boys>.

Gough, D 2000, 'Mixtape: Badly Drawn Boy', *Dazed & Confused*, July, vol. 1, no. 67, p.46

Graphotism 1995, 'Update', *Graphotism*, no. 7, p. 4, viewed 8 August 2019, <https://issuu.com/illadelstylez/docs/graphotism7>.

Graphotism 2000, *GOD SPEED YOU GRAF EMPEROR*, Mo' Wax Please, viewed 8 July 2019, <https://www.mowaxplease.com/futura-2000-mo-wax-book-james-lavelle>.

Gray, L 1994, 'Independents' Day', *New Statesman & Society*, 25 November, vol. 7, no. 330. p.32-33

Greenham, A 2011, *Lack of experience holding you back? UNKLE's James Lavelle started his record label at 18. Here's how...*, Subvert Magazine, viewed 9 May 2019, <https://web.archive.org/web/20130401211319/http://www.subvertmagazine.com/blog/james-lavelle>.

Green Plastic Trees n.d.a, *Radiohead Tour Dates and Gigography*, Green Plastic Trees, viewed 13 June 2019, <http://greenplastic.com/gigography/index.php?year=1992>.

Green Plastic Trees n.d.b, *Radiohead Tour Dates and Gigography*, Green Plastic Trees, viewed 13 June 2019, <http://greenplastic.com/gigography/index.php?year=1997>.

Greenwood, C 2014, 'Colin Greenwood: Radiohead's Top 5 independent venues', *The Guardian*, 31 January, viewed 22 December 2019, <https://www.theguardian.com/music/2014/jan/30/colin-greenwood-radiohead-top-5-independent-venues>.

Gregory, A (ed) 2002, *The International Who's Who in Popular Music 2002*, 4th edn, Europa Publications Limited, London.

Grundy, G 1997, 'The Man From UNKLE', *The Face*, vol. 3, no. 9, pp. 252-255

Grundy, G 1998, 'The Rebel Alliance', *Select*, September, p. 80.

Grundy, G 2012, *DJ Shadow: soundtrack of my life*, The Guardian, viewed 25 June 2019, <https://www.theguardian.com/music/2012/sep/02/dj-shadow-soundtrack-my-life>.

Guinness World Records 2019, *First album made completely from samples*, Guinness World Records, viewed 13 July 2019, <https://www.guinnessworldrecords.com/world-records/first-album-made-completely-from-samples>.

Gundersen, E 1998, 'U.N.K.L.E. Psyence Fiction', *USA Today*, 13 October, viewed 26 July 2019, ProQuest Database

Hahn, L 2006, *Nigo Talkasia Transcript*, CNN, viewed 13 July 2019, <http://edition.cnn.com/2006/WORLD/asiapcf/02/28/talkasia.nigo.script/index.html>.

Halasa, M 1996, 'Rebel with a cause', *The Guardian*, 1 Nov, pp. 14-15.

Harcourt, N 1998, *Morning Becomes Electric*, 29 September, KCRW, radio programme, viewed 31 January 2020, <https://www.kcrw.com/music/shows/morning-becomes-eclectic/james-lavelle>.

Harris, D 1994, 'Mo Wax', *DJ*, March 3-16 1994, vol. 1, no. 109, pp. 24-25.

Harris, L 2011, *Baker's Dozen: UNKLE'S James Lavelle On His 13 Favourite Records*, The Quietus, viewed 26 July 2019, <https://thequietus.com/articles/06129-james-lavelle-unkle-favourite-records?page=2>.

Hay, C 1999a, 'Retail: MTV Awards Will Boost Martin', *Billboard*, 7 August, vol. 111, no. 32, p. 73

Hay, C 1999b, 'Squarepusher Pulls In Three At MVPA Music Video Awards', *Billboard*, 24 April, vol. 111, no. 17, p. 76

Heimlich, A 1998, 'UNKLE - Sweet Science', *Alternative Press*, November, viewed 27 July 2019, ProQuest Database.

Hermes, W 1997, 'Various Artists – Heads 2A', *Spin*, April, vol. 13, no. 1, p.160-161

Hermes, W, 1998, 'Dance Music Enlists A New Sound: Voices', *New York Times*, 22 November, viewed 26 July 2019, ProQuest Database.

Hermes, W 2002, 'DJ Shadow – Head Case', *Spin*, July vol. 18, no. 7, p.96-98

Higgins, M 1998, 'The boy from Unkle How did young James Lavelle persuade Richard Ashcroft and Thom Yorke to do a record for him? Mike Higgins finds out', *The Independent*, 26 July, viewed 26 July 2019, ProQuest Database.

Hilleary, M 2017, 'Mario Caldato Jnr. ; That's a Record 'Cause of Mario', *Mike Hilleary*, viewed March 28 2020, <http://www.mikehilleary.com/mario-caldato-jr>.

HipHopCrack, nd, *Quannum: Featured Indie Label @HIPHOPCRACK.COM,* Solesides, viewed 23 December 2019, <http://www.solesides.com/quannum-featured-indie-label-at-hiphopcrackcom.html>.

Hirway, H 2016, *DJ Shadow - Mutual Slump*, podcast, Song Exploder, 8 December, viewed 5 February 2020, <http://songexploder.net/dj-shadow>.

Hodgkinson, Will 2002, 'Review: HOME ENTERTAINMENT: JAMES LAVELLE', *The Guardian*, 18 October, viewed 9 May 2019, ProQuest database.

Hogan, M 2015, *Did Vinyl Really Die in the '90s? Well, Sort Of...*, Spin, viewed 13 June 2019, <https://www.spin.com/2014/05/did-vinyl-really-die-in-the-90s-death-resurgence-sales>.

Horan, T 1999, 'Mr Fixit's latest coup - a live show without the performers', *The Telegraph*, 28 January, viewed 15 July 2019, <https://www.telegraph.co.uk/culture/4716720/Mr-Fixits-latest-coup-a-live-show-without-the-performers.html>.

Howe, R 2019, *Bob Marley, Johnny Rotten and the story of the Punky Reggae Party*, ABC News, viewed 25 June 2019, <https://www.abc.net.au/news/2019-03-20/punk-reggae-johnny-rotten-bob-marley-trading-places/10879022>.

Hsu, H 2018, 'The Spectacular Personal Mythology of Rammellzee', *The New Yorker*, viewed 12 July 2019, <https://www.newyorker.com/magazine/2018/05/28/the-spectacular-personal-mythology-of-rammellzee>.

Hughes, T 2008, 'Now it's the O2 Academy', *Oxford Mail*, 11 November, viewed 22 December 2019, <https://www.oxfordmail.co.uk/news/3834959.now-o2-academy>.

IMDB 2019a, *Rammellzee*, Internet Movie Database, viewed 27 July 2019, <https://www.imdb.com/name/nm0708440>.

IMDB 2019b, *UNKLE Feat. Thom Yorke: Rabbit in Your Headlights*, Internet Movie Database, viewed 14 July 2019, <https://www.imdb.com/title/tt6802114>.

IMDB 2020a, *Don Francks*, Internet Movie Database, viewed 26 February 2020, <https://www.imdb.com/name/nm0290475/?ref_=nv_sr_srsg_0>.

IMDB 2020b, Malachi Throne, Internet Movie Database, viewed 25 January 2020, <https://www.imdb.com/name/nm0861943>.

Inoue, T 2002, 'Made in the Shade', *Metro*, viewed 16 February 2020, <http://www.metroactive.com/papers/metro/05.23.02/dj-shadow-0221.html>.

in't Veld, H & Weber, S 1998, 'The path over the burnt bridge', *Within Without*, viewed 25 February 2020, <https://web.archive.org/web/20140202025158fw_/http://users.cybercity.dk/~bcc11425/IntSUBAUDIO.html>.

James Lavelle Interview 1996, *Header#1*, CD-Rom Multimedia Video, Header, UK.

James Lavelle Interview 2005, *Director's Series Vol. 5 - Work of Director Jonathan Glazer*, DVD, Palm Pictures, New York.

James, M 1997, "Star Wars' Twenty Years On...', *Muzik*, April, pp.145-145

James, M 1999, 'Pop: The bones of hip hop bleached white', *The Independent*, 12 Janurary, viewed 15 July 2019, <https://www.independent.co.uk/arts-entertainment/pop-the-bones-of-hip-hop-bleached-white-1046566.html>.

Jazzbo, 1998, *Talking headz: UNKLE*, Paper, viewed 15 July 2019, <http://www.papermag.com/talking-headz-unkle-1425143070.html>.

Jenkins, L 2013, *Too Good To Be True: Tom Roninson's Favourite Albums - Eg And Alice - 24 Years of Hunger*, The Quietus, viewed 14 July 2019, <https://thequietus.com/articles/13005-tom-robinson-favourite-albums?page=8>.

Jennings, D 2003, MULTIMEDIA SOUNDTOYS 1996/2003, *DJ Alchemi*, viewed 12 July 2019, <alchemi.co.uk/archives/mus/multimedia_soundtoys_19962003.html>.

jimmyjrg 2020, *What was Mo' Wax Records' best year?*, U77 Forum, 23 March, viewed 23 March 2020, <https://unkle77.proboards.com/thread/12810/mo-wax-records-best-year>.

Jockey Slut 2002, *Under The Influence (Jockey Slut 2002)*, Red Lines, viewed 13 June 2019, <http://red-lines.co.uk/reading/undertheinfluence.htm>.

Johnson, P 1997, *Straight Outa Bristol*, Hodder and Stoughton, London.

Jordon, R 1998, 'Television Wednesday', *The Guardian*, 9 September, p. 20.

Kan, T 2014, 'Urban Archaeology Questionaire', in Lavelle, J 2014, *Mo'Wax : Urban Archaeology: 21 Years Of Mo'Wax Recordings*, Rizzoli, New York.

Kane, D 2014, 'James Lavelle Interview', *Bonafide Mag*, 10 June, viewed 12 February 2020, <http://www.bonafidemag.com/james-lavelle-interview-56>.

Kaufman, G 1998, 'Ashcroft, Yorke, Mike D Give Voice To UNKLE', *MTV*, viewed 13 July 2019, <http://www.mtv.com/news/450038/ashcroft-yorke-mike-d-give-voice-to-unkle>.

Keefe, M <MARKEEFE@aol.com> 1998, 'Fwd: [Marbles] PolyGram-Universal merger (Mo Wax content)', *Acid Jazz Archive*, 14 December, viewed 26 July 2019, <http://www.boralv.se/AcidJazz/Backup/1998-Dec/0153.html>.

Keller, J 2010, 'An Adagio for Strings, and for the Ages', *The New York Times*, 5 March, viewed 26 February 2020, <https://www.nytimes.com/2010/03/07/arts/music/07barber.html>.

Kellman, A 2019, *Sleeping with the Enemy - Paris*, All Music, viewed 25 June 2019, <https://www.allmusic.com/album/sleeping-with-the-enemy-mw0000093210>.

KidCaL <calvin@hklink.net> 1998, 'The Death of MoWax', *Acid Jazz Archive*, 11 December, viewed 26 July 2019, <http://www.boralv.se/AcidJazz/Backup/1998-Dec/0111.html>.

Kirwin, P 2003, 'Guide to...DJ Shadow', *Muzik*, March, p.107.

Kreps, D 2017, 'David Axelrod, Influential Producer and Composer, Dead at 83', *Rolling Stone*, viewed 12 July 2019, <https://www.rollingstone.com/music/music-news/david-axelrod-influential-producer-and-composer-dead-at-83-110459>.

Kulkarni, N 1995, 'Singles', *Melody Maker*, viewed 12 July 2019, <https://djshadow.com/archives/melody-maker-what-does-your-soul-look-like-review-1995>.

Lavelle, A n.d., *Biography – Aidan Lavelle*, Aidan Lavelle, viewed 9 May 2019, < https://www.aidan-lavelle.com/biography>.

Lavelle, H n.d., *Henry Lavelle LinkedIn*, Linkedin, viewed 25 May 2019, <https://www.linkedin.com/in/henry-lavelle-7a450929>.

Lavelle, J 1992a, 'Mo' Wax', *Straight No Chaser*, vol. 1, no. 15, p. 58

Lavelle, J 1992b, 'Mo' Wax', *Straight No Chaser*, vol. 1, no. 16, p. 62

Lavelle, J 1992c, 'Mo' Wax', *Straight No Chaser*, vol. 1, no. 17, p. 58

Lavelle, J 1993, 'Mo' Wax', *Straight No Chaser*, vol. 1, no. 20, p. 53

Lavelle, J 2014, *Mo'Wax : Urban Archaeology: 21 Years Of Mo'Wax Recordings*, Rizzoli, New York

Lavelle, J 2016, *In the studio mixing and remixing tracks...*, Facebook, 22 July, viewed 12 January 2020, <https://www.facebook.com/JamesLavelleOfficial/posts/1100166910098150:0>.

Lavelle, J 2018a, *James Lavelle's Living In My Headphones (21/02/2018)*, radio program, Soho Radio, 21 February, viewed 5 February 2020, <https://www.mixcloud.com/sohoradio/living-in-my-headphones-21022018>.

Lavelle, J 2018b, *James Lavelle's Living In My Headphones (16/05/2018)*, radio program, Soho Radio, 16 May, viewed 5 February 2020, <https://www.mixcloud.com/sohoradio/james-lavelles-living-in-my-headphones-16052018>.

Lavelle, J 2019a, *James Lavelle's Living In My Headphones (04/09/2019)*, radio program, Soho Radio, 4 September, viewed 5 February 2020, <https://www.mixcloud.com/sohoradio/living-in-my-headphones-04092019>.

Lavelle, J 2019b, *James Lavelle's Living In My Headphones (23/01/2019)*, radio program, Soho Radio, 23 January, viewed 5 February 2020, <https://www.mixcloud.com/sohoradio/living-in-my-headphones-with-james-lavelle-23012019>.

Lazarus, D 1995, 'The Man From U.N.K.L.E.', *Dazed and Confused*, vol. 1, no. 16, pp. 68-69

Leedham, R 1994, 'Massive Attack', *Dazed & Confused*, vol. 1, no. 9, p47-49

Lemmens, P n.d., *Supersister - PART 3 - from PUDDING EN GISTEREN to ISKANDER*, Metamorphosis, viewed 24 December 2019, <https://retsisrepus.nl/metamorphosis/SUPERSISTERSTORY%20part%20three.html>.

Le Républicain Lorrain, 2019, 'NYC Rap Tour : en 1982, la France et Metz découvrent la culture hip hop US', *Le Républicain Lorrain*, 25 January, viewed July 8 2019, <https://www.republicain-lorrain.fr/actualite/2019/01/25/nyc-rap-tour-en-1982-la-france-et-metz-decouvrent-la-culture-hip-hop-us>.

Levine, M 2019, *DJ Shadow*, Grove Music Online, viewed 24 June 2019, <https://www.oxfordmusiconline.com/grovemusic/view/10.1093/gmo/9781561592630.001.0001/omo-9781561592630-e-1002218982>.

Lewis, S 1998, 'Psyence Fiction', *Uncut*, October, p. 83

Li, R 2016, *A Brief History of NOWHERE and the Rise of Japanese Street Culture*, Grailed, viewed 24 June 2019, <https://www.grailed.com/drycleanonly/nowhere-history-of-japanese-street-culture>.

Li, R 2019, *Godfather of Streetwear: The Life and Legacy of Hiroshi Fujiwara*, Grailed, viewed 24 June 2019, <https://www.grailed.com/drycleanonly/hiroshi-fujiwara-fashion-history>.

Llewellyn Smith, C 1994, 'Grooving With The Holygoof - Casper Llewellyn Smith meets James Lavelle, a DJ and label supremo with a new compilation coming our way', *The Daily Telegraph*, 12 November 1994, p. 14.

Llewellyn Smith, C 1996, 'Shadow's cast of thousands', *The Telegraph*, viewed 13 July 2019, <https://www.telegraph.co.uk/culture/4703549/Shadows-cast-of-thousands.html>.

Long Live Vinyl, 2017, *James Lavelle interview – the man from UNKLE*, Long Live Vinyl, viewed 13 June 2019, <https://www.longlivevinyl.net/man-unkle-james-lavelle-interview>.

Lorraine, A 1998, 'Psyence Fiction', *Rolling Stone*, 15 October, no. 797, viewed 16 July 2019, ProQuest Database.

Love, L 2018, *The Rise of UK Hip Hop 1980-2018*, Feminist Union of Creativity and Knowledge, viewed July 8 2019, <https://fuckinliberty.com/2018/10/31/the-history-of-uk-hip-hop-1980-2018>.

Lowe, Z 2002, DJ Shadow on Kiss FM, *Build and Destroy*, viewed 26 July 2019, <https://web.archive.org/web/20021222042538/http://homepage.ntlworld.com/andrewlochhead/articles/djshadowxfm.htm>.

L R <lr68@hotmail.com> 1998, 'Re: Comments/UNKLE', *Acid Jazz Archive*, 2 October, viewed 26 July 2019, <http://www.boralv.se/AcidJazz/Backup/1998-Oct/0024.html>.

Ludovic, H-T 1998, 'Lavelle's wise investment pays musical dividends', *Financial Times*, 21 August, viewed 26 July 2019, ProQuest Database

Ma, D 2017, 'In The Beginning', *Wax Poetics*, vol. 1, no. 66, pp. 60-81

Macias, C 2016, Iconic Sacramento record store to close due to rent hike, says owner, *The Sacramento Bee*, viewed 12 July 2019, <https://www.sacbee.com/entertainment/music-news-reviews/article122500379.html>.

Maconie, S 1998, 'UNKLE: Psyence Fiction (Mo'Wax)', *Q Magazine*, September, viewed 26 July 2019, <https://www.rocksbackpages.com/Library/Article/unkle-ipsyence-fictioni-mowax>.

Magazine Canteen 2020, *I-D Magazine 36 – Alice Temple May 1986*, Magazine Canteen, viewed 26 February 2020, <https://magazinecanteen.com/collections/i-d-magazine/products/i-d-magazine-1986-36-alice-temple>.

Manning, T 2003, 'Things to do before you're 30', *Jockey Slut*, May, vol. 6, no. 4, p. 30-34

Margasak, P 1996, 'Mo' Wax Captures the Trip-Hop Vibe', *Rolling Stone*, Jul 11-25, viewed 8 February 2019. Proquest Database.

Mark, O 1998, 'CV: James Lavelle FOUNDER OF MO WAX RECORDS', *The Independent*, viewed 25 May 2019, <https://www.independent.co.uk/life-style/cv-james-lavelle-founder-of-mo-wax-records-1164095.html>.

Marx, W 2015, *Ametora: How Japan Saved American Style*, Google Books, viewed 27 February 2020, <https://books.google.com.au/books?id=I6VVDgAAQBAJ&lpg=PT11&dq=stash%20mo%20wax&pg=PT150#v=onepage&q=Lavelle&f=false>.

MassiveAttack.ie, 2019a, *Blue Lines*, viewed 14 June 2019, <https://massiveattack.ie/discography/blue-lines>.

MassiveAttack.ie, 2019b, *Karmacoma*, viewed 14 June 2019, <https://massiveattack.ie/info/karmacoma>.

MassiveAttack.ie, 2019c, *Unfinished Sympathy*, viewed 14 June 2019, <https://massiveattack.ie/info/unfinished-sympathy>.

May, C 2015, *The 10 records that helped British hip hop find its own voice*, Vinyl Factory, <https://thevinylfactory.com/features/the-10-records-that-helped-british-hip-hop-find-its-own-voice>.

Mccray, JL 2013, *Hidden Gem: Public Enemy Invades London, 1987*, The Source, viewed July 8 2019, <http://thesource.com/2013/11/01/hidden-gem-public-enemy-invades-london-1987>.

McKormick, N 2009, 'Francis 'Eg' White interview: the craftsman behind pop's perfect songs', *The Telegraph*, 21 May, viewed 26 February 2020, <https://www.telegraph.co.uk/journalists/neil-mccormick/5360406/Francis-Eg-White-interview-the-craftsman-behind-pops-perfect-songs.html>.

McLean, C 1995a, 'This Is Spinal Rap', *The Face*, December 1995, vol. 2, no. 87, pp. 103-106.

McLean, C 1995b, 'Waxing Lyrical', *GQ*, November 1995, pp. 154-158.

McLean, C 1998, 'We've just made the biggest, most expensive/action/sex/entertainment shit in the world!', *The Face*, August 1998, vol. 3, no. 19, pp. 62-69.

McLellan, M 2017, *BLADE RUNNER CAR: CLOSER LOOK AT THE FUTURISTIC BLADE RUNNER FLYING CAR FROM THE ORIGINAL & SEQUEL*, Shear Comfort, viewed 28 March 2020, <https://www.shearcomfort.com/blog/blade-runner-car>.

McLeod, K 2000, *Bristol Stomp*, The Village Voice, viewed 12 July 2019, <https://www.villagevoice.com/2000/02/08/bristol-stomp>.

Meadley, P 1996, *Futura 2000: Cult Graffiti Artist*, Fly, viewed 15 July 2019, <https://web.archive.org/web/20040216063832/http://www.fly.co.uk:80/futura.htm>.

Mego Collector 2014, *Mego Star Trek Series 1 – Guide*, Mego Collector, viewed 14 July 2019, < https://www.megocollector.com/mego/mego-star-trek-series-i-guide>.

Messenger 2011, *ERSTE WELTMEISTERSCHAFT DER FAHRRADKURIERE IN BERLIN 1993*, messenger, viewed 12 December 2019, <https://messenger.de/erste-weltmeisterschaft-der-fahrradkuriere-in-berlin-1993>.

Metaxas, N 2014, *An Extended Evening With... James Lavelle*, Nem speaks to James Lavelle, radio program, BBC Radio 6, 7 June, viewed 12 January 2020, <https://www.bbc.co.uk/programmes/p020ybht>.

Micallef, K 1998, 'The Men From U.N.K.L.E.', *CMJ New Music Monthly*, November, no. 63, p.14

Mitchum, R 2011, *Gorillaz - The SIngles Collection 2011-2011*, Pitchfork, viewed 15 July 2019, <https://pitchfork.com/reviews/albums/16077-gorillaz-singles-collection>.

MixesDB 2019, *1999-02-01 - UNKLE vs Scratch Perverts - Breezeblock - Headline Set*, MixesDB, viewed 26 July 2019, <https://www.mixesdb.com/w/1999-02-01_-_UNKLE_vs_Scratch_Perverts_-_Breezeblock_-_Headline_Set>.

Mixmag, 2003, 'UNKLE Reloaded', *Mixmag*, July, p. 36-40.

Mo'Wax Bulletin Board 2000, *Mo'Wax Bulletin Board*, viewed 15 July 2019, <https://web.archive.org/web/20010109044500/http://disc.server.com:80/Indices/105452.html>.

Mo'Wax Official 2020, *About*, Facebook, n.d., viewed, 12 January 2020, <https://www.facebook.com/pg/MoWaxOfficial/about/?ref=page_internal>.

Mo' Wax Discography 2011a, *MW002 Raw Stylus - Many Ways*, Mo' Wax Discography, viewed 29 July 2019, <https://www.mowaxdiscography.com/mw-01-101/2>

Mo' Wax Discography 2011b, *MW003 - palm skin productions - getting out of hell*, Mo' Wax Discography, viewed 29 July 2019, <https://www.mowaxdiscography.com/mw003.html>

Mo' Wax Discography 2011d, *MW021 - MW030 - Music for mad lifted beat junkies*, Mo' Wax Discography, viewed 29 July 2019, <https://www.mowaxdiscography.com/mw-21-30.html>

Mo' Wax Discography 2011d, *MWMF*, Mo' Wax Discography, viewed 29 July 2019, <https://www.mowaxdiscography.com/mwmfw.html>

Mo' Wax Discography 2011e, *Postcards & Flyers*, Mo' Wax Discography, viewed 24 February 2020, <https://www.mowaxdiscography.com/postcards--flyers.html>

MTV News 1998, 'RADIOHEAD'S THOM YORKE, VERVE, KOOL G RAP COME OUT FOR DJ SHADOW', *MTV*, viewed 13 July 2019, <http://www.mtv.com/news/1425034/radioheads-thom-yorke-verve-kool-g-rap-come-out-for-dj-shadow>.

MTV News 1999, 'Ian Brown Joins UNKLE Onstage', *MTV News*, viewed 15 July 2019, <http://www.mtv.com/news/511657/ian-brown-joins-unkle-onstage>.

Mubi 2019, Be There, *Mubi*, viewed 15 July 2019, <https://mubi.com/films/be-there>.

Mulvey, J 1998, 'UNKLE - Psyence Fiction (Mo'Wax)', *NME*, viewed 15 July 2019, <https://web.archive.org/web/19991117114245/http://www.nme.com:80/reviews/reviews/19980719150825reviews.html>.

Murphy, T 2013, DJ Shadow isn't so sure that Endtroducing was the first 100 percent sample-based record, *Westworld*, viewed 12 July 2019, <https://www.westword.com/music/dj-shadow-isnt-so-sure-that-endtroducing-was-the-first-100-percent-sample-based-record-5692493>.

Murray, R 2018, 'Legendary Bristol club The Dug Out is making a return for one night only', *Bristol Post*, <https://www.bristolpost.co.uk/whats-on/music-nightlife/legendary-bristol-club-dug-out-1108194>.

Music Business Worldwide, 2018, *Nick Huggett Named Chief Creative Officer at Because Music in the UK*, Music Business Worldwide, viewed 15 July 2019, <https://www.musicbusinessworldwide.com/nick-huggett-named-chief-creative-officer-at-because-music-in-the-uk>.

Music Careers, 2019, *A&R – Artists and Repertoire*, Music Careers, viewed 14 November 2019, <https://www.musiccareers.net/industry-terms/a-and-r>.

Music Week 1998a, 'Brown to vocal new track', *Music Week*, 5 December, viewed 26 July 2019, ProQuest Database.

Music Week 1998b, 'Osman's A&M Reign Ends', *Music Week*, 9 May, viewed 26 July 2019, Gale Fine Arts and Music Collection Database.

Music Week 1998c, 'THE OFFICIAL UK CHARTS - ALBUMS – 5 SEPTEMBER 1998', *Music Week*, December, viewed 26 July 2019, ProQuest Database.

Muzik 1995, 'Dream Date - Howie B dives into the realms of fantasy for his dream DJ slot', *Muzik*, July 1995, p. 85.

Muzik 1999, Mo' Wax artists to boycott new label', *Muzik*, February 1999, p. 10.

Nagshineh, A 2013, 'James Lavelle's 5 favourite record covers', *Bonafide Mag*, viewed 31 January 2020, <http://www.bonafidemag.com/james-lavelles-top-5-record-covers>.

National Portrait Gallery, n.d., *Zoe Bedeaux, Fashion stylist, designer and singer*, National Portrait Gallery, viewed 12 July 2019, <https://www.npg.org.uk/collections/search/person/mp72132/zoe-bedeaux>.

Naylor, T 1998, 'Badly Drawn Boy', *Melody Maker*, Jan 31, vol. 75, no. 5, page 8, viewed 26 November 2017, ProQuest Database.

Neil, 2010, *Early Shynola videos*, The Lost Continent, viewed 13 July 2019, <http://ukanimation.blogspot.com/2010/04/early-shynola-videos.html>.

Nigo 2000, *One World Mix*, radio program, BBC radio 1, 13 October, viewed 31 January 2020, <https://www.mixcloud.com/UnkleArchive/nigo-one-world-mix-12-october-2000-pt-1>.

Nigo 2014, 'Urban Archaeology Questionaire', in Lavelle, J 2014, *Mo'Wax : Urban Archaeology: 21 Years Of Mo'Wax Recordings*, Rizzoli, New York.

NME 1981, 'Directory Of Sounds', *NME*, 21 February, viewed July 8 2019, <http://uncarved.org/dub/splash/directory.html>.

NME 1994, 'Flux Dance, Let's Art', *DJ Shadow*, viewed 29 July 2019, <https://djshadow.com/archives/flux-dance-lets-art-nme-1994>.

NME 1995, 'Sudden Farewell From The Verve', *Music Saves*, viewed 13 July 2019, <http://musicsaves.org/verve/interviews/17.shtml>.

NME 1996, 'DJ Shadow : Endtroducing...', *NME*, viewed 13 July 2019, <https://web.archive.org/web/20021015200744/http://www.nme.com:80/reviews/111.htm>.

NME 1997, 'Thom's umbra is up', *Citizen Insane*, viewed 27 July 2019, <https://citizeninsane.eu/media/uk/nme/03/pt_1997-07-19_nme.htm>.

NME 1998a, 'A Monkey's UNKLE', *NME*, viewed 15 July 2019, <https://web.archive.org/web/20020612025909/http://www.nme.com:80/news/714.htm>.

NME 1998b, 'LAVELLE'S UNKLE MAKES AUGUST VISIT', *NME*, viewed 27 March 2020, <https://web.archive.org/web/20020708133605/http://www.nme.com:80/news/381.htm>.

NME 1998c, 'Ian Brown's Mid-Air Monkey Business Unfinished', *NME*, viewed 24 February 2020, <https://www.nme.com/news/music/ian-brown-182-1393481>.

NME 1998d, 'Ian Brown: Inside Story, Out At Last', *NME*, viewed 15 July 2019, <https://www.nme.com/news/music/ian-brown-150-1398957>.

NME 1998e, 'Strangeways Here I Come (Again)', *NME*, viewed 15 July 2019, <https://www.nme.com/news/music/ian-brown-159-1384883>.

NME 1998f, 'The Manna From UNKLE!', *NME*, viewed 13 July 2019, <https://www.nme.com/news/music/unkle-26-1387850>.

NME 1999a, *NME.Com*, NME, viewed 15 July 2019, <https://web.archive.org/web/20000616210420/http://www.nme.com:80/reviews/top401998.html>.

NME 1999b, 'UNKLE / IDLEWILD / DELAKOTA / LLAMA FARMERS - London WC1 Astoria', *NME*, viewed 15 July 2019, <https://web.archive.org/web/20000609063251/http://www.nme.com:80/reviews/reviews/19990025121108reviews.html>.

NME 2001, 'DJ SHADOW NO LONGER THE MAN FROM UNKLE', *NME*, viewed 15 July 2019, <https://www.nme.com/news/music/unkle-25-1387355>.

Nowinski, A 1999, 'Durban Poison's Namboos Fuse Rhythms On Debut', *Billboard*, 20 November, vol. 111, no. 47, p.33

Official UK Charts Company 2019a, *Air*, Official Charts, viewed 26 July 2019, <https://www.officialcharts.com/artist/30264/air>.

Official UK Charts Company 2019b, *DJ Shadow*, Official Charts, viewed 26 July 2019, <https://www.officialcharts.com/artist/31363/dj-shadow>

Official UK Charts Company 2019c, *Emergency On Planet Earth*, Official Charts, viewed 26 July 2019, <https://www.officialcharts.com/search/albums/emergency-on-planet-earth>.

Official UK Charts Company 2019d, *Gabrielle*, Official Charts, viewed 26 July 2019, <https://www.officialcharts.com/artist/3775/gabrielle>.

Official UK Charts Company 2019e, *Jamiroquai*, Official Charts, viewed 26 July 2019, <https://www.officialcharts.com/artist/28264/jamiroquai>.

Official UK Charts Company 2019f, *License To Ill*, Official Charts, viewed 26 July 2019, <https://www.officialcharts.com/search/albums/license-to-ill>.

Official UK Charts Company 2019g, *Money Mark*, Official Charts, viewed 26 July 2019, <https://www.officialcharts.com/artist/34072/money-mark>.

Official UK Charts Company 2019h, *Official Compilations Chart Top 100 05 June 1994 - 11 June 1994*, Official Charts, viewed 26 July 2019, <https://www.officialcharts.com/charts/official-compilations-chart/19940605/7503/>.

Official UK Charts Company 2019i, *Portishead*, Official Charts, viewed 26 July 2019, <https://www.officialcharts.com/artist/30605/portishead>.

Official UK Charts Company 2019j, *Psyence Fiction*, Official Charts, viewed 26 July 2019, <http://www.officialcharts.com/search/albums/psyence-fiction>.

Official UK Charts Company 2019k, *Tricky*, Official Charts, viewed 26 July 2019, <http://www.officialcharts.com/artist/29831/tricky>.

Official UK Charts Company 2019l, *U.N.K.L.E.*, Official Charts, viewed 26 July 2019, <https://www.officialcharts.com/artist/706/unkle>.

Official UK Charts Company 2019m, *UNKLE Feat. Ian Brown*, Official Charts, viewed 26 July 2019, <http://www.officialcharts.com/artist/7425/unkle-ft-ian-brown>.

Official UK Charts Company 2019n, *What Does Your Soul Look Like*, Official Charts, viewed 26 July 2019,

<https://www.officialcharts.com/search/singles/what-does-your-soul-look-like>.

Official UK Charts Company 2020, *OK Computer*, Official Charts, viewed 24 February 2020, <https://www.officialcharts.com/artist/30605/portishead>.

Omae, K 2018, *The Records That Changed DJ KRUSH's Life*, Donuts Magazine, viewed 24 June 2019, <https://donutsmagazine.com/en/interview/dj-krush-full>.

Onedotzero 2004, *Motion Blur: Graphic Moving Imagemakers*, pp. 160-169, Laurence King Publish, UK.

O'Connor, F 1995, 'Re:LA Recording Budget', in Lavelle, J 2014, *Mo'Wax : Urban Archaeology: 21 Years Of Mo'Wax Recordings*, Rizzoli, New York.

Parkes, T 1993, 'Influx', *Melody Maker*, November 20, p.31

Passey, M 1996, *The Mo' Wax Story*, radio program, BBC Radio 1, April 21, viewed 28 December 2019, <https://www.mowaxplease.com/james-lavelle-story-mo-wax-1996>.

Pattenden, M 1998, 'Relative Success', *The Times*, 22 August, viewed 26 July 2019, ProQuest Database.

Patterson, S 2007, 'The Salvation Army', *Mixmag*, August, pp. 50-53

Pemberton, A 1994, *Trip Hop*, Mixmag, viewed 24 June 2019, <http://www.solesides.com/various-trip-hop-mixmag.html>.

Penman, I 1994, 'Various Artists – Royalties Overdue', *The Wire*, vol. 1, no. 126, p.66

Penn, A 2014, *Toby Feltwell,* Sex Magazine, viewed 15 July 2019, <http://sexmagazine.us/articles/toby-feltwell/1>.

Peterson, G 2017, *Gilles Peterson Worldwide 2017-09-23 with James Lavelle & Kevin Saunderson*, radio program, BBC, 23 September, viewed 30 September 2018, <https://www.mixcloud.com/corenewsuploads/gilles-peterson-worldwide-2017-09-23-with-james-lavelle-kevin-saunderson>.

Pfenninger, L 2019, *Mo' Wax Recordings History*, On A&M Records, viewed 15 July 2019, <www.onamrecords.com/Mo_Wax.html>.

Phenian, 1995, *From Acid Jazz to Trip Hop - A Bluffers Guide*, Acid Jazz, viewed July 8 2019, <http://boralv.se/AcidJazz/FAQ/Fly/>.

Phillips, M 2017, *Run DMC & Beastie Boys @ Brixton Academy: 30 Years Ago Today*, Moving The River, viewed July 8 2019, <https://movingtheriver.com/2017/05/24/run-dmc-beastie-boys-brixton-academy-30-years-ago-today>.

Philster 1997, *Source Lab - Gallic Butter*, The Fly!, viewed 14 July 2019, <https://web.archive.org/web/19980530002845/http://www.fly.co.uk/source/SOURCE4.html>.

Pitchfork, 2003, 'Top 100 Albums of the 1990s', *Pitchfork*, viewed 17 June 2019, <https://pitchfork.com/features/lists-and-guides/5923-top-100-albums-of-the-1990s/?page=2>.

Pollard, A 2018, *James Lavelle THE MAN FROM MO'WAX*, Starburst, viewed 15 July 2019, <https://www.starburstmagazine.com/features/james-lavelle-man-mowax>.

Polynominal, n.d., *Akai MPC-60 II*, Polynominal, viewed 25 June 2019, <www.polynominal.com/akai-mpc60-II/index.html>.

Poole, Gary 1985, *BMX Rider*, p. 60, Modern Publishing, New York.

Potato Head 2017, *James Lavelle talks trip-hop, record labels and solo albums*, Potato Head, viewed 25 May 2019, <https://www.ptthead.com/james-lavelle-talks-trip-hop-record-labels-solo-albums>.

Prasad, A 1998, *Massive Aggressive*, Red Lines, September 26, viewed July 8 2019, <http://www.red-lines.co.uk/reading/massiveaggressive.htm>

Pride, D 1995, 'Trip Hop Steps Out', *Billboard*, April 15, vol. 107, no.15, pp. 1, 80.

Pustianaz, M 2010, 'Justin Winks aka Casio Social Club (Mullet Records)', *CHAIN D.L.K.*, viewed 22 December 2019, <http://www.chaindlk.com/interviews/justin-winks-aka-casio-social-club-mullet-records>.

Rage 2017, *James Lavelle - Guests & Specials - Rage*, viewed 13 June 2019, <https://www.abc.net.au/rage/guest/james-lavelle/9651406>.

Rare Records, n.d., *White Label Promo – Promotional Records*, Rare Records, viewed June 13, 2019, < https://www.rarerecords.net/record-info/white-label-promo-promotional-records/>.

Ray, J 2018, RAMM:ΣLL:ZΣΣ, *Super Weird Substance*, viewed 12 July 2019, <www.superweirdsubstance.com/rammellzee>.

Raygun, 1998, *James Lavelle - Top 50 Most Influential People in Pop Culture*, Solesides, viewed 15 July 2019, <https://web.archive.org/web/20030924051731fw_/http://www.solesides.com:80/winblad/james%20lavelle/lavellerg0898.html>.

Rayner, A 1999, 'The Empire Strikes Back', *Straight No Chaser*, vol. 2, no. 4, p.24-25

Red Lines, n.d., The Wild Bunch, viewed July 8 2019, <http://www.red-lines.co.uk/thewildbunch.html>.

Raz, G 2012, 'DJ Shadow On Sampling As A 'Collage Of Mistakes'', *NPR*, 17 November, viewed 26 February 2020, <https://www.npr.org/2012/11/17/165145271/dj-shadow-on-sampling-as-a-collage-of-mistakes>.

Reeves, M 1999, *Quannum: Interview - Platform Network August 1999*, Solesides, viewed 23 December 2019, <http://www.solesides.com/quannum-interv-platform-network-081099.html>.

Reid, T <t-bird@salata.com> 1999, 'Re: DJ Shadow in San Francisco', *Acid Jazz Archive*, 2 March, viewed 26 July 2019, <http://www.boralv.se/AcidJazz/Backup/1998-Oct/0071.html>.

Reighley, K 1999, 'The Scene Is Now - Father Afrika Bambaataa', *CMJ New Music Monthly*, December, vol. 1, no. 76, p.72.

Riese 2016, 'How Olivia Became The Most Successful Lesbian Business Of All Time', *Autostraddle*, viewed 28 March 2020, <https://www.autostraddle.com/how-olivia-became-the-most-successful-lesbian-business-of-all-time-355248>.

ResFest 1999a, *1999 Tour Dates*, ResFest, viewed 13 July 2019, <https://web.archive.org/web/20000816094826fw_/http://www.resfest.com/04_tour_dates/1999_tour.html>.

ResFest 1999b, *ResFest 1999 Cinema Electronica*, ResFest, viewed 13 July 2019, <https://web.archive.org/web/20000815060354fw_/http://www.resfest.com/02_films/1999_ce.html>.

Resident Advisor, n.d., *Giles Peterson*, Resident Advisor, viewed 14 June 2019, <https://www.residentadvisor.net/dj/gillespeterson/biography>.

Reynolds, S 1994a, 'Trip Hop Don't Stop: Massive Attack and Portishead', *Melody Maker*, 17 September, viewed July 8 2019, <https://www.rocksbackpages.com/Library/Article/trip-hop-dont-stop-massive-attack-and-portishead>.

Reynolds, S 1994b, 'Wax factor -- Royalties Overdue by various artists', *Melody Maker*, 18 June, vol. 71, no. 24, p. 34, viewed 17 May 2018, <http://reynoldsretro.blogspot.com/2018/03/mo-wax-compilation-x-2.html>.

Reynolds, S 1994c, 'West Country time warp blues. The world centre of ambient rap is...Bristol. Simon Reynolds meets local heroes and trip hop pioneers Massive Attack, Tricky and Portishead', *The Guardian*, 11 September, viewed 17 May 2018, ProQuest database.

Reynolds, S 1996, 'State of the Artisan', *The Wire*, January, vol. 1, no. 143, pp.24-27

RIAA 2020, *Gold & Platinum*, RIAA, viewed 24 February 2020, <https://www.riaa.com/gold-platinum/?tab_active=default-award&ar=Radiohead&ti=OK+Computer#search_section>.

Roberts, M 1997, 'The Shadow Knows', *Westworld*, 3 April, viewed 23 December 2019, <https://www.westword.com/music/the-shadow-knows-5057324>.

Roberts, M 1998, 'Say Unkle', *Westworld*, 12 July, viewed 23 December 2019, <https://www.westword.com/music/say-unkle-5059094>.

Roeder, M 1998, *DJ Shadow News*, Endtroducing, viewed 14 July 2019, <https://web.archive.org/web/19990508145134/http://www.endtroducing.com/djs_news98.html>.

Roeder, M 1999, *DJ Shadow Chat April 10, 1999*, Endtroducing, viewed 13 July 2019, <https://web.archive.org/web/20010614184118/http://www.endtroducing.com:80/chatlogs/041099chat.html>.

Rose, C 1994, 'Young Free And Turning Out Singles', *The Times*, 9 Apr 1994, viewed 13 June 2019, ProQuest database.

Rose, C 1999, *Trade Secrets : Young British Talents Talk Business*, Thames & Hudson, UK.

Abdallah, R 2016, 'Why A Storm In Heaven Is The Verve's Masterpiece', *Drowned in Sound*, 16 August, viewed 27 February 2020, <http://drownedinsound.com/in_depth/4150293-why-a-storm-in-heaven-is-the-verves-masterpiece>.

Rule, G 1997, 'DJ Shadow + Akai MPC= History', *Keyboard*, October, vol. 23, no. 10, viewed 13 June 2019, ProQuest database.

Rutter, P 2016, 'The recorded music industry sector', in P Rutter (ed.), *The Music Industry Handbook*, 2nd edn, Routledge, Abingdon, UK, n.p.

Saeed, A 2012, *An In-Depth Interview With DJ Shadow*, Noisey, viewed 13 July 2019, <https://www.vice.com/en_us/article/8qm7zz/an-in-depth-interview-with-dj-shadow>.

Scanlon, A 2000, 'Sleeve Notes', *The Times*, 15 July, viewed 26 July 2019, ProQuest Database.

Scaping, P, ed.,1984, *BPI Year Book 1984*, British Phonographic Industry, pp. 42–43.

Schwartzberg, L 2015, *Double Dutch's Forgotten Hip-Hop Origins*, Vice, viewed 8 July 2019, <https://www.vice.com/en_au/article/nn974m/double-dutchs-forgotten-hip-hop-origins-456>.

Scott, D 2017, *Chuck D Reflects On Clyde Stubblefield's Impact As Hip Hop's Most Sampled Drummer*, HiphopDX, viewed 25 June 2019, <https://hiphopdx.com/news/id.42506/title.chuck-d-reflects-on-clyde-stubblefields-impact-as-hip-hops-most-sampled-drummer>.

Scott, S 2009, *Toys and American Culture: An Encyclopedia*, ABC-CLIO, California.

Select, 1992, 'Blue Lines, Massive Attack', *Select*, January, p. 51.

Shadow 1991, 'Letters', *The Source*, May, no. 20, p. 10

Shambro, J 2019, All About DAT, *LiveAbout*, viewed 12 July 2019, <https://www.liveabout.com/all-about-dat-1817874>.

Shapiro, P 1999, 'in brief critical beats', *The Wire*, November, no. 189, p.68

Sherburne, P 2019, *UNKLE's James Lavelle on Resilience*, Spotify, viewed 15 July 2019, <https://artists.spotify.com/blog/unkles-james-lavelle-on-resilience>.

shivo 2004, *first off i don't think the sample*, U77 Forum, 8 December, viewed 12 January 2020, <http://unkle77.proboards.com/post/71374>.

shivo 2018, *Keep wishing. It was done by Pablo*, U77 Forum, 25 January, viewed 12 January 2020, <http://unkle77.proboards.com/post/131625>.

Simpson, D 1995, *Northern Soul Asylum, Melody Maker*, Music Saves, viewed 13 July 2019, <http://musicsaves.org/verve/interviews/2.shtml>.

Slow, 1999, *Slow Magazine Interview - UNKLE*, Slow, viewed 15 July 2019, <http://slowmagazine.com/slow/interviews/03_Unkle.asp>.

SLurg, 2006, *DJ Shadow Sortir de l'ombre*, Just Like Hip Hop, viewed July 8 2019, <https://web.archive.org/web/20070921220835/http://www.justlikehiphop.com/interview.php?id_interview=44&page=1>.

Smart, CK 1996, *Emancipation Hallucination - Fear and Loathing with the original Dust Brothers*, Fly, viewed 15 July 2019, <https://web.archive.org/web/20040218082328/http://www.fly.co.uk:80/dust.htm>.

Smith, A 1998, 'The men from Unkle', *Sunday Times*, 26 July, viewed 27 July 2019, ProQuest Database.

Smith, R 2017, 'Hidden Tracks : Nowhere Left To Hide', *Tedium*, viewed 25 January 2020, <https://tedium.co/2017/11/09/hidden-tracks-album-history>.

Snaporaz100 2010, *Unkle Intro (Optional) Samples (with subs),* Youtube, 14 August, viewed 5 February 2020, <https://www.youtube.com/watch?v=oRwnUM10mf4>.

Snell, T 1998a, 'Mo Wax signs deal with XL in return to its indie roots', *Music Week*, 14 November, viewed 26 July 2019, ProQuest Database.

Snell, T 1998b, 'SLIMMING DOWN FOR SURVIVAL', *Music Week*, 27 June, viewed 26 July 2019, ProQuest Database.

Snell, T 1998c, 'Staff face uncertainty as A&M shuts up shop', *Music Week*, 27 June, viewed 26 July 2019, ProQuest Database.

Speigel, L 2011, 'Whitley Strieber, 'Communion' Author, Describes Bizarre Encounter With Mystery Man', *Huffington Post*, <https://www.huffingtonpost.com.au/2011/09/07/communion-author-whitley-strieber_n_943681.html>.

Spence, S 2001, 'Futura 2000 is now - A hip-hop superhero returns', *The Japan Times*, viewed 15 July 2019, <https://www.japantimes.co.jp/culture/2001/05/30/arts/futura-2000-is-now/#.Wph1amaB06U>.

Spencer, R 2012, 'The Classic Album: UNKLE - Psyence Fiction', *Future Music*, January, no. 248, p.14-16

Spine Magazine 2002?, *Futura*, Spine Magazine, viewed 24 June 2019, <https://web.archive.org/web/20021122172359/http://www.spinemagazine.com/features/visual/futura_interview_01.html>.

Spine Magazine n.d. a, *DJ Shadow - Flashback*, Spine Magazine, viewed 24 June 2019, <https://web.archive.org/web/20040503040449/http://www.spinemagazine.com/features/music/djshadow.html>.

Spine Magazine n.d. b, *DJ Shadow - Flashback*, Spine Magazine, viewed 24 June 2019, <https://web.archive.org/web/20021223000951/http://www.spinemagazine.com/features/music/djshadow02.html>.

Spine Magazine n.d. c, *DJ Shadow - Flashback*, Spine Magazine, viewed 24 June 2019, <https://web.archive.org/web/20030226134106/http://www.spinemagazine.com:80/features/music/djshadow03.html>.

Spray Daily, 2014, *Bombin' – 1987 Documentary About British Graffiti and Hip-Hop*, Spray Daily, viewed 29 July 2019, <https://www.spraydaily.com/bombin-1987-documentary-about-british-graffiti-and-hip-hop>.

Stenman, E 1998, 'DJ Shadow', *Tape Op*, vol. 1, no. 11, pp.17-18.

Sterling, S 2006, *DJ Shadow: REMIXMAG September 2006*, Solesides, viewed 15 July 2019, <http://www.solesides.com/dj-shadow-remixmag-september-2006-full-blast.html>.

Stokes, N 2008, *Interview: James Lavelle*, Natasha Stokes, viewed 17 June 2019, <https://natashastokes.com/2008/04/25/interview-james-lavelle>.

Street Sounds, 2015, *Electro*, Street Sounds, viewed 29 July 2019, <https://web.archive.org/web/20150331205909/http://www.streetsounds.co/Electro.htm>.

Stubbs, D 1996, 'DJ Shadow: The Penumbra of the Beast', *Melody Maker*, 26 October, pp.28-30

Sturges, F 1998, 'Welcome to the man from Unkle', *The Independent – The Friday Review*, 24 July 1998, p.15

Sturges, F 2003, 'Richard Ashcroft: Grand designs', *The Independent*, viewed 26 October 2018, <https://www.independent.co.uk/arts-entertainment/music/features/richard-ashcroft-grand-designs-113592.html>.

Sturges, F 2014, 'James Lavelle interview: The man from UNKLE', *The Independent*, 8 June, viewed 12 July 2019, <https://www.independent.co.uk/arts-entertainment/music/features/james-lavelle-interview-the-man-from-unkle-9499748.html>.

Sun Ra, 2014, *Lanquidity*, Sun Ra, viewed July 8 2019, <https://sunramusic.bandcamp.com/album/lanquidity>.

Sutherland, A 1994, 'Urban Fashion Labs', *The Wire*, November, vol. 1, no. 129, pp. 30-32, 65.

Sutherland, M 1997, 'Return of the Mac!', *Melody Maker*, 31 May, Green Plastic Bags, viewed 14 July 2019, <http://www.greenplastic.com/coldstorage/articles/melodymaker053197.html>.

Swenson, K 2002, *DJ Shadow: Collage Constructionist - Remix Magazine, July 2002,* Solesides, viewed 23 December 2019, <http://www.solesides.com/dj-shadow-collage-constructionist-remix-july-2002.html>.

Swift, I 2013, *Very early flyer : sticker for #djshadow ...*, Instagram, 29 March, viewed 25 June 2019, <https://www.instagram.com/p/XaEN3rmW-S>.

Swihart, S 2019a, 24 Years of Hunger – Eg & Alice, *All Music*, viewed 23 December 2019, <https://www.allmusic.com/album/24-years-of-hunger-mw0000987477>.

Swihart, S 2019b, Eg & Alice Biography, *All Music*, viewed 23 December 2019, <https://www.allmusic.com/artist/eg-alice-mn0001859629>.

Takayama, Y 2013, *MAJOR FORCE 25th Anniversary Interview*, Wax Poetics Japan, viewed 24 Japan, <https://www.waxpoetics.jp/news/major-force-25th-anniversary-interview>.

Tate, G and Light, A, 2019, *Hip-hop*, Encyclopedia Britannica, viewed 25 June 2019, <https://www.britannica.com/art/hip-hop>.

Teen Machine 1985, *Alice Temple with Boy George*, The Blitz Kids, viewed 14 July 2019, <https://web.archive.org/web/20160324010511/http://theblitzkids.com/site_archive/kaosbrazil/aliceboy.html>.

Thatcher, D & Lavelle, J 1998, 'Trip Hop', *Muzik*, March, vol. 1, no. 34, p.66

The Face, 1997, *Dark Star*, Music Saves, viewed 13 July 2019, <http://musicsaves.org/verve/interviews/33.shtml>.

The Fashion Post, 2013, *Toby Feltwell*, The Fashion Post, viewed 13 July 2019, <https://fashionpost.jp/portraits/23430>.

The Guardian 1994, 'In The Mix: James Lavelle', *The Guardian*, 11 November 1994, page 45.

The Irish Times, 2009, 'Eg White comes out of his shell', *The Irish Times*, 1 August, viewed 14 July 2019, <https://www.irishtimes.com/news/eg-white-comes-out-of-his-shell-1.711562>.

The Light Surgeons, 2019, *U.N.K.L.E. Tour Visuals*, The Light Surgeons, viewed 15 July 2019, <http://www.lightsurgeons.com/com/unkle-tour-visuals>.

The List 1996, 'Hip-Hop DJs – Breakaway', *The List*, September 20 - October 3, no. 289, p. 70, viewed 26 March 2020, <https://archive.list.co.uk/the-list/1996-09-20/72>.

The Man from Mo' Wax 2018, DVD, BFI, London, directed by Matthew Jones.

The Mo'Wax Vaults: Asthetic Origins 2018, *The Man from Mo' Wax*, DVD, BFI, London.

The Mo'Wax Vaults: Extended interview with James Lavelle and DJ Shadow 2018, *The Man from Mo' Wax*, DVD, BFI, London.

The Mo'Wax Vaults: The Lost Men from Unkle 2018, *The Man from Mo' Wax*, DVD, BFI, London.

The New York Times 1982, 'Toy Selection Undid Mego', *The New York Times*, June 16, viewed 14 July 2019, <https://www.nytimes.com/1982/06/16/business/toy-selection-undid-mego.html>.

The Sample Source Wiki 2019, *Event Horizon*, The Sample Source Wiki, viewed 23 December 2019, <https://samplelist.fandom.com/wiki/Event_Horizon#UNKLE>.

The Star Wars Holiday Special 2018, *Boba Fett*, The Star Wars Holiday Special, viewed 14 July 2019, <http://www.starwarsholidayspecial.com/characters/boba-fett>.

The Sun, 1998, 'How Refreshing', *The Sun*, 24 December, viewed 26 July 2019, ProQuest Database.

The Times 1992, 'Reasons to be cheerful; Pop', *The Times*, 6 December, viewed 14 July 2019, ProQuest Database.

Thomas, B 2017, *Happy Birthday to Boy George! Culture Club's "Move Away" was one of 1986's most requested videos*, Night Flight, viewed 14 July 2019, <nightflight.com/happy-birthday-today-to-boy-george-culture-clubs-move-away-was-one-of-our-most-requested-videos-in-1986>.

Thompson, A 2002, *James Lavelle Biography*, Floor Filler, viewed 13 June 2019, <http://www.digitall.com.gr/floorfiller/lavelle-bio.htm>.

Thompson, B 1995, 'ARTS: Twenty something', *The Independent*, 19 November, viewed 12 July 2019, <https://www.independent.co.uk/arts-entertainment/arts-twenty-something-1582705.html>.

Thompson, B 2001, 'Pop: Rescued from the record bins Discerning hip-hop artists love to sample David Axelrod. Now he's sampling himself. Ben Thompson on a new future for music's past', *The Independent*, 20 July, viewed 12 July 2019, ProQuest Database.

Timo Fett 2019, *I am very pleased to announce that we excitingly have an update for you*, U77 Forum, 16 January, viewed 12 January 2020, <http://unkle77.proboards.com/post/133342>.

Tingen, P 2006, *Jim Abbiss*, Sound on Sound, viewed 13 July 2019, <https://www.soundonsound.com/people/jim-abbiss>.

Tingen, P 2007, *Jim Abbiss*, Mix Online, viewed 13 July 2019, <https://www.mixonline.com/recording/jim-abbiss-365764>.

Titmus, S 2013, *Interview: Morgan Khan*, Red Bull Music Academy Daily, viewed 25 June 2019, <https://daily.redbullmusicacademy.com/2013/06/morgan-khan-interview>.

Toop, D 1984, 'Electro', *The Face*, May, vol. 1, no. 49, pp.40-48.

Toop, D 1991, *Rap Attack 2: African Rap To Global Hip Hop*, Serpent's Tail, London.

Toop, D 1994, 'The dream-makers return; New Waves', *The Times*, 28 October, viewed July 8 2019, ProQuest Database.

Toop, D 1995, 'Mo' Wax clears the ears; New Waves: The Sounds Of Tomorrow, Today', *The Times*, 17 June, viewed July 8 2019. ProQuest Database.

Toy's Factory 1998, *Mo' Wax Night At Yellow - Heart of Darkness*, Toy's Factory, viewed 26 July 2019, <https://web.archive.org/web/20000312054932fw_/http://www.toysfactory.co.jp/bpm/mo_wax/party/980922.html>.

Toy's Factory 1999, *JAMES'S SELECTION*, Toy's Factory, viewed 27 July 2019, <https://web.archive.org/web/19991112205539fw_/http://www.toysfactory.co.jp/bpm/mo_wax/japan/j_james.html>.

Toy's Factory 2000a, *Last Orgy 3 Super Remix*, Toy's Factory, viewed 26 July 2019, <https://web.archive.org/web/20000613234120fw_/http://www.toysfactory.co.jp:80/bpm/mo_wax/japan/j_unkle03.html>.

Toy's Factory 2000b, *mo' wax*, Toy's Factory, viewed 26 July 2019, <hhttps://web.archive.org/web/20000310152123fw_/http://www.toysfactory.co.jp:80/bpm/mo_wax/disco.html>.

Trebay, G 2016, 'Tokyo's Underground Shopping Paradise', *The New York Times*, viewed 13 July 2019, <https://www.nytimes.com/2016/07/08/fashion/mens-style/tokyo-shopping-park-ing-ginza.html>.

Tubbs, Christopher 2013, *Christopher Tubbs interviews DJ and UNKLE producer James Lavelle*, Vimeo, 4 October, Christopher Tubbs, viewed 10 January 2020, <https://vimeo.com/76140183>.

Tuffrey, L 2012, *DJ Shadow's Reconstructed: An Oral History*, The Quietus, viewed 14 July 2019, <https://thequietus.com/articles/10446-dj-shadow-reconstructed-best-of-interview>.

Tui 2001, Daft Punk scoop 'Online Innovation' award, *Tui Interactive Media*, viewed 12 July 2019, <https://web.archive.org/web/20040724184739/http://www.tui.co.uk/pages/press/daftpunk_press01.html>.

Tuzio, A 2020, *"Last Orgy": the foundations of streetwear*, Collater.al, viewed 27 March 2020, <https://www.collater.al/en/last-orgy-foundations-streetwear-style>.

Twells, J and Fintoni, L 2015, *The 50 best trip-hop albums of all time*, FACT, viewed 25 June 2019, <https://www.factmag.com/2015/07/30/50-best-trip-hop-albums>.

Tycoon To$h Kingdom n.d., *Who's T*, Tycoon To$h Kingdom, viewed 24 June 2019, <http://www4.airnet.ne.jp/mor/tosh/whos.html>.

UNKLE 1998, *Interview With James Lavelle*, sound recording, Mo' Wax, UK.

unkle98 2019, *Watching The Man From MoWax bonus features and I noticed behind DJ Shadow is a poster for the German Tour from 1993...*, Instagram, 2 September, viewed 23 March 2020, <https://www.instagram.com/p/B16M8p1FW4O>.

URB, 1998, *Pop Will Eat Itself - The Men From UNKLE*, Solesides, viewed 12 July 2019, <http://www.solesides.com/various-pop-will-eat-itself-the-men-from-unkle-urb-1098.html>.

UKBMXHistory, 2017, *Craig Campbell at the Wembley Lada Speedway International Indoor 1982 – BMX Weekly*, UKBMXHistory, viewed 14 July 2019, <https://www.ukbmxhistory.com/craig-campbell-at-the-wembley-lada-speedway-international-indoor-event-1982-bmx-weekly>.

Valadez, A 2018, *TuneIn Conversation: James Lavelle*, TuneIn, podcast, 20 November, viewed 12 January 2020, <https://tunein.com/podcasts/Music-Talk/TuneIn-Conversation-p1011712/?topicId=127214416>.

Vaziri, A 2006, *DJ Shadow: URB Magazine, July 2006*, Solesides, viewed 23 December 2019, <http://www.solesides.com/dj-shadow-article-urb-magazine-july-2006.html>.

Veekhoven, T 2014, *WAMPAS AND TAUNTAUNS AND DIANOGAS, OH MY: KENNER'S STAR WARS CREATURE TOYS*, Star Wars, viewed 12 July 2019, <https://www.starwars.com/news/wampas-tauntauns-dianogas-oh-my-kenner-star-wars-creature-toys>.

VOGUE Paris 2017, 'ATLANTIQUE, NOUVELLE VAGUE', *Press Reader*, 24 August, p. 178, viewed 25 February, <https://pressreader.com/article/281715499728164>.

Vintage Synth Explorer 2020, *E-mu SP-1200*, Vintage Synth Explorer, viewed 16 February 2020, <http://www.vintagesynth.com/emu/sp1200.php>.

Vital Distribution, 1994, *Forthcoming Shit!*, Vital Distribution, viewed 26 July 2019, <https://www.instagram.com/p/YsW28WEqlx>

Walters, B 1998, 'UNKLE', *Spin*, November, vol. 14, no. 11, pp.135-136.

Wang, G 2018, *Ancient to future: Interplanetary sounds in Straight No Chaser magazine*, Stack, viewed 13 June 2019, <https://www.stackmagazines.com/music/straight-no-chaser-magazine-paul-bradshaw>.

Warren, RB, 2014, 'The Flaw In The Force: The Star Wars Holiday Special', *The Weeklings*, viewed 25 January 2020, <https://theweeklings.com/rbwarren/2014/12/15/the-flaw-in-the-force-the-star-wars-holiday-special>

Waterman, R 1994, *Career Guide For Losers*, State 51, viewed 13 June 2019, <https://web.archive.org/web/19991011170349/http://www.state51.co.uk:80/phat/career0.html>.

Webb, P 2007, 'Once Upon A Time In Bristol', *The Wire*, October, no. 284, pp.36-43.

Weingarten, C 2017, *Kool G Rap on the Highly Technical Rap Style That Influenced Generations*, Rolling Stone, viewed 13 July 2019, <https://www.rollingstone.com/music/music-features/kool-g-rap-on-the-highly-technical-rap-style-that-influenced-generations-112844>.

Weiss, J 2017, 'The Human Abstract Poetic: A Tribute to David Axelrod', *Passion of the Weiss*, viewed 12 January 2020, <https://www.passionweiss.com/2017/02/06/david-axelrod-tribute>.

Werde, B 2002, 'The Shadow Knows', *CMJ New Music Monthly*, June, no. 102, pp.32-39

White, P 2010, '25 Products That Changed Recording - Alesis ADAT', *Sound on Sound*, viewed 12 July 2019, <https://www.soundonsound.com/reviews/25-products-changed-recording>.

WhoSampled 2019a, *Bloodstain by UNKLE feat. Alice Temple*, WhoSampled, viewed 11 November 2019, <https://www.whosampled.com/UNKLE/Bloodstain>.

WhoSampled 2019b, *Calling on the Dream Team by L.A. Dream Team*, WhoSampled, viewed 11 November 2019, <https://www.whosampled.com/L.A.-Dream-Team/Calling-on-the-Dream-Team>.

WhoSampled 2019c, *Countdown by Alan Hawkshaw*, WhoSampled, viewed 11 November 2019, <https://www.whosampled.com/Alan-Hawkshaw/Countdown>.

WhoSampled 2019d, *Garage Piano by UNKLE*, WhoSampled, viewed 11 November 2019, <https://www.whosampled.com/UNKLE/Garage-Piano>.

WhoSampled 2019e, *Guns Blazing (Drums of Death Pt. 1) by UNKLE feat. Kool G Rap*, WhoSampled, viewed 11 November 2019, <https://www.whosampled.com/UNKLE/Guns-Blazing-(Drums-of-Death-Pt.-1)>.

WhoSampled 2019f, *Kool G Rap feat. MF Grimm and B1 – 'Take 'Em to War' sample of David Alxelrod's 'A Divine Image'*, WhoSampled, viewed 12 January 2020, <https://www.whosampled.com/sample/24279/Kool-G-Rap-MF-Grimm-B1-Take-%27Em-to-War-David-Axelrod-A-Divine-Image>.

WhoSampled 2019g, *Nursery Rhyme/Breather by UNKLE feat. Badly Drawn Boy*, WhoSampled, viewed 11 November 2019, <https://www.whosampled.com/UNKLE/Nursery-RhymeBreather>.

WhoSampled 2019h, *Rabbit in Your Headlights by UNKLE feat. Thom Yorke*, WhoSampled, viewed 11 November 2019, <https://www.whosampled.com/UNKLE/Rabbit-in-Your-Headlights>.

WhoSampled 2019i, *Rock On by UNKLE*, WhoSampled, viewed 11 November 2019, <https://www.whosampled.com/UNKLE/Rock-On>.

WhoSampled 2019j, *Tracks Sampled in 'Best Foot Forward' by DJ Shadow*, WhoSampled, viewed 11 November 2019,

<https://www.whosampled.com/DJ-Shadow/Best-Foot-Forward/samples>.

WhoSampled 2019k, *Tracks Sampled in 'Celestial Annihilation' by UNKLE*, WhoSampled, viewed 11 November 2019, <https://www.whosampled.com/UNKLE/Celestial-Annihilation/samples>.

WhoSampled 2019l, *Tracks Sampled in 'Midnight in a Perfect World' by DJ Shadow*, WhoSampled, viewed 11 November 2019, <https://www.whosampled.com/DJ-Shadow/Midnight-in-a-Perfect-World/samples>

WhoSampled 2019m, *Tracks Sampled in 'The Knock (Drums of Death Pt. 2)' by UNKLE feat. Mike D*, WhoSampled, viewed 11 November 2019, <https://www.whosampled.com/UNKLE/The-Knock-(Drums-of-Death-Pt.-2)/samples>.

WhoSampled 2019n, *Tracks Sampled in 'Unkle (Main Title Theme)' by UNKLE*, WhoSampled, viewed 11 November 2019, <https://www.whosampled.com/UNKLE/Unkle-(Main-Title-Theme)/samples>.

WhoSampled 2019o, *UNKLE feat. Alice Temple's 'Bloodstain' sample of The The Grodeck Whipperjenny's 'Evidence for the Existance of the Unconscious'*, WhoSampled, viewed 11 November 2019, <https://www.whosampled.com/sample/22836/UNKLE-Alice-Temple-Bloodstain-The-Grodeck-Whipperjenny-Evidence-for-the-Existance-of-the-Unconscious>.

WhoSampled 2019p, *UNKLE feat. Kool G Rap's 'Guns Blazing (Drums of Death Pt. 1)' sample of Alan Hawkshaw's 'Countdown'*, WhoSampled, viewed 11 November 2019, <https://www.whosampled.com/sample/45436/UNKLE-Kool-G-Rap-Guns-Blazing-(Drums-of-Death-Pt.-1)-Alan-Hawkshaw-Countdown>.

WhoSampled 2019q, *UNKLE feat. Kool G Rap's 'Guns Blazing (Drums of Death Pt. 1)' sample of Frank Zappa's 'Apostrophe'*, WhoSampled, viewed 11 November 2019, <https://www.whosampled.com/sample/56487/UNKLE-Kool-G-Rap-Guns-Blazing-(Drums-of-Death-Pt.-1)-Frank-Zappa-Apostrophe>.

WhoSampled 2019r, *UNKLE feat. Kool G Rap's 'Guns Blazing (Drums of Death Pt. 1)' sample of Namco's 'Galaxian'*, WhoSampled, viewed 11 November 2019, <https://www.whosampled.com/sample/60912/UNKLE-Kool-G-Rap-Guns-Blazing-(Drums-of-Death-Pt.-1)-Namco-Galaxian>.

WhoSampled 2019s, *UNKLE feat. Kool G Rap's 'Guns Blazing (Drums of Death Pt. 1)' sample of Tullio De Piscopo's 'Medium Rock'*, WhoSampled, viewed 11 November 2019, <https://www.whosampled.com/sample/34729/UNKLE-Kool-G-Rap-Guns-Blazing-(Drums-of-Death-Pt.-1)-Tullio-De-Piscopo-Medium-Rock>.

WhoSampled 2019t, *UNKLE feat. Kool G Rap's 'Guns Blazing (Drums of Death Pt. 1)' sample of Wizard's 'Buffalo Station/Get on Down to Memphis'*, WhoSampled, viewed 11 November 2019, <https://www.whosampled.com/sample/150293/UNKLE-Kool-G-Rap-Guns-Blazing-(Drums-of-Death-Pt.-1)-Wizzard-Buffalo-StationGet-on-Down-to-Memphis>.

WhoSampled 2019u, *UNKLE feat. Richard Ashcroft's 'Lonely Soul' sample of Carmine Coppola's 'Do Lung Bridge'*, WhoSampled, viewed 11 November 2019, <https://www.whosampled.com/sample/197758/UNKLE-Richard-Ashcroft-Lonely-Soul-Carmine-Coppola-Do-Lung-Bridge>.

WhoSampled 2019v, *UNKLE feat. Richard Ashcroft's 'Lonely Soul' sample of Lionel Morton's 'Fearless Fred's Amazing Animal Band'*, WhoSampled, viewed 11 November 2019, <https://www.whosampled.com/sample/71663/UNKLE-Richard-Ashcroft-Lonely-Soul-Lionel-Morton-Fearless-Fred%27s-Amazing-Animal-Band>.

WhoSampled 2019w, *UNKLE feat. Richard Ashcroft's 'Lonely Soul' sample of Renaissance's 'Bullet'*, WhoSampled, viewed 11 November 2019, <https://www.whosampled.com/sample/484587/UNKLE-Richard-Ashcroft-Lonely-Soul-Renaissance-Bullet>.

WhoSampled 2019x, *UNKLE feat. Richard Ashcroft's 'Lonely Soul' sample of Shanti's 'Innocence'*, WhoSampled, viewed 11 November 2019, <https://www.whosampled.com/sample/253192/UNKLE-Richard-Ashcroft-Lonely-Soul-Shanti-Innocence>.

WhoSampled 2019y, *UNKLE feat. Thom Yorke's 'Rabbit in Your Headlights' sample of Arriving at the Machine scene in Contact*, WhoSampled, viewed 11 November 2019, <https://www.whosampled.com/sample/354487/UNKLE-Thom-Yorke-Rabbit-in-Your-Headlights-Contact-Arriving-at-the-Machine>.

WhoSampled 2019z, *UNKLE feat. Thom Yorke's 'Rabbit in Your Headlights' sample of Doctor's Speech scene in Jacob's Ladder*, WhoSampled, viewed 11 November 2019, <https://www.whosampled.com/sample/337771/UNKLE-Thom-Yorke-Rabbit-in-Your-Headlights-Jacob%27s-Ladder-Doctor%27s-Speech>.

WhoSampled 2019aa, *UNKLE feat. Thom Yorke's 'Rabbit in Your Headlights' sample of Dom & Ravel's 'Essa Menina Tá Ficando Moça'*, WhoSampled, viewed 11 November 2019, <https://www.whosampled.com/sample/586613/UNKLE-Thom-Yorke-Rabbit-in-Your-Headlights-Dom-%26-Ravel-Essa-Menina-Tá-Ficando-Moça>.

WhoSampled 2019bb, UNKLE's *'Berry Meditation' sample of Tonto's Expanding Head Band's 'Riversong'*, WhoSampled, viewed 11 November 2019, <https://www.whosampled.com/sample/200136/UNKLE-Berry-Meditation-Tonto%27s-Expanding-Head-Band-Riversong>.

WhoSampled 2019cc, *UNKLE's 'Celestial Annihilation' sample of Byron Davis & the Fresh Krew's 'Now Dance'*, WhoSampled, viewed 11 November 2019, <https://www.whosampled.com/sample/56581/UNKLE-Celestial-Annihilation-Byron-Davis-%26-the-Fresh-Krew-Now-Dance>.

WhoSampled 2019dd, *UNKLE's 'Celestial Annihilation' sample of Newcleus's 'Let's Jam'*, WhoSampled, viewed 11 November 2019, <https://www.whosampled.com/sample/56580/UNKLE-Celestial-Annihilation-Newcleus-Let%27s-Jam>.

WhoSampled 2019ee, *UNKLE's 'Unkle (Main Title Theme)' sample of Bass Dominators feat. M.C.C.'s 'Go Head, Go Head (Yo! Yo!)'*, WhoSampled, viewed 11 November 2019, <https://www.whosampled.com/sample/133281/UNKLE-Unkle-(Main-Title-Theme)-Bass-Dominators-M.C.C.-Go-Head,-Go-Head-(Yo!-Yo!)>.

WhoSampled 2019ff, *UNKLE's 'Unkle (Main Title Theme)' sample of There Were Too Many of Us scene in Hearts of Darkness: A Filmmaker's Apocalypse*, WhoSampled, viewed 11 November 2019, <https://www.whosampled.com/sample/286246/UNKLE-Unkle-(Main-Title-Theme)-Hearts-of-Darkness%3A-A-Filmmaker%27s-Apocalypse-There-Were-Too-Many-of-Us>.

WhoSampled 2019gg, *UNKLE's 'Unkle (Main Title Theme)' sample of Hubert J. Bernhard's 'The Planetarium Lecture Series: No. 3: The UFO's (Side 1)'*, WhoSampled, viewed 11 November 2019, <https://www.whosampled.com/sample/74655/UNKLE-Unkle-(Main-Title-Theme)-Hubert-J.-Bernhard-The-Planetarium-Lecture-Series%3A-No.-3%3A-The-UFO%27s-(Side-1)>.

WhoSampled 2019hh, *UNKLE's 'Unkle (Main Title Theme)' sample of Rage's 'A Pilgrim's Path'*, WhoSampled, viewed 11 November 2019, <https://www.whosampled.com/sample/160111/UNKLE-Unkle-(Main-Title-Theme)-Rage-A-Pilgrim%27s-Path>.

WhoSampled 2019ii, *UNKLE's 'Unkle (Main Title Theme)' sample of The Luv Bandits's 'Mizzer Bahd'*, WhoSampled, viewed 11 November 2019, <https://www.whosampled.com/sample/58710/UNKLE-Unkle-(Main-Title-Theme)-The-Luv-Bandits-Mizzer-Bahd>.

WhoSampled 2019jj, *UNKLE's 'Unkle (Main Title Theme)' sample of TV Promo scene in The Twilight Zone*, WhoSampled, viewed 11 November 2019, <https://www.whosampled.com/sample/348105/UNKLE-Unkle-(Main-Title-Theme)-The-Twilight-Zone-TV-Promo>.

WhoSampled 2019kk, *UNKLE's 'Unreal' sample of The Eclectic Mouse's 'Pre-Dawn Retrospective Chant'*, WhoSampled, viewed 11 November 2019, <https://www.whosampled.com/sample/34730/UNKLE-Unreal-The-Eclectic-Mouse-Pre-Dawn-Retrospective-Chant>.

WhoSampled 2019ll, *UNKLE's 'Unreal' sample of The Jules Blattner Group's 'Birth'*, WhoSampled, viewed 11 November 2019, <https://www.whosampled.com/sample/34736/UNKLE-Unreal-The-Jules-Blattner-Group-Birth>.

WhoSampled 2020a, *Ape Shall Never Kill Ape by UNKLE*, WhoSampled, viewed 27 March 2020, <https://www.whosampled.com/UNKLE/Ape-Shall-Never-Kill-Ape/>.

WhoSampled 2020b, *Judy Goes on Holiday by Supersister*, WhoSampled, viewed 9 February 2020, <https://www.whosampled.com/Supersister/Judy-Goes-on-Holiday>.

WhoSampled 2020c, *Spinners by UNKLE*, WhoSampled, viewed 23 March 2020, < https://www.whosampled.com/UNKLE/Spinners>.

WhoSampled 2020d, *UNKLE feat. Ian Brown's 'Be There' sample of sample of Terry Callier's 'Dancing Girl'*, WhoSampled, viewed 24 February 2020, <https://www.whosampled.com/sample/55654/UNKLE-Ian-Brown-Be-There-Terry-Callier-Dancing-Girl>.

WhoSampled 2020e, *UNKLE's 'Unkle (Main Title Theme)' sample of Fiery the Angels Fell scene in Blade Runner*, WhoSampled, viewed 9 February 2020, <https://www.whosampled.com/sample/347646/UNKLE-Unkle-(Main-Title-Theme)-Blade-Runner-Fiery-the-Angels-Fell>.

WhoSampled 2020f, *Unreal by UNKLE*, WhoSampled, viewed 26 February 2020, <https://www.whosampled.com/UNKLE/Unreal>.

Wikipedia 2019, *Coast to Coast AM*, Wikipedia, viewed 24 December 2019, <https://en.wikipedia.org/w/index.php?title=Coast_to_Coast_AM&oldid=930744130>.

Wikipedia 2020, *1983 in British music*, Wikipedia, viewed 25 January 2020, <https://en.wikipedia.org/w/index.php?title=1983_in_British_music&oldid=928073989>.

Wilder, E 2017, *Endtroducing*, Bloomsbury, New York.

Williams, E 2017, *James Lavelle on Mo' Wax, UNKLE and the importance of design*, Creative Review, viewed 9 May 2019, <https://www.creativereview.co.uk/james-lavelle-importantce-of-design>.

Willoughby, G n.d., *BladeZone Presents: Deconstructing the Spinner*, BladZone, viewed March 28 2020, <http://media.bladezone.com/contents/film/interviews/gene-winfield>.

Willmott, B 1996, 'Talkin' about Mo' generation', *Vox*, March, p. 44-50

Wines, B 2016, *Interview / Jean-Benoit Dunckel / AIR*, Test Pressing, viewed 15 July 2019, <http://testpressing.org/2016/06/interview-jean-benoit-dunckel-air>.

Winston, D 2017, 'Breakbeat Samurai', *Wax Poetics*, vol. 1, no. 66, pp.51-59

Wilson, R 2014, *Route One October 2014*, Route One, viewed 10 April 2018, <http://direct.routeone.co.uk/files/data/search.xml>.

Wookieepedia 2019, *Dewback*, Wookieepedia, viewed 27 July 2019, <https://starwars.fandom.com/wiki/Dewback?oldid=8337651>.

Worldwide BAPE Heads Show 1998, *YouTube*, viewed 18 February 2020, <https://youtu.be/U04dvCiSZRY>.

Wustemann, L 2019, 'James Lavelle: living with contemporary art', *Financial Times*, 5 April, viewed 12 February 2020, <https://www.ft.com/content/0c776a98-548f-11e9-8b71-f5b0066105fe>.

Wu'Matt 2008, *Unkle Samples for download*, U77 Forum, 3 March, viewed 12 January 2020, <http://unkle77.proboards.com/post/34683>.

Wright, R 2017, 'James Lavelle', *Q Magazine*, September, pp. 87-91.

Yellow Peril, 1995, 'Straight To The Headz', *Snarl Texts*, viewed July 8 2019, <http://www.snarl.org/texts/features/James.htm>.

Yoshioka, K 2018, *高木完&K.U.D.O、メジャー・フォース「30年目の真実」（前編）*, Honeyee, viewed 24 June 2019, <https://www.honeyee.com/feature/art-culture/001911>.

Young, R 1998, 'UNKLE – Psyence Fiction', The Wire, August, vol. 1, no. 174, p.69

Yu, S 2019, *How Hiroshi Fujiwara Set The Template For Streetwear Culture*, Farfetch, viewed 24 June 2019, <https://www.farfetch.com/hk/style-guide/icons-influencers/hiroshi-fujiwara-streetwear-culture>.

Zen <solesides@aol.com> 1996, 'DJ Shadow - Trip Hop?', Google Groups, March 20, *rec.music.hip-hop*, viewed 25 June 2019, <https://groups.google.com/d/msg/rec.music.hip-hop/2Bh_tkFHuOA/4ffRNpsQwx8J>.

Appendix: Timeline 1973-2003

1973

January 1 1973 - Josh Davis born, Hayward California, USA.

1974

February 22 1974 - James Lavelle born Oxford, England.

1982

James Lavelle first hears Hip Hop played in his school hall accompanied by a breakdance performance.

1983

James Lavelle buys his first hip hop cassettes, Slick Rick and Grandmaster Flash.

1984

James Lavelle meets and befriends Tim Goldsworthy who is 12 years old, two years older than Lavelle.

1986

James Lavelle's parents separate, and he starts skipping school.

James Lavelle watches Stanley Kubrick's *2001 A Space Odyssey* for the first time.

1987

James Lavelle watches the documentary *Bombin* on Channel 4.

1988

James Lavelle's grandmother Dorothy enrols him at the Oxford Cello School for a one-week course, as she wanted some help with his teaching.

Lavelle starts DJing as part of a sound system in Oxford called The Underground Movement.

Lavelle begins work experience with Bluebird Records for one week, this extends for two years working on weekends until their shops closed down.

Lavelle goes to see Soul II Soul versus Shock Sound System, a gig he later described as "the most important gig I went to see…when I was 14."

1989

January - Swifty starts working as Art Director at *Straight No Chaser Magazine.*

James Lavelle Starts calling himself Holygoof after reading Jack Kerouac's *The Road*.

1990

Bluebird Records closes down.

James Lavelle begins Business Studies at the Oxford College of Further Education.

Lavelle begins work experience at Honest Jon's Records.

Lavelle leaves college and gets full time work at Honest Jon's Records.

Lavelle first hears DJ Shadow's remix of *Zimbabwe Legit*.

1991

James Lavelle contributes Jazz Charts to *Echoes* for Honest Johns.

Lavelle begins writing for *Straight No Chaser* and contributes to *I-D Magazine*.

Lavelle starts the Mo' Wax Please nights at The Venue, Oxford and reconnects with Tim Goldsworthy on the clubs opening night.

DJ Shadow releases *Lesson Four*.

May - Shadow has a letter regarding racial politics in hip hop music published in *Source Magazine*.

May 23 - Galliano plays at Mo' Wax Please.

June - Shadow appears in *Source Magazine*'s Unsigned Hype section after he sends them a mixtape.

November 19 - Mo' Wax Please Presents The Talking Loud Sessions, featuring Patrick Forge, James Lavelle, and Mathew Kershaw.

1992

James Lavelle borrows £1000 and Mo' Wax Records is founded, with the first three releases coming out in 1992.

Tycoon Tosh aka Nakanishi Toshio moves to England with Masayuki Kudo, and they meet Lavelle at Honest Jon's.

First Men From UNKLE remix released.

DJ Shadow meets Dan the Automator.

February - James Lavelle turns 18 years old.

May - Solesides Records formed with DJ Shadow and friends.

May 26 - Shadow buys his first sampler, the MPC 60 mk II.

June 19 - James Lavelle plays The Groove Academy, New York.

August 22 - Lavelle DJs at Talkin' Summer at The Fridge.

October - The first Mo' Wax release by Repercussions comes out.

November - Lavelle calls DJ Shadow and they talk about music and movies.

1993

That's How It Is! club night started by Gilles Peterson and James Lavelle at Bar Rumba, London.

Mo' Wax has sixteen releases across 1993.

James Lavelle flies to LA and meets DJ Shadow in person for the first time. Shadow plays him a cassette of David Axelrod.

London Records offers Lavelle £25,000 for a licensing deal with Mo' Wax. Lavelle declines.

February – DJ Shadow releases *Entropy* on his Solesides label, credited to DJ Shadow & The Groove Robbers.

August 27 - Lavelle plays Mo' Wax night in Berlin.

August 27-29 - Futura takes part in the 1st Cycle Messenger Championship Berlin. He also takes part in a graffiti demonstration with Stash, and meets James Lavelle.

October – Lavelle features in Issue 3 of *Phat Magazine*, with the article 'Career Guide To Losers'. Lavelle meets Ben Drury because of this article.

November 15 – DJ Shadow's *In/Flux* released on Mo' Wax.

November - Shadow and Lavelle tour Germany. Shadow is studying communications at the time and has to fax his homework back to America.

November 22 - DJ Shadow guests at That's How It Is.

December - Lavelle Goes to Japan as part of Straight No Chaser's "Skoolin' Da Jaz" Tour and meets members of Major Force and DJ Krush.

1994

Mo' Wax address: 73-75 Mortimer Street, London W1N 7TB.

Mo' Wax release 45 items this yea.

Mo' Wax makes its first profit on Federation's album *Flower to the Sun*.

James Lavelle meets Richard File in Brighton.

James Lavelle features on a cassette promoting nightclub That's How It Is with Giles Peterson.

Lavelle stops using the name Holygoof.

May 12 - Lavelle DJs at 'The Shape of Things To Come - Chapter 2", also features DJ Shadow, and DJ Krush who has signed to Mo' Wax.

May 28 - *Melody Maker* announces Lavelle has set up a new label called Smoke Filled Thoughts with London Records.

June - DJ Shadow's *What Does Your Soul Look Like EP* released.

June 20 - *The Time Has Come* released as Major Force EMS Orchestra VS UNKLE. It reaches #1 on the British Indie Charts.

June 22 - James Lavelle DJs at Beastie Boys gig at The Astoria, London.

October 1 - *LOST AND FOUND (S.F.L.)/KEMURI* by DJ Shadow/DJ Krush will enter the UK Singles Charts at #84, before dropping back out again.

October 31 - *Headz* released.

November 20-25 - Lavelle set to DJ for Beastie Boys but show is cancelled due to injury of Eric Bobo, the Beastie Boys percussionist. Rescheduled for 3rd and 4th of March 1995

November 23 - Lavelle DJs at LFO gig, with Autechre and Nightmares on Wax at the Leisure Lounge.

November 25 - "Independants Day" article in *New Statesman & Society* says that Lavelle has signed a deal with Virgin that will allow him to start new labels for them, both major and independent.

November 26 - *Headz* enters the UK Compilation Charts at #36 before dropping out again.

1995

Mo' Wax address: 167 Caledonian Road, London, N1.

MW releases around 50 items this year.

Futura visits London to work on paintings for Mo' Wax.

Lavelle introduces Nigo to Futura and Stash.

Lavelle starts Dusted club night.

January 21 - *The Time Has Come EP* is the first Mo' Wax release to enter the Album Charts, spending one week at #73 before dropping out again.

January 31 - Mike D sends Lavelle a fax regarding a *Mo' Wax Vs Grand Royal* album.

March 3-4 - Lavelle DJ's at the rescheduled Beastie Boys gigs.

March 16 - *Dewback* released on *110 Below, Volume 2: Trip to the cHIP sHOP*.

March 20 - Massive Attack - *Karmacoma (UNKLE remix)* released. Credited by Goldsworthy, Kudo and Lavelle, and featuring scratches by DJ shadow.

March 25 - DJ Shadow's *What Does Your Soul Look Like* enters the Singles Top 100 at #59, before dropping to #97 in its second week, and then out of the charts.

April - Mo' Wax move in to new offices, includes three studios for Major Force West, Tim Goldsworthy, and Howie B. Plans for recording an Unkle album in LA begin.

April / May - DJ Shadow, DJ Krush and James Lavelle start their BATTLE ROYAL tour of Japan.

June - The July issue of *Muzik* features an advertisement for the UNKLE album.

June - Rammellzee is flown to UK to record UNKLE's *Rock On*.

June 28 - Rammellzee is interviewed at Mo' Wax offices.

August - Paperwork was signed for Steve Finan to take 50% ownership of MoWax Headz Limited.

August 14 - A&M approve budget for UNKLE sessions in LA.

September - UNKLE sessions begin in LA. Tim Goldsworthy brings a tape by The Psychonauts to LA and Lavelle decides to sign them to Mo' Wax. Goldsworthy also plays The Verve's *History* and Lavelle decides he wants to work with Richard Ashcroft.

September - Lavelle models t-shirts in September issue of I-D alongside his brother Henry.

September 23 - Lavelle hosts DJ Krush's *Meiso* album launch party at his Dusted club night.

October - Lavelle approaches Richard Ashcroft about collaborating.

December - Lavelle appears in 'A Year In The Life' in *Muzik* Jan 1996, says "It was great to hear there's a new Star Wars film on the way."

December - DJ Shadow DJ's at Australian Summersault Tour alongside the Mo' Wax Headz Tour featuring Money Mark, Shadow and Lavelle.

1996

Mo' Wax Arts started early 1996 as an unofficial arm of Mo' Wax.

Mo' Wax release a merchandise catalogue including t-shirts, and a record bag.

Mo' Wax places an advertisement in Grand Royal Magazine #3 (page 8) announcing *Mo' Wax Vs Grand Royal* is coming soon.

Lavelle models in a fashion show for Yoshi Yamamoto in Paris.

Mo' Wax puts out over 100 releases, including CD's, Cassette's, Records and promos.

January - Australian Summersault Tour & Mo' Wax Headz Tour continues. Featuring DJ Shadow, James Lavelle, Charlie from Atticus Blue, and Money Mark.

January - After Australian tour Shadow goes back to finishing *Endtroducing.....*

April - In the May issue of *Muzik* (released in April) Lavelle announces he is closing his Excursions subsidiary label after it's 10th release. He also announced they will license the Dr Octagon album and have recently signed drum and bass artist Preshay.

April 21 - *BBC Radio 1* airs "The Mo'Wax Story".

April 29 - The Dust Brothers announce their intention to sign with Mo' Wax due to the attraction of the "total freedom" Lavelle gives his artists, but no album ever eventuates.

May 20 - *The Time Has Come EP* is reissued on LP and CD by Mo' Wax as part of a Reissue Series.

June - DJ Shadow finishes *Endtroducing.....*

June 7 - Shadow and Lavelle play the opening of Lavelle's new club night Basiks. The night runs the first Friday of every month at Gossips Nightclub.

June 24 - *Cream Live II* released.

July 13 - Lavelle starts Dusted 2 'The Bounty Hunter Sessions' at The Blue Note on Saturdays.

August - Lavelle asks DJ Shadow to produce the UNKLE album.

August 13 - *Endtroducing.....* test pressing pressed.

August 20 - *Headz 2A* (featuring UNKLE's *Garage Piano*) test pressing pressed.

September - Lavelle features on the cover of *Jockey Slut Magazine*.

September - *Lonely Soul* first vocal recorded at Olympic Studios. *Untitled Heavy Beat* also recorded at these sessions.

September 16 - *Endtroducing.....* released in UK

September 28 - *Endtroducing* enters UK Album Charts.

September - Lavelle is mocked in the October issue of *Muzik* for sporting a red mohawk hairstyle.

October 4 - Lavelle DJs at Voyager for *Tribal Gathering 96* CD Launch.

November - Alice Temple records *Bloodstain* demo at The Strongroom, East London.

November - Interviews with Lavelle appear on *Mushroom Jazz* CD-ROM.

November 9 - *NME* reports Noel Gallagher has been asked by DJ Shadow to remix one of his songs.

November 14 - Test Pressing of *Berry Meditation* pressed.

November 19 - *Endtroducing...* released in US.

December - Tim Goldsworthy leaves UNKLE.

December 12 - Nature Boy (KUDO & Tim From U·N·K·L·E Remix) released on Kodama & Gota's *Something Remix* album.

1997

Mo' Wax address: 96/98 Baker Street, London, W1M 1LA.

In early 1997 James Lavelle plays a "Best of 96" set on GLR 94.9FM, the predecessor to *BBC London Radio*.

In mid 97 Mo' Wax send an 8 page newsletter promotional booklet out to fans. It contains announcements for future releases such as Luke Vibert, Attica Blues, Dj Shadow, Deborah Anderson, and hints of a *Grand Royal vs Mo' Wax* release, as well as *Headz 3*.

Grand Royal Magazine #5 page 58, features article by DJ Shadow on Miami Bass.

Lavelle becomes a father to Llyla-Blue with partner Janet Fischgrund.

Nigo starts recording his solo album in the Major Force West studio, recording one track each time he visits London.

January - Mo' Wax takes part in a Video Game tournament in *Muzik* Magazine's February issue. Their team is called 'MoWax Bounty Hunters'. Others competing include Massive Attack's 3D,

Carl Cox, Liam Howlett of The Prodigy, Metalheadz, and Dave Clark.

January 9 - Test Pressing for UNKLE's *Rock On* pressed.

February - Lavelle celebrates his 24th birthday at London's Met Bar with Noel Gallagher, Richard Ashcroft, Ian Brown, Carl Craig, Alexander McQueen, and "an Everest of cocaine."

February - *Berry Meditation* released.

March - Lavelle announces in April's issue of *Muzik* that he wants to record at Skywalker Sound Studios.

March 8 - *Endtroducing* enters the Billboard Heatseekers Top 50 at #50.

March 15 - *Berry Meditation* peaks at #77 and spends one week in UK Singles Charts.

March 15 - *Endtroducing* rises to #46 in the Billboard Heatseekers Top 50.

March 22 - *Endtroducing* falls to #47 in the Billboard Heatseekers Top 50.

March 30 - DJ Shadow tours USA. He plays unreleased UNKLE work. The tour is shared with Jeru The Damaja, and later De La Soul in April.

April 5 - *Endtroducing* rises to #43 to re-enter to Billboard Heatseekers Top 50.

April 12 - *Endtroducing* drops to #44 in the Billboard Heatseekers Top 50.

April 19 - *Endtroducing* rises to #43 in the Billboard Heatseekers Top 50.

April 21 - DJ Shadow appears at a record store in NYC for a set and invites fans to bring in records that will be difficult for him to mix. Before the set *MTV* set up a meeting between Shadow and Grandmaster Flash.

April 26 - *Endtroducing* rises to #37 in the Billboard Heatseekers Top 50. This is its highest position and the last time it charts.

May 20 - UNKLE's Can remix of *Vitamin C* released on remix album *Sacrelige*.

June - For the July issue of *Muzik* Lavelle reviews two Star Wars games on PlayStation.

June 8 - Thom Yorke meets with DJ Shadow.

July - Ian Brown calls Lavelle to say he won't appear on the UNKLE album.

July - Thom Yorke records vocals for *Rabbit In Your Headlights* between Radiohead's tour dates.

August - *Bloodstain* and *Chaos* vocals recorded at Metropolis Studios, Chiswick.

August 7 - Mo' Wax and Japanese label Toy's Factory hold a Mo' Wax Japan party featuring DJ sets by James Lavelle with Kan Takagi, Nigo, and DJ Shadow with Lyrics Born and Latif.

September - Will Malone arranges strings for *Lonely Soul* which are recorded at CTS North-West London with the London Session Orchestra.

September - The piano on *Chaos* is recorded.

September 29 - DJ Shadow's *High Noon* is released as a single in the UK.

October - *Guns Blazing (Drums of Death Part 1)* vocals recorded with Kool G Rap in San Francisco.

October 1 - *James vs. Nigo – A Bathing Ape Vs Mo'Wax* released in Japan.

November 17 - Lavelle and Shadow open for Radiohead. Shadow plays UNKLE demos in his set.

December 8 - DJ Shadow and QBert's *Camel Bobsled Race* is released in the UK.

1998

January - DJ Shadows's Solesides label closes, reborn as Quannum.

January - Shadow rumoured to be involved in a Prince Paul album entitled *The Good The Bad and The Ugly*, with Dan The Automator and Mike Simpson from the Dust Brothers. Also rumoured to include RZA, Beck, De La Soul and Björk. The album ends up being shelved.

January 13 - *Pre-emptive Strike* released in US.

January 31 - *Preemptive Strike* enters the Billboard Heatseekers Top 50 at #1.

February - Badly Drawn Boy records vocals for *Nursery Rhyme* at Brilliant, San Francisco.

February - Jason Newstead records bass and Theremin for *The Kock* at The Plant, San Francisco.

February 7 - *Preemptive Strike* drops to #4 in the Billboard Heatseekers Top 50.

February 9 - Shadow is nominated for "Best International Male" at the Brit Awards. Running against Jon Bon Jovi, Coolio, LL Cool J, and DJ Sash.

February 14 - *Preemptive Strike* drops to #11 in the Billboard Heatseekers Top 50.

February 18 - Shadow receives a fax from his manager about working on a solo album for Zach De La Rocha. The sessions eventually happen in 2003.

February 21 - Lavelle and The Psychonauts host a Mo' Wax Night at Nitsa Club in Barcelona.

February 21 - *Rock On, Ape Shall Never Kill Ape, Last Orgy 3* CDs released in Japan.

February 21 - *Preemptive Strike* drops to #14 in the Billboard Heatseekers Top 50. This is its final appearance in the charts.

March - Mike D's *The Knock (Drums of Death Part 2)* vocals arrive from New York.

March - Shadow tells Lavelle they need to finish the album now as he has other things he wants to work on.

March - Ian Brown mentions in *Mojo Magazine* that he intends to work with UNKLE.

March 20 - *Billboard* reports that Shadow has started a new label called Quannum, after shutting Solesides.

March 21 - *Trilogy Box Set* released in Japan, containing *Rock On, Ape Shall Never Kill Ape, Last Orgy 3*.

March 27 - MTV Europe host a two-hour program dedicated to Mo' Wax, featuring interviews with Shadow and Lavelle.

April - Money Mark figure releases as promo for Marks' *Push The Button* album releasing May 4.

April - The May issue of *Spin* names Shadow as #26 in the Top 40 DJs, up from #29 in 1997.

April - *Celestial Annihilation* and *UNKLE Main Title Theme* recorded at DJ Shadows home studio near San Francisco.

May 9 - *Music Week* reports that Osman Eralp has left A&M. His resigning causes a domino effect that ends with Mo' Wax falling apart.

May 24 - Shadow and Lavelle support The Verve as DJs at Wigan England Haigh Hall.

June 2 - *Psyence Fiction* is being sequenced. Lavelle and Shadow then fly to Japan to promote *Psyence Fiction* and take part in a photoshoot.

June - Lavelle DJs at a Beastie Boys UK tour aftershow and plays *Guns Blazing*. After the set, Lavelle hands out a finished copy of the album to a reporter from *Jockey Slut* who has been interviewing him for a feature on the album.

June 16 - *Psyence Fiction's* release date of August 24th announced by *NME*.

June 22 - *BBC* debut *Lonely Soul* on the radio.

June 29 - *Psyence Fiction Survival Kit* promo 12" released with *Rabbit in the Headlights*, *Guns Blazing*, *Unreal*, and a 5" vinyl included in the pop-up format with *Nursery Rhyme*.

July - *Psyence Fiction* album is played in public for the first time at the Viper Room club in LA. Promos of the album start to be received by press.

July - *Straight No Chaser's* Great Day in Hoxton photo taken one Sunday.

July 23 - Lavelle and Shadow appear at the New York release/listening party for *Psyence Fiction* at Lot 61.

July 23 - *Pre-emptive Strike* released in Japan.

August - *Grand Royal Vs Mo' Wax* release was scheduled for August 1998, but never happened.

August 5 - Lavelle and Shadow co-present *The Evening Session* on *BBC Radio 1*.

August 21 - *Psyence Fiction* released in Japan.

August 23 - *Psyence Fiction* UK launch party at HMV. Album played in full at 10pm, Lavelle and Shadow performing solo DJ sets from 11pm. Futura2000 creates a live painting during the night, and at midnight the album is available to buy. Lavelle and Shadow stay till 3am to sign copies.

August 24 - *Psyence Fiction* released in UK.

August 25 - *Rabbit In Your Headlights* single released in UK. The 12" UK version came with an UNKLE dot to dot activity sheet, labelled as #1 of 3.

September - UNKLE American Tour Announced.

September - *Psyence Fiction* is nominated for Best Album by readers of *Muzik Magazine*. Going up against Air, Massive Attack, and Beastie Boys.

September 1 - Lavelle DJ's at Viper Room alongside Mario C, and The Psychonauts.

September 2 - Latryx releases *Lady Don't Tek No*, produced by DJ Shadow.

September 5 - *Psyence Fiction* enters UK Album Charts, peaks at #4 and spends 14 weeks in UK Top 100 charts.

September 8 - James Lavelle appears on *The Breezeblock* program on *BBC Radio 1*.

September 9 - *MTV2* in UK show a documentary entitled *The UNKLE Probe*.

September 12 - *Psyence Fiction* #12 on UK Top 100 charts.

September 13 - *The Knock* is featured in the Saporro Beer Tokio Hot 100 at #16.

September 19 - *Psyence Fiction* #26 on UK Top 100 charts.

September 22 - Mo' Wax Night in Tokyo. Lavelle brings out Kan Takagi to perform *Last Orgy 3* and Shadow plays a reconstructed version of *Psyence Fiction* using the tour vinyl.

September 25 - *MTV.com* post an interview with Lavelle and Shadow from their *MTV News* program.

September 26 - *Psyence Fiction* #32 on UK Top 100 charts.

September 28 - *Psyence Fiction* American five date tour begins in L.A. at the Virgin Sunset at midnight. During the set Shadow threw copies of the 12"'s he was using into the crowd. They contained instrumental and accapella versions of the songs on the album. He told a fan there were only 25 of these made.

September 29 - 1998 *Psyence Fiction* released in America.

September 29 - Lavelle appears on *KCRW* to promote the UNKLE album and tour.

October - MTV Europe start playing the *Rabbit In Your Headlights* video.

October 2 - UNKLE US Tour ends in Austin, Texas.

October 3, *Psyence Fiction* #44 on UK Top 100 charts.

October 9 - *Rabbit In Your Headlights* CD single released in UK.

October 10 - *Psyence Fiction* #65 on UK Top 100 charts.

October 12 - *Guns Blazing* promo released in USA.

October 17 - *Psyence Fiction* enters the Billboard Heatseekers Chart at #1, and #107 in the Billboard Top 200.

October 17 - *Psyence Fiction* #82 UK Top 100 charts.

October 19 - DJ Shadow DJs at the Grog Shop, Cleveland Heights. Latyrx and Blackalicious open.

October 21 - Noel Gallagher works on his remix of *Drums of Death*.

October 23 - Ian Brown sent back to prison. He recorded his vocals for *Be There* in his home studio right before this after Lavelle sent him a DAT with the instrumental.

October 24 - *Psyence Fiction* drops to #11 in the Billboard Heatseekers Chart in its second week, and to #171 in the Billboard Top 200. This is its final appearance in the Billboard Top 200.

October 24 - *Psyence Fiction* #64 in UK Top 100 charts.

October 31 - *Psyence Fiction* drops to #15 in the Heatseekers Chart in its third week.

October 31 - *Psyence Fiction* #76 UK Top 100 charts. This is its final week charting in the UK in 1998. It will re-enter the charts again in February 1999.

November - *Rabbit In Your Headlights* gets awarded Video Of The Month in *Muzik's* December issue.

November 7 - *Psyence Fiction* drops to #19 in the Heatseekers Chart in its fourth week.

November 14 - *Psyence Fiction* drops to # 28 in the Heatseekers Chart in it's 5th week.

November 14 - *Music Week* announce Mo' Wax have signed long term deal with XL Recordings, the Beggars Banquet subsidiary that is home to artists including Prodigy and Badly Drawn Boy. Elsewhere in the magazine, James Lavelle and Scratch Perverts discuss touring.

November 21 - *Psyence Fiction* Drops to #41 in the Billboard Heatseekers Chart. This is its final appearance in the chart.

November 21 - *Rabbit In Your Headlights* single released in Japan.

November 30 - Major Force West *93-97* album scheduled to be released.

December 1 - BBC start playing *Be There*.

December - The January 1999 Issue of *Muzik* claims Lavelle was paid £400,000 as part of the XL / Mo 'Wax deal.

December - The Jungle Brothers announce their next album will feature beats from DJ Shadow. In 1999 they release their album *VIP* which does not feature Shadow.

December 12 - Lavelle plays the *Worldwide Bapeheads Show* with Cornelius, Scha Dara Parr, Ben Lee, Money Mark in Tokyo. Their set features a live performance of *Last Orgy 3*.

1999

Mo' Wax address: Ground Floor 25 Heathmans Road, London, SW6 4TJ.

Nigo's *Ape Sounds* released by Toy's Factory, and Nigo starts his own record label.

January - In the February issue of *Muzik*, James Lavelle is named #31 in their list of the 50 Most Powerful People In Dance Music.

January 9 - UNKLE nominated for best Dance Act and Best Album at 1999 NME Brat Awards.

January 10-24 - UNKLE take part in the NME National Tour supported by Llama Farmers, Delakota, and Idlewild.

January 16 - *Music Week* announces Domino have signed Tim and Kudo under the name Flacco.

January 18 - *Be There* released on two CD singles in UK.

January 24 - UNKLE's play at The Astoria on the last night of the NME National Tour which features the first live appearance of Ian Brown since his arrest last year.

January 26 - *The NME Premiere Review*, a one-hour TV program from *Channel 4*, is shown at five Virgin Cinemas in UK. The program features a recording of live performances from various acts, including UNKLE. James Lavelle is also interviewed, with the clip available to stream from the NME website in 1999.

January 27 - *The NME Premiere Review* airs on *Channel 4* at 11:30pm.

February 1 - The Scratch Perverts and Lavelle perform on *Breezeblock*. The mix later appears on the 2004 bootleg *WWIII*.

February 2 - *Be There* enters UK Singles Top 100 Chart at #8 where it peaks. It spends 6 weeks in the Top 100 all together before leaving again.

February 4 - The fifth Heineken Weekender in Galway features a Mo' Wax Records Night featuring UNKLE, James Lavelle and The Scratch Perverts. DJ Shadow also makes a cameo appearance during the night.

February 6 - *Psyence Fiction* re-enters UK Top 100 Album Charts at #57

February 6 - *BBC 4* airs UNKLE's performance from January at the Astoria at 12:35am.

February 13 - *Psyence Fiction* #71 UK Top 100 charts.

February 18 - Shadow and Lavelle take part in a live chat on the *Top Of The Pops* website at 5pm.

February 19 - James Lavelle, DJ Shadow, and Ian Brown perform *Be There* on *Top of the Pops*.

February 20 - *Psyence Fiction* #80 UK Top 100 charts.

February 20 - DJ Shadow plays with Latyrx and Blackalicious at Justice League in San Francisco.

February 26 - Shadow and Cut Chemist play The 45 Sessions, which spawns their later *Brainfreeze* release and tour.

February 27 - *Psyence Fiction* #81 UK Top 100 charts. *Be There* #20 UK Singles Top 100 Chart.

March 6 - *Psyence Fiction* #84 UK Top 100 charts. This is its last appearance in the UK Album Charts. *Be There* #29 UK Singles Top 100 Chart.

March 13 - *Be There* #45 UK Singles Top 100 Chart.

March 20 - *Be There* #67 UK Singles Top 100 Chart.

March 27 - *Be There* #75 UK Singles Top 100 Chart. This is its final appearance in the UK charts.

April 3 - Lavelle plays at Nowere 6th Birthday party, Japan.

April 10 - Shadow takes part in a webchat for the fansite *Entroducing.com*, he mentions that UNKLE got in trouble for some uncleared samples on *Psyence Fiction* but doesn't elaborate.

April 21 - Quannum/Latyrx/Shadow begin UK tour with set in Bristol at Blue Mountain.

April 21 - *Be There* released in Japan

April 23 - *Art of War* show featuring Lavelle, Blackalicious, Shadow, Latyrx, The Psychonauts, Scratch Perverts, Mo' Wax Night at the Scala club, London.

May - MWA (Mo' Wax Arts) renamed Mo' Wax Associated and fully incorporated into Mo' Wax Labels Ltd.

May 4 - Lavelle and Nigo host an Ape VS Mo' Wax night at Kyoto Lab Tribe, Japan.

May 29 - DJ Shadow and UNKLE both play Homelands.

July 27 - Quannum's *Spectrum* compilation is released featuring Shadow.

July 31 - Shadow takes part in a second webchat with members of *Entroducing.com*. He mentions that he decided he wouldn't cut his hair until the UNKLE album was complete, and Lyrics Born sent a photo of Shadow with his long hair to be included in the artwork for Quannum's *Spectrum* album.

September 9 - *Rabbit In Your Headlights* is nominated for Breakthrough Video at the 1999 MTV Music Video Awards in New York. It loses to Fatboy Slim's *Praise You*.

September 17 - Lavelle starts new club called Vecta with The Psychonauts at the Electrowerkz in Islington, London.

October 18 - DJ Shadow and Cut Chemist play Philedelphia. Cut Chemist has his records stolen and is unable to play. They are later returned in December.

October 19 - Handsome Boy Modelling School's *So..Hows your Girl* album released in US. The album features DJ Shadow.

December 7 - Lavelle plays *Be There* on Ian Brown's tour at the Brixton Academy.

2000

James Lavelle moves in with Richard File, in a flat on Old Street, London.

Mo' Wax release the Futura book.

January 18 - DJ Shadow and Cut Chemist perform a "farewell" show in LA as part of their Brainfreeze tour. The show is recorded, and the video is streamed live as a webcast on the Jurassic 5 website.

February - In the March issue of *Muzik*, Lavelle is named #51 in their list of most powerful people in Dance Music (down from #31 last year). Blurb notes that UNKLE's *Psyence Fiction* album has sold half a million copies.

February 1 - UNKLE nominated at BRIT Awards as Best British Newcomer.

March - Lavelle records the soundtrack to Jonathan Glazer's *Sexy Beast* film. The soundtrack was recorded between Lavelle and members of the band South over eight days.

June - Lavelle announces residency at Fabric with The Scratch Perverts.

July 1 - DJ Shadow plays at Thud Rumble in San Fran. The show is later released on VHS.

August 23 - *Art of War* mix released, features DJ Shadow's UNKLE demo *Untitled Heavy Beat*.

September - It is announced that the *Entroducing* album has entered the 2001 Guinness World Records. The album is awarded First Completely Sampled Album.

September 17 - Vecta club night launched by James Lavelle.

September 25 - Nigo's *Ape Sounds* released in UK by Mo' Wax.

September 29 - *Dark Days* film begins showing in US. The soundtrack features DJ Shadow and includes new and old tracks.

October 13 - Lavelle presents the introduction to NIGO's *One World Mix* on *BBC Radio One*.

November 1-8 - The Bape Heads Tour 2000 tours Japan and features DJ sets from James Lavelle, Nigo, and Kudo.

November 16 – Lavelle and Nigo DJ at Futura and Stash's Command Z afterpart.

November 28 - The Verve bring out Rich File and Lavelle to perform *Lonely Soul* during a performance.

2001

Mo' Wax address: The Clockhouse, 1st Floor 220 Latimer Road, London, W10 6QY (287).

David Axelrod releases a new self titled album on Mo' Wax. It is awarded a Guinness World Record for the longest time taken to complete an album.

Nigo releases *Ape Sounds Remixed*.

March - UNKLE and SLAM release *Narco Tourists*.

July 6 – Nigo and James Lavelle DJ at Nigo's *Shadow of The Ape Sounds - Directors Cut* - Release Party held at Club Womb, Shibuya, Japan.

2002

UNKLE Sounds - Do Androids Dream of Electric Beats released

June - DJ Shadow's *Private Press* released.

September 11 - UNKLE premiere *Eye For An Eye* at 12:30am on Channel 4.

October 15 – James Lavelle's *Global Underground 023: Barcelona* released.

2003

James Lavelle is 29 years old.

Mo' Wax is £270,000 in debt.

Lavelle is forced to sell his Basquiat painting.

September 22 - UNKLE release *Never, Never Land* as Mo' Wax Records shuts down.

August 28 – DJ Shadow's performance at the Institute of Contemporary Arts London includes *Lonley Soul* live with Richard Ashcroft, and a remix of *Nursery Rhyme*.

Index

3D, 6, 44, 46, 155
A Northern Soul, 94, 95, 131
A Tribe Called Quest, 7, 11, 114
A&M, 59, 60, 61, 62, 68, 72, 73, 108, 193, 194, 195, 282, 290
Abstract Soul, 78, 82
Acid Jazz, 14, 30, 45, 46, 55, 56
Adagio For Strings, 131, 143
Alan Scholefield, 10, 12
Alice Temple, 98, 124, 126, 284
Alien, 171
Andrea Parker, 60, 61
Antony Genn, 198
Anything You Like, 76
Ape Shall Never Kill Ape, 102, 104, 105, 106, 189, 289, 290
Ape Sounds, 101, 104, 295, 300, 301
Apocalypse Now, 122, 132, 179
Atlantique Khan, 148, 149
Attica Blues, 55, 57, 61, 69, 285
Baby Ford, 73, 80
Badly Drawn Boy, 135, 137, 142, 164, 288, 294
Ball Busters, 136
Bape, 29, 101, 103, 189
Basic Mega-Mix, 35, 229
Be There, 130, 161, 162, 165, 189, 191, 192, 198, 294, 295, 296, 297, 298, 299

Beastie Boys, 7, 28, 44, 56, 57, 73, 74, 76, 79, 81, 114, 145, 178, 197, 280, 281, 290, 292
Beat Bop, 71, 115
Belmondo, 69, 73
Ben Drury, 53, 62, 76, 120, 172, 186, 201, 226, 235, 279
Berry Meditation, 76, 77, 80, 82, 285, 286
Beth Ornton, 164
Bitter Sweet Symphony, 98, 189
Björk, 46, 47, 58, 111, 114, 288
Blackalicious, 38, 90, 178, 196, 205, 293, 297, 298
Blade Runner, 84, 122, 163, 218, 271
Blood Stain (UNKLE Reconstruction), 129
Bloodstain, 98, 107, 124, 127, 128, 130, 164, 284, 287
Blue Lines, 18, 46, 93, 166
Blue Note, 23, 284
Bluebird, 9, 10, 11, 14, 29, 276
Bombin, 6
Breather, 137, 139
Breezeblock, 192, 296
Celestial Annihilation, 131, 141, 142, 165
Chaos, 148, 149, 150, 287
Charlie Dark, 14, 61, 69, 83
Cherry Pie, 78
Chico Jam, 79
Chief Xcel, 38

Concerto for Strings and Beats, 143
Cornelius, 106, 114
Cream, 83, 84, 284
Cream Live Two, 83
Cycle Messenger World Championships, 52
Cynthia Rose, 14
Dan The Automator, 38, 60, 106, 109, 182
Dave Thomson, 7
David Axelrod, 37, 67, 115, 155, 196
David Toop, 50, 51
Dazed & Confused, 46, 50, 79, 139, 151, 225, 239, 245
De La Soul, 7, 55, 106, 114, 286, 288
Deborah Anderson, 80, 164, 285
Denis Lavant, 157, 225
Dewback, 69, 281
Dissatisfied, 124, 148
DJ Krush, 30, 39, 52, 53, 56, 57, 114, 280, 282
DJ Milo, 44
DJ Spooky, 73, 80, 171
DJ Zen, 38
Dust Brothers, 71, 106, 197, 283, 288
Ed Hartman, 66
Eg & Alice, 125
Electro, 5, 46
Endtroducing, 65, 66, 68, 87, 88, 90, 96, 110, 147, 170, 181, 194
Entropy, 38, 227, 278
Fleetwood Mac, 141, 142, 164, 166
Frances O'Connor, 72
Fraser Cooke, 25

Fujiwara Hiroshi, 27, 30, 101, 105
Funkenklein, 34, 37
Futura, 51, 52, 54, 80, 103, 171, 172, 176, 185, 197, 279, 281, 299
Garage Piano, 76, 77, 82, 284
Getting Ahead in the Lucrative Field of Artist Management, 135, 186
Gift of Gab, 38, 88
Gilles Peterson, 9, 13, 14, 19, 30, 254, 278
Global Underground, 129, 301
Gorillaz, 182
Grand Royal, 56, 145, 197, 281, 283, 285, 291
Grandmaster Flash, 7, 31, 41, 115, 275, 287
Grant Marshall, 43
Greek Mythology, 7
G-Son, 73
Guinness World Record, 88
Guns Blazing, 116, 119, 146, 147, 191, 288, 290, 293
Handsome Boy Modelling School, 182, 298
Header, 71, 72
Headz, 55, 77, 107, 197, 280, 282, 283, 284, 285
Hearts of Darkness, 122, 176, 270
High Noon, 88, 91, 109, 233, 288
Hollywood BASIC, 20, 34, 37, 57
Holygoof, 15, 24, 276, 279
Honest Jon's, 9, 10, 11, 12, 14, 20, 25, 27, 29, 277
Howie B, 29, 49, 50, 54, 55, 281

Ian Brown, 130, 161, 191, 286, 287, 289, 294, 296, 297
If You Find Earth Boring (UNKLE Mix), 53
In/Flux, 30, 38, 39, 65
Intro (Optional), 113, 163, 259
Island Records, 15, 19, 24, 193
James vs. Nigo, 103
Jason Newstead, 146, 147, 288
Jean-Michel Basquiat, 59, 70, 218
Jeremy Healey, 9
Jeru The Damaja, 107, 286
Jim Abbiss, 110
John King, 71, 106
Johnny Dollar, 18, 166, 167
Jon Clare, 10
Jonathan Glazer, 155
Jurassic 5, 113, 178, 299
Justin Winks, 7
Kan Takagi, 27, 28, 30, 80, 101, 104, 105, 106, 176, 189, 204, 207, 292
Karmacoma (U.N.K.L.E. Situation), 69
KDVS, 31, 228
KMEL, 33
Kool G Rap, 116, 117, 118, 146
Kung Fu, 7
Last Orgy 3, 105, 106, 189, 289, 290
Lateef, 38, 90, 119, 204
Latryx, 178, 292
Lesson 4, 34, 228, 235
Lisa Haugen, 88, 228
Living In My Headphones, 79, 245

London Records, 55, 59, 128, 177, 278, 280
Lonely Soul, 98, 99, 107, 124, 131, 132, 133, 135, 148, 164, 169, 181, 182, 284, 287, 290, 300
Lost and Found, 51, 52, 53, 65
Love TKO, 29, 49
Lyrics Born, 38, 88, 89, 119, 178, 204, 287, 298
Major Force, 27, 28, 29, 30, 44, 49, 53, 63, 70, 82, 102, 104, 105, 114, 279, 280, 281, 285, 295
Major Force West, 49, 63, 70, 82, 104, 105, 114, 277, 281, 285, 295
Malcolm McLaren, 28, 43, 115
Malcom Catto, 196
March of The General, 104, 105
Mario C, 68, 73, 74, 75, 76, 77, 78, 80, 81, 82, 205, 292
Mark Burgess, 7
Mark Hollis, 149, 150
Masayuki Kudo, 27, 29, 49, 63, 68, 69, 82, 100, 102, 164, 183, 199
Massive Attack, 6, 7, 17, 18, 44, 46, 58, 59, 60, 69, 76, 93, 111, 113, 114, 131, 155
Matthew Puffet, 7
Max Burgos, 74, 80, 206
Melody Maker, 37, 39, 48, 55, 56, 137, 222, 223, 244, 251, 254, 257, 259, 261, 280
Men From U.N.K.L.E., 23, 24, 25, 213, 238, 249

Metallica, 114, 146, 147
Michael Kopelman, 9, 29
Midnight In A Perfect World, 67, 235
Mike D, 1, 56, 81, 118, 121, 145, 146, 147, 169, 182, 197, 206, 244, 268, 281, 289
Mo' Wax Arts, 198
Mo' Wax Please, 12, 13, 15, 277
Mo' Wax Please Records, 19
Mo' Wax Vs Grand Royal, 56
Money Mark, 60, 73, 74, 76, 77, 78, 79, 80, 82, 104, 145, 173, 182, 195, 203, 204, 205, 206, 207, 229, 233, 253, 282, 283, 290, 295
MPC, 36, 66, 107, 109, 141, 278
Nakanishi Toshio, 27, 29, 49, 51, 63, 82, 102, 204, 207, 277
Nellee Hooper, 27, 44, 46, 48
Never Never Land, 193, 198
Nightmares on Wax, 9, 280
Nigo, 101, 102, 103, 104, 105, 189, 196, 281, 285, 287, 288, 295, 300
NME, 14, 18, 37, 39, 56, 81, 89, 95, 96, 99, 110, 126, 149, 179, 183, 185, 189, 190, 191, 198, 224, 285, 290, 295, 296
Norman Jay, 9
Nursery Rhyme, 135, 137, 138, 291, 301
OK Computer, 107, 151, 152, 154, 181
Oras Washington, 31
Organ Donor, 87, 153
Osman Eralp, 193

Outro (Mandatory), 159, 238
Oxford, 3, 4, 5, 6, 7, 8, 10, 12, 13, 25, 151, 176, 190, 222, 225, 242, 275, 276, 277
Pablo Clements, 84
Palm Skin Productions, 22, 85
Paris, 35, 36, 161, 283
Patrick Forge, 13, 17, 277
Paul Bradshaw, 14, 30, 46
Paul McMahon, 7
Pete Tong, 9, 14
Philippe Ascoli, 149
Photek, 73, 80
Plaid, 54, 73, 80
Planet of the Apes, 102, 103, 104
Planet Telex (Karma Sunra Mix), 151
Pointmen, 54, 171, 172
Portishead, 46, 54, 58, 69, 93, 114
Prime Cuts, 189, 190
Psyence Fiction Director's Cut, 199
Public Enemy, 7, 32, 44, 114
Push The Button, 173, 229, 290
Quannum, 113, 178, 196, 288, 289, 297
Rabbit In Your Headlights, 108, 109, 152, 155, 176, 182, 287, 291, 293, 294, 295
Radiohead, 12, 55, 107, 108, 109, 114, 151, 152, 154, 288
Rammellzee, 5, 52, 70, 71, 105, 202, 208, 238, 239, 242, 282
Rare Records, 66
Raw Stylus, 22, 249

Real Deal (Shadow Remix), 35, 228
Repercussions, 20, 21, 278
Rich File, 133, 141, 142, 157, 162, 163, 164, 165, 166, 167, 198, 209, 211, 300, 301
Richard Ashcroft, 94, 95, 99, 107, 131, 132, 133, 135, 181, 185, 199, 282, 286, 301
Rock On, 71, 72, 105, 106, 208, 213, 230, 234, 267, 282, 286, 289, 290
Ronny Jordon, 24
Royaltie$ Overdue, 56
Run DMC, 7, 28, 31, 44
Scha Dara Parr, 106
Scratch Perverts, 104, 189, 192, 294, 296, 299
Shadow's Legitimate Mix, 16, 35, 37
Shynola, 119, 120, 191
Skylab, 51, 207, 229
Skywalker Sound Studios, 108, 286
Sleeping With The Enemy, 35
Smoke-Filled Thoughts, 59
Solesides, 38, 56, 90, 119, 179, 205, 238, 242, 256, 260, 261, 265, 278, 288, 289
Songs Of Experience, 67
Soul II Soul, 7, 44, 114
Soup or Salads, 78, 82
Source Lab Vs. Mo' Wax, 149, 232
Source Magazine, 33, 277
Source Records, 149
South, 196
Spike Stent, 162
Spinners, 84

Stanley Kubrick, 133, 156, 170, 186, 238
Star Wars, 69, 102, 103, 108, 116, 127, 128, 136, 282, 287
Stash, 52, 103, 106, 279, 281
Steve Finan, 59
Stone Roses, 114, 130, 161
Straight No Chaser, 13, 14, 15, 19, 21, 23, 26, 30, 190, 276, 277, 279
Street Sounds, 5, 7, 8, 43
Stüssy Tribe, 29, 101
Style Wars, 70
Sweatmouth, 19
Swifty, 15, 23, 25, 53, 62, 276
Symphony No. 25910 - Escape From Planet Of The Apes-, 105
Takarajima, 101
Talk Talk, 114, 149, 150
Talkin' Loud, 14, 17, 19
Talkin' Summer, 17, 278
Terry Callier, 115, 164
The Abyss, 185
The Baby Namboos, 75, 211, 229
The Bends, 107, 151, 154
The Escapade of Futura 2000, 52
The Face, 25, 33, 73, 75, 76, 96, 153, 240, 248, 262, 264
The Fridge, 14, 17, 278
The Knock, 145, 146, 147, 289, 292
The Light Surgeons, 191
The Man From U.N.C.L.E., 25, 67, 116
The Neptunes, 197
The Oxford Venue, 12

The Private Press, 196
The Psychonauts, 83, 84, 197
The Time Has Come, 49, 50, 53, 54, 57, 93, 124, 171
The Underground Movement, 7
The Venus Project, 19
The Wire, 50
Thom Yorke, 65, 98, 99, 107, 108, 138, 151, 152, 154, 181, 287
Tim Goldsworthy, 13, 49, 68, 69, 74, 80, 94, 99, 100, 124, 164, 181, 183, 204, 275
Tim Simenon, 9
Tim Westwood, 14, 45
Tiny Panx, 27, 28, 105
Tommy Boy, 35, 37
Tommy Guerrero, 196
Tony Vegas, 104, 105, 189
Top Of The Pops, 192
Toy's Factory, 103, 104, 105, 106, 173, 176, 236, 237, 264, 287
Tricky, 44, 58, 75, 93
Trilogy Box Set, 105, 290
Trip Hop, 41, 69
Tui Interactive Media, 72, 265

Unfinished Sympathy, 114, 131
UNKLE Main Title Theme, 121, 122, 123, 290
UNKLE vs. Scratch Perverts, 192
Unreal, 98, 107, 128, 130, 161, 162, 163, 164, 291
Untitled Heavy Beat, 99, 164, 284, 299
Urban Hymns, 98, 181
Virgin, 59, 60, 61, 62, 176, 194, 195, 280, 293, 296
Virgin Records, 61, 176, 177, 195
War Is Hell, 164
What Does Your Soul Look Like, 57, 65, 90, 280, 281
Where Do You Go?, 76
Why Hip-Hop Sucks in '96, 89
Wild Bunch, 6, 7, 18, 27, 43, 44, 75
Will Bankhead, 53, 62, 76, 141, 172
Will Malone, 18, 131, 143, 287
Worldwide Bape Tour 1998, 189
XL, 195, 196, 198, 294, 295
Zimbabwe Legit, 16, 35, 277
Zoe Bedeaux, 75, 76, 94

Acknowledgments

I'd like to thank all of the Libraries, Museums and Archives of the world for archiving yesterday's knowledge for the future. Specifically, I'd like to thank the following who helped in the creation of this book: State Library of Victoria, State Library of South Australia, RMIT University Library, HYMEN Archive, and the Internet Archive.

I'd also like to thank all of the people out there who photograph, upload and discuss their extensive collections online. From fan-sites like MoWaxPlease.com, to user-created databases such as Discogs, and forums like Unkle77.com, there's such a great community of people online who have taken the time to share information and images which have in turn helped with the creation of this book.

Thank you also to those who took the time to read through early drafts of this book for me, especially Brian who continued to send through tips and information that has helped me greatly.

Finally, thank *you* for reading this book. I hope it was an enjoyable and informative experience, and I hope it inspires people to write their own books.

If you have any thoughts or feedback regarding the book, please feel free to get in touch and I'll do my best to respond: jimmyjrg@gmail.com or see www.unklewiki.com for updates.

- James Gaunt
  March 2020

Printed in Great Britain
by Amazon